Writing
Resource Book

First Steps Second Edition was developed by STEPS Professional Development
(proudly owned by Edith Cowan University) on behalf of the
Department of Education and Training (Western Australia).

It was written by:

Kevlynn Annandale

Ross Bindon

Julie Broz

Jenny Dougan

Kerry Handley

Annette Johnston

Lynn Lockett

Philippa Lynch

Rebecca Rourke

Second Edition

Addressing Current Literacy Challenges

First Steps Writing Resource Book

Published in the United Kingdom by Steps Professional Development
Unit 78 Shrivenham 100 Business Park
Majors Road, Watchfield
Oxon SN6 8 TY

Steps Professional Development is a wholly owned subsidiary of Edith Cowan University in Perth, Western Australia. As a not-for-profit organisation, Steps Professional Development provides professional development and publishes resources for teachers in the areas of literacy (R-Y12), mathematics (R-Y9), and fundamental movement skills (R-Y3). Steps Professional Development has offices in Australia, the United Kingdom and the United States.

Originally published in Australia by Rigby Heinemann, a division of Reed International Books Australia Pty Ltd.

ISBN 1-905232-22-5 Writing Map of Development
                   Writing Resource Book   (pack)
ISBN 1-9052322-23-3 CD-ROM

05 WMoD&R 10 9 8 7 6 5 4 3 2 1

Text by Kevlynn Annandale, Ross Bindon, Julie Broz, Jenny Dougan, Kerry Handley, Annette Johnston, Lynn Lockett, Philippa Lynch and Rebecca Rourke
Edited by Philip Bryan
Text designed by Anna Cesaro
Cover designed by Anna Cesaro and Kathryn Greenough
Typeset by Alena Jencik
Printed and bound by Craft Print

Acknowledgements
The authors and the publishers would like to thank the following people and organisations for granting their permission to reproduce copyright material.

For texts:
Association of Independent Schools of Western Australia for permission to reproduce a 'brochure from the Sustainability Conference', p. 156; Australian Sports Commission for permission to reproduce 'Your rating as a coach', p. 83 (bottom right); Avis Australia for permission to reproduce 'Double Qantas Frequent Flyer Points', p. 103 (bottom right); City of Subiaco for permission to reproduce 'Leadlight festival', © City of Subiaco, p. 129; Philip Gore and Australian Table for permission to reproduce 'Movies', ACP Publishing, p. 116 (top right); James Hasick, Antarctic Journal © 1993, first published by Era Publications, Australia, pp. 116 (top left), 118 (top); John Curtin College of the Arts for permission to reproduce 'A Circle in a Room Full of Squares (2004), Western Australia, p. 151; King Features Syndicate Inc NY for permission to reproduce 'The Phantom' © King Features Syndicate Inc NY, 1951, 2005-09-19, p. 63; Murdoch Books Pty Limited for permission to reproduce Little Aussie Cookbook, courtesy of Murdoch Books Pty Limited (cover), p. 93 (top left); 'Newsday' for permission to reproduce 'A perfect princess', © Newsday, p. 85 (bottom); PanMacmillan, Australia, for permission to reproduce '47 things you might not know about Morris Gleitzman' © PanMacmillan, Australia, p. 83 (left); Penguin Group Australia for permission to reproduce Unreal (cover) by Paul Jennings, published by Penguin Group Australia, p. 61 (top right); Dr Paul Swan for permission to reproduce 'Getting Closer', p. 94; Transperth for permission to reproduce the transperth timetable; the information regarding Transperth services is effective as at 10/2005. To access up-to-date timetable information, please visit the Transperth website at www.transperth.wa.gov.au or call Transperth InfoLine on 13 62 13 (TTY: 08 9428 1999), p. 74 (middle); WA Independent Grocers' Association for permission to reproduce 'The referendum on longer shopping hours', © WA Independent Grocers' Association, p. 103 (top left); WA Institute of Sport for permission to reproduce 'Following big brother', © WA Institute of Sport, p. 83 (top); West Australian Health Department for permission to reproduce 'Parent Questions 18–21 months', © West Australian Health Department, Child Care Record Card CH511 (2000), p. 84; The West Australian Newspapers Limited for permission to reproduce 'Trio's freeway bravery saved officer' by Daniel Emerson, p. 116 (middle)

For photographs:
Lindsay Edwards, pps. 3, 10, 13, 16, 19, 22, 26, 137, 159; all other photographs supplied by the Department of Education of Western Australia

Every attempt has been made to trace and acknowledge copyright. Where an attempt has been unsuccessful, the publisher would be pleased to hear from the copyright owner so any omission or error can be rectified.

Thank you to Hillsmeade Primary School.

Contents

Authors' Acknowledgements

The *First Steps* Team from STEPS Professional Development acknowledges the contributions made by the following people. We give our grateful thanks to:

All teachers and students who were involved in trialling the materials and offering feedback, either as Critical Readers, Test Pilots or Navigator Schools.

Those students and teachers who provided us with great samples of work to enhance the text. A special thanks to Louise Swain for her work in the creation and collection of many of these work samples.

The authors of the original *First Steps* edition, developed by the Education Department of Western Australia, and the efforts of the many individuals who contributed to that resource.

Introduction

The *First Steps Writing Resource Book* Second Edition builds on the original *First Steps* writing text (formerly known as the *Writing Resource Book*) by drawing on contemporary research and developments in the field of writing instruction. The new *Writing Resource Book*, used in conjunction with the *First Steps Writing Map of Development* Second Edition, has a strong focus on supporting teachers as they implement a multi-dimensional approach to teaching writing.

The *First Steps Writing Resource Book* will help teachers focus on the explicit teaching of different forms of text; writing processes, strategies and conventions; and the contextual aspects associated with the act of composing texts. Teachers will find the information relevant for all phases of writing development, and will be able to apply the ideas and suggestions with all students in their classroom.

CD-ROM icons appear throughout the *First Steps Writing Resource Book*. They indicate that a practical format is available on the Writing Strand CD-ROM (included in the *First Steps Writing Map of Development* Second Edition). The CD-ROM is an electronic treasure chest of activity formats, recording sheets, resource lists and teaching, learning and assessment frameworks. The *First Steps Linking Assessment Teaching and Learning* book is also a useful companion resource.

The Explicit Teaching of Writing

Teaching students to become effective, lifelong writers cannot be simplified into one method or a set of steps; the act of writing consists of multiple processes, strategies and conventions that intertwine and overlap. Teachers need to be explicit in demonstrating and talking to students about what effective writers do. Teachers also need to provide opportunities for students to apply new understandings in their own authentic writing contexts.

A successful writing program requires a daily block of time, with time allocated for explicit instruction on selected aspects of writing, time for students to write independently, and opportunities for students to receive and provide feedback.

The table in Figure 1 provides a basic structure for examining a block of time dedicated to the teaching of writing. The basic structure is flexible and can change on a daily basis, as needed. The needs of the students will drive decisions teachers make about how much time to spend on each element in a day or a week.

ESSENTIAL ELEMENTS OF A WRITING BLOCK	ROLE OF THE TEACHER	ROLE OF THE STUDENTS
Time for Explicit Instruction (5–20 minutes) This time provides a forum for whole class or small group instruction. Students' phases of development and identified Major Teaching Emphases from the *Writing Map of Development* will help teachers determine the focus of mini-lessons. These may focus on classroom routines or any selected aspects of writing. • Use of Texts, e.g. Introducing a new form. *(Refer to Chapter 1, Section 2.)* • Contextual Understanding, e.g. Use of devices. *(Refer to Chapter 2.)* • Conventions, e.g. Use of grammar. *(Refer to Chapter 3, Section 2.)* • Processes and Strategies, e.g. How to plan for writing. *(Refer to Chapter 4.)*	Introduce a selected focus using Practices or Procedures to teach writing. These might include: **Procedures** *(Refer to Chapter 1, Section 1.)* Modelled Writing Shared Writing Interactive Writing Guided Writing Language Experience **Practices** Familiarising Analysing Discussing	Listen and actively participate in mini-lessons. Complete Guided Practice activities– (Refer to *First Steps Writing Map of Development*.) Make connections from mini-lesson to their own writing.
Time for Independent Writing (20–40 minutes) This time provides students with the opportunity to apply the processes of writing to compose texts for authentic purposes and real audiences. Students might be involved in any of the following: • Self-selected writing projects and topics. • Jointly decided short-term writing projects, e.g. Teacher and students decide on the need to write a thank-you letter to a guest speaker. • Self-selected topics within parameters provided, e.g. a particular form.	Provide time for students to apply new learning through writing. Observe and record what stage of the writing process each student is up to. Confer with individuals or small groups of students. Provide small group instruction as necessary.	Actively write; may be involved in planning, drafting, refining or publishing. Participate in individual or group conferences. Participate in small group instruction if required.
Time for Feedback (5–15 minutes) Time for students to share their writing either in whole-class, small-group or partner forums. This provides a real audience for students to share draft attempts and to receive valuable feedback on how to improve their writing.	Facilitate the sharing of writing, e.g. Author's Chair. Participate as an audience member in sharing sessions. Provide constructive feedback to students.	Volunteer to share writing with others, e.g. read writing aloud to an audience. Seek specific feedback from audience. Provide constructive feedback to peers. Make choices about what feedback will be incorporated.

Figure 1 Basic Structure of a Writing Block

CHAPTER 1

Use of Texts

Overview

The Use of Texts substrand focuses on the composition of a range of texts. Texts are defined as any form of communication from which meaning is created. This can be spoken, written or visual.

Many categories are used to sort the enormous range of texts that students might compose; for example, fiction and non-fiction, narrative and informational, narrative and expository, literature and mass media. Texts in the *First Steps* resource are classified in three categories — written, spoken or visual. Each category can be further separated into printed, live and electronic, with some texts falling into one or more categories, e.g. a video is a combination of electronic, spoken and visual text.

Students can become both composers and comprehenders of text if they can identify the primary purpose of a text, rather than its category. The overview in Figure 1.2 categorises texts according to their purpose.

This chapter provides information about ways to develop students' knowledge and understandings of texts. The two sections are as follows:

- **Section 1 — Instructional Procedures for Teaching Writing**
- **Section 2 — Understanding Different Forms of Writing**

Figure 1.1

An Overview of Texts

Tending Towards Literary Text → Tending Towards Informational Text

Modes	MEDIA	Entertain	Recount	Socialise	Inquire	Describe	Persuade	Explain	Instruct	FORMATS
Written	Printed	Narrative, e.g. *Fairytale*, *Fable*, *Fantasy*, Poem, e.g. *Haiku*, *Limerick*, *Free Verse*, Song Lyric, Word Puzzle	Biography, Autobiography, Diary, Journal, Retells *direct or indirect experiences*, Minutes of meetings, Review	Invitation, Apology, Message, Note, Personal correspondence, Announcement	Survey, Questionnaire, Interview	Report, Label, Menu, Contents page, Index, Glossary, Bibliography, Blurb, Description	Exposition, Menu, Job application, Editorial, Headlines, Competition entry, Slogan, Advertisement	Explanation, Affidavit, Memo, Rules, Policy, Journal, Timetable, Complaint	Directions, Timetable, Recipe, Manual, Invoice, List, Experiment, Summons, Blueprint, Map	Magazine, Letter, Book, Brochure, Pamphlet, Newspaper, Newsletter, Chart, Journal, Itinerary
Written	Electronic	Joke		Chat room, Conversation						CD-ROM, Text Message, Email, Fax, Card
Spoken	Live	Joke, Story, Song lyric	Conversation	Greeting, Apology, Telephone conversation	Interview	Oral report	Debate, Discussion	Oral explanation	Oral directions	Performance, Speech
Spoken	Electronic	Talking book, Song lyric		Voicemail message			Talkback radio, Song lyric			Audio cassette, Radio, Television, CD-ROM, Video
Visual	Live	Play, Theatre								Clothing, Tattoo, Gesture
Visual	Printed	Painting, Photograph, Cartoon	Picture book, Photograph			Travel brochure	Logo, Advertisement, Catalogue	Timeline, Graph, Table, Flowchart	Road sign	Button, Flyer, Poster, Magazine, Graffiti, Sticker
Visual	Electronic	Television sitcom, Film					Advertisement	Documentary, News report		CD-ROM, Video cassette, Web page

PURPOSES

Figure 1.2 An Overview of Texts

4

Instructional Procedures for Teaching Writing

Using a Range of Instructional Procedures

The strategic use of a range of instructional procedures creates a strong foundation for a comprehensive approach to teaching writing. Each procedure involves varying degrees of responsibility for both the teacher and student. Using a selective range of teaching procedures ensures that explicit instruction and guidance, when needed, is balanced with regular opportunities for independent application of understandings, strategies and processes. Once teachers are familiar with a range of procedures, they can determine which procedure will be the most effective to use according to students' needs, familiarity with the task or the purpose of the writing.

What Are Procedures for Teaching Writing?

Instructional procedures provide meaningful contexts for focusing on selected parts of the writing process. They are characterised by a number of widely accepted steps or stages, conducted frequently and are generally applicable to all phases of development. Six procedures have been selected as a comprehensive approach to writing. The six procedures are as follows:

- **Modelled Writing**
- **Language Experience**
- **Shared and Interactive Writing**
- **Guided Writing**
- **Independent Writing**
- **Author's Chair**

The inclusion of each procedure has been influenced by the Gradual Release of Responsibility Model (Pearson and Gallagher, 1983). Procedures such as Modelled Writing and Language Experience allow the teacher to demonstrate how writing can be used to construct texts for different purposes and audiences. Shared and Interactive Writing and Guided Writing provide opportunities for students to practise the process of writing with guidance and support. Independent Writing sessions allow students to apply what they have learnt about writing, and Author's Chair provides opportunities for them to give and receive feedback on their writing.

Teachers need to be aware of the essential elements of each procedure; this will ensure consistency in understanding and use. This awareness will also allow teachers to select the most appropriate instructional procedure to meet individual students' needs.

Selecting Instructional Procedures

When selecting instructional procedures, the following questions can help ensure that students gain the maximum benefit from each session.

- What is the purpose of this session?
- Which instructional procedure will allow for the appropriate degree of student participation? e.g. **Do students need explicit teaching or time for purposeful practice?**
- What resources will be required?
- How will students be grouped?
- What will be planned for other students while working with a small group?
- What classroom routines are in place to enable students to work independently?

An overview of the procedures appears on the following page (Figure 1.3) and all procedures are discussed in detail in this section.

Overview of Instructional Procedures

	Modelled Writing	Language Experience	Shared Writing	Interactive Writing
Definition	Demonstrating writing behaviours and verbalising the thinking processes involved with those behaviours	Using a shared experience as a basis for jointly composing a text	Working with students to compose and construct a piece of writing, with the teacher acting as scribe	Working with students to compose and construct a text collaboratively, using a 'shared pen'
Key Features	• Brief sessions from 5 to 10 minutes • Each session has a clear, singular focus • Use clear 'think aloud' statements • Writing occurs in front of students • The composed text can be seen by all students	• Based on a shared experience • Text composed as a result of the experience • Use students' language when creating the text	• Sessions kept brief and lively, from 10 to 20 minutes • Teacher scribes, students contribute ideas • Teacher thinks aloud, invites questions and discussion • Each session has a planned explicit focus based on students' needs	• Sessions kept brief and lively, from 10 to 20 minutes • Usually small group • Teacher and students share the pen • Each session has a planned explicit focus based on students' needs • Students participate actively

	Guided Writing	Independent Writing	Author's Chair
Definition	Teacher scaffolds and supports a group of students with similar needs as they develop writing behaviours and understandings	• Students independently apply previously learnt writing processes, understandings and strategies to own texts	An opportunity for students to voluntarily share their writing and receive constructive feedback
Key Features	• Students grouped to focus on an identified need • Most writing is done as individuals • Teacher is the guide and supporter • Sessions are about 10 to 20 minutes • Students receive support and feedback when required	• Students take responsibility for their writing • Students apply previous learning • All students engaged in a writing-related task • Sustained period for writing • Students write for authentic purposes	• Writing is shared with peers • Feedback is explicit and constructive • Sessions are 10 to 15 minutes • Can be used daily at the end of writing sessions

Figure 1.3 Overview of Instructional Procedures

Modelled Writing

Definition: The explicit demonstration of writing behaviours and the verbalisation of the thinking processes involved.

Description

The focus of Modelled Writing is on the explicit planning and demonstration of selected writing behaviours. Demonstrating the interactive nature of the writing process shows how writers continually make decisions as they construct texts. The teacher holds the pen and makes decisions about the writing; students observe the process and the product, rather than contribute towards it.

Modelled Writing is most effective when the teaching focus is based on observation of students' learning needs, then builds on their experiences, current understandings and prior knowledge. Students might need many repeated demonstrations before they can apply the understandings to their own writing.

It is important to explicitly model all substrands of writing. It may be beneficial to work on the same text over several Modelled Writing sessions, demonstrating the many interrelated processes associated with writing.

Key Features

- Sessions are brief: five to ten minutes.
- Sessions have a clear, singular focus.
- Clear Think-Aloud statements are used.
- The writing is composed as the students watch.
- The text being composed can be seen by all students.

Benefits for Students

Modelled Writing helps students to:
- understand how effective writers compose texts
- understand that writing is composed for a specific audience and purpose
- develop an understanding of the process of writing
- understand the relationship between spoken and written language
- understand how particular text forms are explicitly constructed
- use a piece of writing as a reference point for their own writing.

Suggestions for Using Modelled Writing in the Classroom

Planning for *Modelled Writing*

- Determine the purpose, audience and form for the writing.
- Determine an explicit focus for the session based on students' needs.
- Decide on the explicit language that will be used during the Think-Alouds.
- Select the required writing tools and materials, e.g. large sheet of paper and a thick marker, overhead projector, interactive whiteboard, large computer screen.

Conducting *Modelled Writing* Sessions

- Clearly explain the chosen writing focus, making links to students' experiences and prior learning.
- Explain the purpose, audience and form of the writing.
- Begin to write, pausing often to demonstrate the specific focus by 'thinking aloud'. Students can ask questions and offer suggestions; however, the teacher is in charge of the pen and thinking aloud is the focal point of the session.
- Invite students to verbally rephrase the session focus.
- Display the Modelled Writing sample prominently to provide a clear reference point for students' own writing.
- Involve students in recording the Modelled Writing behaviours.

After *Modelled Writing*

- Provide opportunities for students to practise and apply their understandings by taking part in Shared, Interactive, Guided or Independent Writing sessions.
- Repeat Modelled Writing sessions on the same focus using different contexts, as required, until students can independently apply their understandings to their writing.

Ideas for Assessment

There are few opportunities to gather information about students during a Modelled Writing session. It is sometimes possible to gauge students' understandings by the questions they ask, or through the comments they make during demonstrations. Observe and monitor students' use of the modelled behaviours during Shared, Interactive, Guided and Independent Writing.

**Reflecting on the Effective Use
of the Modelled Writing Procedure**

- Did I keep the session short and sharp (five to ten minutes)?
- Was my focus clear and explicitly stated?
- Did I use Think-Alouds clearly as part of my demonstration?
- Did the students stay focused and attend to the demonstration?

Figure 1.4

Language Experience

Definition: To use a shared experience as a basis for jointly composing a text.

Description

The focus of Language Experience is to involve students in a shared experience, then use students' language to jointly construct a written text. The teacher scribes the text and students are supported as active participants in the writing process.

Language Experience opportunities can be created in a range of ways.

- Planned activities inside the classroom, e.g. cooking, blowing bubbles, hatching chickens, bringing in an animal or object to observe and discuss, inviting a guest speaker.
- Planned activities outside the classroom, e.g. taking a trip to an interesting location such as a park, museum or zoo.
- Unplanned events, e.g. a thunderstorm, a crane across the road.

Key Features

- Text composed is based on a shared experience.
- Students' oral language forms the basis for the creation of the written text.
- Use of Shared Writing procedure to compose the text.
- Participation of the whole class.

Benefits for Students

Language Experience helps students to:

- understand the similarities and differences between spoken and written language
- talk and write about events in which they have participated
- develop understandings about print
- produce meaningful and supportive texts for reading
- have ownership of the texts produced
- develop vocabulary and expand concepts
- understand the relationship between thinking, speaking, writing and reading.

Suggestions for Using Language Experience in the Classroom

Planning for *Language Experience*

- Decide on a purposeful experience that will interest the students.
- Involve students in the planning, preparation and organisation of the experience, where possible, e.g. writing invitations to parents for a special class event, making bookings for an excursion, preparing questions for a guest speaker.

Conducting *Language Experience* Sessions

- Share the experience. If appropriate, take photographs to record the event.
- Ensure students are as involved as possible and that there are lots of opportunities for conversations during the experience.
- After the experience, discuss the event as a whole class, encouraging students to use vocabulary related to the experience.
- Involve students in a Shared Writing session to record the experience. Use students' ideas and language to demonstrate the relationships between thinking, talking and writing.
- Jointly re-read the text as it is being constructed to check and maintain its meaning.
- Refine the text together until it is ready to be published.
- Publish the text with photos or student drawings, e.g. make a big book, a chart, a wall display.
- Involve students in purposeful reading and re-reading of the text.
- Make connections between this text and other texts that the class has written or read together.

After *Language Experience*

- Display the text so that students can use it as a future writing reference.
- Involve students in further writing activities related to the experience, e.g. reports for school newsletter, thank-you letters.
- Use the text as a springboard for other writing and reading activities.
- Use the text in Modelled, Shared or Guided Reading sessions.

Ideas for Assessment

Language Experience sessions allow the teacher to observe students at work as part of the whole class. Teachers are able to gather valuable information by observing individual students' involvement and contribution to the Shared Writing session.

Reflecting on the Effective Use of the Language Experience Procedure

- Did I provide an experience that was interesting and relevant to the students?
- Did I stimulate enough discussion to generate rich oral language?
- Did I ask open-ended questions?
- Did I value the students' own oral language in the creation of the written text?
- Did I use the opportunity to extend students' vocabularies?

Figure 1.5

Shared and Interactive Writing

Definition: Teacher-managed process in which a piece of text is composed and constructed collaboratively.

Description

Shared and Interactive Writing are supportive writing procedures that involve the teacher and students working together to make joint decisions about planning, drafting, refining and publishing a text.

In Shared Writing, the teacher acts as the scribe, allowing students to participate in the creation of a text without having to actually write it. Students are actively involved, as they are invited to contribute, develop and organise ideas. The teacher responds to students' contributions with comments and questions, using the results to shape the written text.

In Interactive Writing, the teacher makes decisions about where students can take over the pen to write parts of the text. Students are invited to 'share the pen' at strategic points so that they can actively participate at their instructional level. Interactive Writing usually works best with a small group of students, as each student has the opportunity to write; however, it can also be done with individuals or the whole class.

Shared and Interactive Writing enable students to collaboratively compose texts at a level beyond their normal independent writing. Both procedures can be used to consolidate and extend students' writing behaviours and understandings, and both can be adjusted to meet individual needs.

A short text may be completed in a Shared or Interactive Writing session; however, the same piece of writing might be worked on over several sessions with a different focus each time. The texts can then be used for a variety of follow-up writing and reading activities.

Key Features

- Sessions are most effective when kept brief and lively: ten to twenty minutes.
- The teacher is the scribe during Shared Writing.
- The pen is shared between the teacher and students during Interactive Writing.
- All students actively participate.
- Planned and explicit focus in a session is based on students' needs.

- The teacher questions and 'steers' discussion to engage the students.
- All students can see the text being composed.
- The text is re-read after composing.

Benefits for Students

Shared and Interactive Writing help students to:
- be actively involved in the process of writing in a supported way
- engage in the production of texts that may be beyond their independent writing level
- transfer the behaviours and strategies used by competent writers to their own writing
- develop confidence in writing
- understand how particular text forms are explicitly constructed
- be exposed to a range of text forms.

Suggestions for Using Shared and Interactive Writing in the Classroom

Planning for *Shared Writing* and *Interactive Writing*

- Determine an explicit focus for the session based on students' needs.
- Determine the purpose, audience and form of the writing.
- Select the writing tools and materials that will be used, e.g. a large sheet of paper and a thick marker, a large computer screen, interactive whiteboard.
- When conducting Interactive Writing, carefully consider at which point in the text you can allow specific students to 'share the pen'.

Conducting *Shared Writing* and *Interactive Writing* Sessions

- Explain the purpose, audience and form of the writing.
- Clearly explain the writing focus of the session.
- Explain that joint decisions will be made about the writing.
- Activate students' prior knowledge and experiences of the topic and task.
- Engage students in the construction of the text, e.g. word choices, how to best express ideas, inviting students to 'share the pen' in Interactive Writing.
- As a group, constantly re-read the text as it is constructed to check its meaning.
- Invite students to refine the text, if appropriate.
- Review the selected focus at the end of the session.

After *Shared and Interactive Writing*

- Display the Shared or Interactive Writing text prominently. Remind students to use it as a reference for their own writing.
- Provide opportunities for students to practise and apply the understandings, processes and strategies shared.
- Make the composed text available for independent reading.

Ideas for Assessment

Shared and Interactive Writing sessions allow the teacher to observe students working as part of a group or as part of the whole class. Teachers are able to gather valuable information by observing individual students' participation and contributions during the writing session, and by directing questions to specific students.

Reflecting on the Effective Use of the Shared and Interactive Writing Procedures

- Did students actively participate in the construction of the text?
- Was the session short and focused so that students were attentive, engaged and eager to participate?
- Was the session paced so that a reasonable amount of print was produced in a short time?
- What did students learn from this session that they will be able to use in their own writing?
- Did I make the most appropriate teaching points for the students?
- What do I need to do next to help students with their writing?

Figure 1.6

Guided Writing

Definition: The provision of scaffolded support to a group of students with similar needs, as they develop writing behaviours and understandings

Description

Guided Writing involves guiding and supporting students through the process of writing, providing explicit instruction and feedback through planned mini-lessons and conferences. It is based on assessment of students' needs and behaviours, and leads them towards becoming independent writers. Texts that students write through Guided Writing are usually more complex than texts they would write on their own.

Guided Writing uses — and builds on — behaviours taught in Modelled and Shared Writing. Students with similar needs (or at similar phases of development) work together on a part of the process of writing relevant to their learning needs. Students usually 'hold the pen' and 'own' the writing; however, explicit feedback is given when needed and repeated demonstrations can be provided.

Key Features

• Students are grouped to focus on an identified need.
• Most writing is done as individuals.
• The teacher is the guide and supporter.
• Session length: ten to twenty minutes.
• Students receive support and feedback as required.

Benefits for Students

Guided Writing helps students to:
• independently write texts of increasing difficulty
• make choices and decisions about their writing in consultation with peers and the teacher
• develop as individual writers by practising, exploring, experimenting and taking risks in a supportive environment
• develop writing behaviours that they can apply to all writing
• experience success with writing by receiving immediate feedback
• develop the ability to self-monitor their writing and set writing goals.

Suggestions for Using Guided Writing in the Classroom

Planning for *Guided Writing*

- Identify a small group of students who have a similar need. The identified need will become the focus of the session.
- Determine the purpose, audience and form of the writing event.
- Make sure students come organised and equipped with writing tools, e.g. **writing folder, pens, paper, personal dictionaries, laptop computer.**
- Organise other students to work independently.

Conducting *Guided Writing* Sessions

- Gather the group in an area where they can work easily.
- Tell students the session focus; make sure they understand the purpose, audience and form of the writing event.
- Link the focus back to previous Modelled and Shared writing sessions.
- Invite students to share their ideas or their first sentence before writing. (This ensures students have grasped the focus of the lesson.)
- Allow each student to start writing immediately after this brief discussion.
- Interact with students to develop and clarify their ideas and understandings as they write.
- Provide assistance and explicit feedback as required.
- Assess what students are doing, by observing, taking notes and asking questions.
- Review the selected focus at the end of the session, linking it back to students' writing; reiterate the main points.

After *Guided Writing*

- During Independent Writing, encourage students to continue working on the texts they produced in Guided Writing.
- Provide opportunities for students to share their writing.
- Have students reflect on the writing produced during Guided Writing.
- Encourage students to apply what they learnt in Guided Writing during Independent Writing.
- Use observations and notes taken to direct further teaching and learning experiences.

Ideas for Assessment

Guided Writing allows teachers to question, observe and confer with students as they write, and to note what students are able to do when working with guidance. Use each student's performance to monitor their development, and for planning further teaching and learning experiences that will support and extend each student.

Reflecting on the Effective Use of the Guided Writing Procedure

- Did I select a small group of students with a similar need?
- Was my focus clear and explicitly stated?
- Did I provide explicit feedback and support to the students?
- Did I make the most appropriate teaching points during the session?
- What do these students need next to support their writing?
- Did I see any evidence of students using what I have previously modelled?
- Did I provide sufficient challenges to encourage further development?
- Did the rest of the class stay on task with independent activities?

Figure 1.7

Independent Writing

Definition: The independent application of previously learnt writing understandings, processes and strategies to compose own texts.

Description

Independent Writing focuses on students taking charge of their own writing. Students apply the understandings, processes and strategies learnt through the supported teaching procedures, then take responsibility for working through any challenges they encounter in the process of writing.

During Independent Writing, the writing tasks may be:
• self-selected projects and topics
• jointly decided short-term writing projects
• self-selected topics within given parameters.

Students often refine texts they have previously written, and might revisit them over an extended period to improve them for publication. Ensure that students have sufficient time during Independent Writing to work through processes, think deeply and produce writing that is personally satisfying. Conduct conferences during Independent Writing time to give guidance and feedback to individuals or small groups. It is also possible to monitor and observe students as they work.

Key Features

• Students take responsibility for their writing.
• Students apply previous learning.
• The whole class is engaged in a writing-related task.
• A sustained period is provided for writing.
• Students write for authentic purposes and audiences.

Benefits for Students

Independent Writing helps students to:
• apply writing understandings, processes and strategies in meaningful contexts
• refine and consolidate their learning
• build fluency and confidence with the process of writing
• write for enjoyment, and for their own purposes
• polish texts for publication.

Suggestions for Using Independent Writing in the Classroom

Planning for *Independent Writing*

- Provide adequate time for students to write, so that they are able to think about their task and produce texts that satisfy them as writers.
- Make sure that the understandings, processes and strategies needed to undertake Independent Writing have been previously modelled, shared and discussed.
- Provide a rich variety of writing materials and resources.
- Reinforce key elements of writing previously demonstrated by displaying jointly constructed charts as models and prompts.
- Establish suitable areas for students and groups to work in.
- Establish any necessary routines, e.g. noise level, storage of work, conferencing etiquette.

Conducting *Independent Writing* Sessions

- Reiterate the routines for Independent Writing.
- Make sure that students have a clear understanding of the purpose and audience for writing events.
- Encourage students to refer to, and reflect upon, learning covered in Modelled, Shared, Interactive and Guided Writing.
- Observe students and confer at the point of need by prompting, responding as a reader, and extending their thinking.
- Work with individuals or small groups while the rest of the class is writing.

After Independent Writing

- Provide opportunities for students to share their work and receive feedback.
- Have students share published texts with their intended audience.
- Provide opportunities for students to reflect on their writing.
- Use observations and work samples to guide future teaching and learning experiences.

Ideas for Assessment

Independent Writing sessions provide the opportunity to observe individual students as they write. Note which elements of Modelled, Shared, Interactive and Guided Writing sessions have been understood by students and which elements need further teaching. Assess the process of writing and the writing produced. Collect information about students' selection of writing topics and forms, writing behaviours, understandings, attitudes and interests.

Reflecting on the Effective Use of the Independent Writing Procedure

- Did I set aside sufficient time for Independent Writing?
- Did I introduce the essential understandings and strategies necessary for Independent Writing?
- Did I encourage all students to write independently?
- Did I offer a choice of writing materials?
- Did I celebrate writing successes?
- Did I write too? If not, did I use the time to gather information about the students?
- What can I do to help students extend their writing?

Figure 1.8

Author's Chair

Definition: An opportunity for students to voluntarily share their writing and receive constructive feedback. (Author's Chair is also known as Author's Circle.)

Description

The focus of Author's Chair is for students to share their writing with an audience and receive constructive feedback. They can then incorporate their peers' suggestions into their writing.

A special chair is designated as the 'author's chair'. A student sits in the author's chair and reads a piece of their writing aloud to a group of peers. The writing should be current, and the group should listen carefully and respectfully, then respond as critical friends. Each student in the group thinks of an element of the writing they wish to comment on or develops a question to ask the author. Students in the group are asked to be specific about exactly what worked for them in the writing. Authors are encouraged to respond to the comments they receive or to reflect upon them.

The teacher's initial role is to facilitate sessions and guide audience responses. Model language that is useful for promoting constructive criticism, such as using 'I statements', e.g. **I wondered ...**, **I think ...**, **I could picture ....** Model how to ask questions about specific elements of the writing, e.g. **Why did you represent the character in that way?** Several groups can be operating in the classroom at the same time once students know the procedure; when this happens, the teacher no longer takes an active part, concentrating instead on observing and conferring.

Key Features

- Writing is shared with peers.
- Feedback is explicit and constructive.
- Session length: ten to fifteen minutes.
- Can be used at the end of daily writing sessions.

Benefits for Students

Author's Chair helps students to:
- develop reflective and critical thinking as they talk about their writing with other writers
- give and receive feedback on writing
- develop active listening skills
- ask effective questions about their peers' writing

- develop a sense of a community of writers
- improve their writing based on constructive feedback
- learn that their ideas are valued
- view themselves as authors who write for an audience and make choices about their writing
- become perceptive readers and writers as they shift between author and audience.

Suggestions for Using Author's Chair in the Classroom

Planning for *Author's Chair*

- Establish a cooperative and caring environment that invites students to share and respond constructively.
- Designate a special place in the room and a special chair for the author.
- Model the procedure for Author's Chair several times with the whole class before attempting it with small groups. Use a 'fishbowl' technique, where students sit around the perimeter of the room and observe a group trying out the Author's Chair process. Then discuss the strengths and weaknesses of the process.
- Decide how many students will participate, e.g. whole class, small group.
- Select a student to be the author for the session.

Conducting *Author's Chair* Sessions

- Review the procedure, if needed.
- The selected author sits in the special chair, reads their writing and shares any accompanying illustrations or diagrams.
- On the first reading the audience listens respectfully, trying to get a sense of the piece.
- The author invites the audience to listen as the work is read again and to focus on a specific feature of the writing.
- The author invites the audience to make comments or suggestions, and to ask questions about the specific feature of the writing identified.
- The author can choose to listen to each comment, to respond or to make notes. A second student could make notes on the discussion to give to the author at the end, if required.
- The session ends with the author thanking the audience for their feedback. The author has the final say in accepting or rejecting any of the suggested changes to their text.

After *Author's Chair*

- Gather the class together to reflect on their own involvement in Author's Chair. Discuss the successes of the session and any issues arising from it.
- If needed, schedule an individual conference with the author to discuss any suggested changes to their writing.
- Encourage all students to apply ideas and suggestions from the session to their own writing.
- Record useful sentence stems for providing feedback to peers. Jointly construct cumulative charts of the stems and display them for future reference.

Comments We Use During Author's Chair

- I loved the way that ...
- Your writing reminded me of ...
- One suggestion I would give is ...
- What did you mean by ...
- I was puzzled when ...

Figure 1.9 Useful sentence stems for giving feedback during Author's Chair

Ideas for Assessment

Author's Chair is an opportunity to observe and record students' interest and participation as authors and listeners. Record students' comments and questions and use them to provide the focus for further instruction. During Independent Writing, make note of how students have incorporated audience comments into their own writing.

**Reflecting on the Effective Use
of the Author's Chair Procedure**

- Did I act as facilitator of Author's Chair?
- Could students effectively manage the session independently? If not, what can I do to help them do this in the future?
- Did different students participate as authors?
- Did students provide specific and positive feedback to the author?
- Did I give students time to reflect on their participation in Author's Chair?

Figure 1.10

SECTION 2

Understanding Different Forms of Writing

What Are the Text Forms?

Each text form has a structure and an organisation that flows from its purpose, and from its social and cultural context. Because language is dynamic and fluid, the purpose and shape of different text forms often merge into one another, e.g. a persuasive argument presented in a narrative form.

Very few texts written today are 'pure', with features that immediately identify them as having only one purpose. Most texts are hybrids, because the writer has combined or manipulated forms, formats, media or modes to suit a particular purpose. Being able to identify texts by their primary purpose will allow students to take into account the social and cultural context of the text.

The table below categorises text forms according to their purpose.

Purposes	Example of Text Forms		
To Describe	Report Contents page Bibliography	Label Index Blurb	Menu Glossary Description
To Entertain — prose and poetry	Narrative Word Puzzle	Poem Fable Joke Fairytale	Song lyric
To Explain	Explanation Rules Timetable	Affidavit Policy Complaint	Memo Journal
To Inquire	Survey	Questionnaire	Interview
To Instruct	Directions Manual Experiment	Invoice Summons Recipe	List Blueprint
To Persuade	Exposition Headline	Job application Competition entry	Editorial Slogan
To Recount	Autobiography Review	Diary Minutes of meeting	Retell Journal
To Socialise	Invitation Note	Apology Greeting	Message

Figure 1.11 Text Forms and Purposes

This section of the *First Steps Writing Resource Book* will focus on how to assess students' control of different text forms. It also provides information about how to help students understand the purpose, organisation and language features of common text forms, and to help them consider how these forms can be shaped and adjusted to account for variations in context. The goals for all students are to:

• expand the variety of text forms they compose
• enhance the control they exercise over a range of text forms
• adapt, combine and manipulate texts.

Although it is important for students to be continually involved in composing a range of text forms for different purposes, it is also appropriate to focus a unit of work on a selected text form. This might involve students participating in speaking and listening activities, reading and collecting samples of the text form, analysing model texts, attending to multiple demonstrations, contributing to shared demonstrations, listening to Think-Alouds, completing guided practice activities or creating independent writing across learning areas.

The following pages contain detailed information about the assessment and teaching of different forms. They are organised under eight major social purposes for writing, and will support teachers in creating a unit of work around a selected form of text.

Each social purpose for writing contains the following support information:
• Sample text forms
• Type of information included in text forms
• Sample organisational frameworks for a range of text forms
• Language features
• An assessment guide
• Support activities linked to stages of development.

Figure 1.12 illustrates a suggested pathway for using this information to create a unit of work.

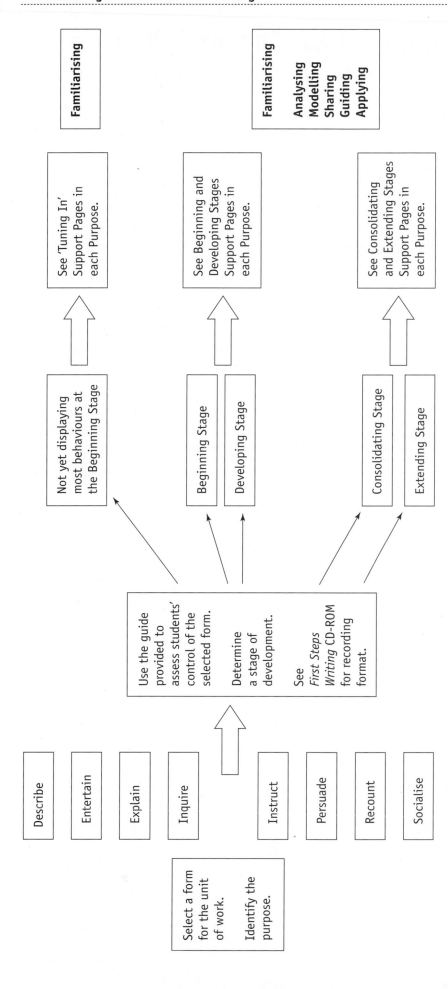

Figure 1.12 Suggested Pathway for Developing a Unit of Work for a Selected Form

Introducing a New Form of Writing

Figure 1.13 is based on The Gradual Release of Responsibility model (Pearson and Gallagher, 1983). Using this model to introduce any new form of text will help teachers to plan a balanced unit of work. This model involves the sequential use of effective teaching practices to introduce a new form of text. The use of different teaching practices moves students from a supportive context where the teacher has a high degree of responsibility for demonstrating the creation of a text (such as modelling and sharing), to a more independent context where the student takes on the responsibility of creating their own text (guiding and applying).

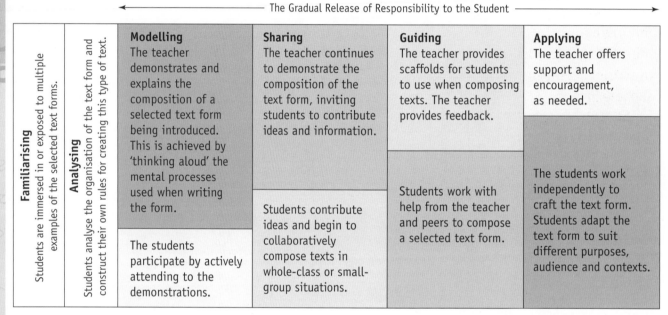

The Gradual Release of Responsibility to the Student

Familiarising	Analysing	Modelling	Sharing	Guiding	Applying
Students are immersed in or exposed to multiple examples of the selected text forms.	Students analyse the organisation of the text form and construct their own rules for creating this type of text.	The teacher demonstrates and explains the composition of a selected text form being introduced. This is achieved by 'thinking aloud' the mental processes used when writing the form.	The teacher continues to demonstrate the composition of the text form, inviting students to contribute ideas and information.	The teacher provides scaffolds for students to use when composing texts. The teacher provides feedback.	The teacher offers support and encouragement, as needed.
		The students participate by actively attending to the demonstrations.	Students contribute ideas and begin to collaboratively compose texts in whole-class or small-group situations.	Students work with help from the teacher and peers to compose a selected text form.	The students work independently to craft the text form. Students adapt the text form to suit different purposes, audience and contexts.

Figure 1.13 Introducing a New Form of Text Using a Gradual Release of Responsibility Model

Familiarising

Familiarising is a collective term. It describes the way in which teachers raise students' awareness and activate students' prior knowledge about a particular form of text. (Familiarising is also known as *immersing* or *exposing*.) When introducing a new text form, familiarising could involve students discussing, reading, listening to or viewing samples of the new form. Familiarising is a critical teaching practice for supporting students' success in the writing of a new text form. Teachers can familiarise students with a new text form in any of the following ways.

1 Sample Displays

Provide opportunities for students to read and view a variety of examples of the chosen text form. These examples can be collected from a range of sources, such as magazines, newspapers, brochures, manuals, comics, catalogues, junk mail, literature, the Internet, student samples from previous years, reading books used in the classroom, books students are reading at home, text books from across learning areas. Encourage students to collect further samples from real-life contexts and contribute them to the display.

Collections of text forms should be discussed and compared, not just displayed. The key to the display is to help students build an awareness of the common features of the selected text form. This can be done by:
- talking about the purpose, e.g. to entertain, to recount
- identifying the possible intended audience
- drawing attention to the text organisation, e.g. headings, subheadings
- highlighting the type of language used, e.g. signal words, adjectives, tense.

2 Reading to and Reading with Students

All writers need to see and hear how other writers compose particular forms of texts. Students need to be read to, and to have quality texts available for them to read independently. Students will benefit from opportunities to discuss the texts read, critically evaluating how real authors achieve their purpose.

An excellent way for the whole class to discuss and explore examples of text forms is through shared reading of texts featuring a specific text form. Students can collaboratively discuss the purpose, use of the form, content presented, structure and organisation of the text and the type of language used.

Guided Reading sessions will also provide a forum for teachers to encourage students, through questioning, to discover the features of the selected text forms.

3 Other Literacy Activities

A wide range of other literacy experiences will help students build their text form knowledge. These could include activities such as:
- reconstructing texts that have been cut into individual paragraphs
- highlighting specific language features within a text, e.g. blue for signal words, yellow for nouns, green for technical vocabulary
- innovating on a text form

A variety of experiences across learning areas are suggested under each writing purpose.

Analysing

Johnson (1988) advocated a problem-solving approach to teaching writing, an approach that can be used effectively to introduce new forms of texts. Analysing is the key practice used during a problem-solving approach, resulting in students 'discovering' the framework of a particular form of text.

Analysing involves students breaking texts into parts to:
- explore the organisation of the text form
- focus on the language features used in the text form
- construct their own rules for writing the text form
- modify and extend their rules in light of further experience.

There are two suggested models for involving students in analysing text forms. Both models will result in the creation of a possible organisational framework, list of rules for crafting that form, and the identification of associated language features.

One-Text Model: one sample of the chosen text form is used.
Multi-Text Model: several samples of the chosen text form are ranked.

One-Text Model

The One-Text Model involves students exploring one sample of the chosen text form. Select a text that is an effective model of the form, then follow these steps.

Step 1: Labelling

The aim of the first step is to arrive at a series of labels that begin to identify the organisational framework of the text form. It is important that students can later refer back to these labels, as they produce their own text.

Discourage generic labels such as 'Introduction' or 'Fact One', as they won't provide much support for students later when they attempt the text form for the first time. If students provide such generic terms, have them clarify the label by stating what information has been included in that part of the text. For example, Introduction will be more explicit if it is labelled as *Who, When, Where, What*.

- Read the sample text with the students. Use an enlarged copy, overhead transparency or big book to make sure that all students can see the text.

- Work together to decide what each paragraph or section is trying to achieve. Ask questions that encourage students to decide. For example:
  — What information has been included in this paragraph?
  — What is this part of the text telling us? e.g. **This part tells us where the animal lives.**
  — Why has the author included this section?
- As students decide on the label for each paragraph, attach that label to the sample text.

Step 2: Language Features

Once the framework is identified, provide time for students to discuss the language features in the sample text. Students will require a great deal of support to identify the language features and use the metalanguage needed to discuss concepts such as verbs, nouns, pronouns and signal words.

- Ask questions that encourage students to explore the language features of the text form. For example:
  — What adjectives are used?
  — What tense is the text written in?
  — What linking words are used?
- Attach labels of the language features to the sample text.

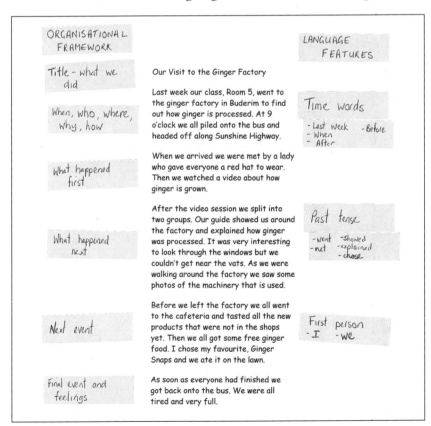

Figure 1.14 A Retell with Organisational Framework and Language Features Labelled

Multi-Text Model

The Multi-Text Model of analysing involves students working with more than one sample of the chosen text form. Students are asked to rank samples of the text form in terms of effectiveness. Students then use the information from their discussions about the rankings to devise 'rules' and a framework for writing the selected form.

Step 1: Ranking

Provide students with up to four samples of the selected text form. For the sake of comparison, it is helpful if the sample texts are about the same topic.

- Discuss the purpose of the text form and the possible audience.
- Read or have students read each sample.
- Provide time for students to individually rank the samples in order, from most effective to least effective.
- Have students work in small groups to discuss their rankings, and to reach consensus about the order. Groups then record the reasons for their choices.
- Record each group's rankings.

Step 2: Justification of Ranking

- Direct students' attention to the text that was ranked as the least effective. Elicit reasons why this text was ranked as the least effective; record students' responses.
- Repeat; this time direct students' attention to the text that was ranked as the most effective. Elicit and record students' reasons for this ranking of this text.

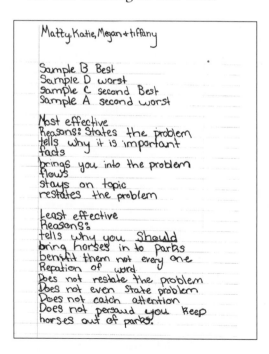

Figure 1.15 Sample Ranking and Justifications

Step 3: Language Features

• Provide time for students to discuss the key language features of the text that was ranked most effective.

• Record the key language features with the justification information above.

Step 4: Create Rules

• Provide time for each group to re-read the information they have collated, and to devise a set of 'rules' for writing the selected text form.

• Invite groups to share their 'rules', then combine the rules to create a class reference chart.

There are probably inaccuracies in students' 'rules' at this stage of the process, but the 'rules' only need to be specific enough to support them in their future attempts at creating the text form. Extend, refine and replace the rules as the students' understanding of the text form develops.

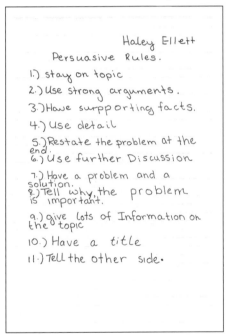

Figure 1.16 Sample of Rules for Writing a Persuasive Text

Modelling

Students will need several demonstrations on how to construct a text using the framework or rules they 'discovered'. Effective modelling should be explicit, have a clear focus and include targeted Think-Aloud statements that provide students with an insight into how proficient writers use frameworks to write. By using the practice of modelling to demonstrate a new framework, teachers are able to articulate what is happening inside their head. Thinking aloud is a vital part of modelling.

The Modelled Writing procedure allows students to observe and clarify their knowledge and understandings of the framework. Before expecting students to apply their new learning, make sure that they have been actively involved in several demonstrations on how to use the framework.

Modelling sessions need to be carefully planned and thought out. It is more effective to think through what needs to be modelled and where in the text that might happen, than to make spontaneous comments as the text is being written.

Display the texts composed during modelling sessions; this will allow students to use them as examples when they are composing their own texts.

Sharing

Follow the analysing and modelling sessions with many sharing sessions, as sharing the accomplishment of a writing task is a cooperative and supportive way of engaging students. These sessions typically follow the procedure of Shared or Interactive Writing.

During the sharing sessions, it's critical that teachers continue to choose one specific focus to highlight.

Guiding

Guiding is a teaching practice that involves the teacher explicitly scaffolding a writing task. Guiding sessions provide continued support for students during their early stages of controlling a new form of text. The student maintains control, but is able to request assistance at any point.

Support for students can be provided in a number of ways:
- Allowing students to work with others to compose a text.
- Providing planning formats.
- Breaking the task into manageable parts.
- Providing practice on specific elements relevant to the form.
- Providing strategic assistance at key points.
- Creating opportunities to practise different forms across learning areas. Teachers can consider which learning areas might provide suitable contexts for writing different forms. A sample 'Writing Across Learning Areas' planning format is provided on the *First Steps Writing* CD-ROM.

Applying

Applying refers to the context and purpose of writing. Such writing tasks are whole and focused, with a purpose and audience, and generally involve the student independently creating texts and making ongoing decisions. During Independent Writing time, students have the opportunity to apply and manipulate what they have learnt about text forms to suit different purposes and audiences. Access to teacher advice is not denied, but neither is it planned or structured in a way that indicates reliance.

The ultimate goal is for students to function in society as literate individuals who can use writing to communicate their ideas, share information, stimulate thinking, formulate questions and influence policy and action.

Social Purpose: Writing to Describe

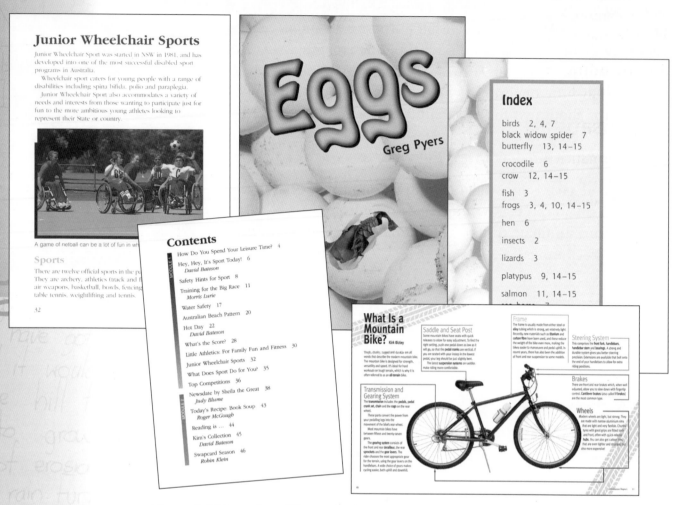

Figure 1.17 Samples of Texts Used to Describe

Understanding Texts That Describe

In texts that describe, information is systematically organised and recorded to classify and describe a whole class of things, e.g. computers, lions, Life on the Victorian Goldfields. Texts that describe can be text forms in their own right, such as reports, menus or travel brochures. They can also be part of other overall texts, e.g. indexes, glossaries, labels, descriptions and contents pages.

The following information is usually included in texts used to describe.

1 Classification or Generalisation

This may take the form of a heading, e.g. **Main Courses**, or a definition of the subject, e.g. **Computers are programmable electronic devices.** This part of the text can also refer to the specific topic to be described, e.g. **Lions are one of the many carnivorous mammals that inhabit the plains of Africa.**

2 Description

Provides a detailed description of various components of the topic. These components are sequenced in a specific way, depending on the text topic.

3 Concluding or Summarising Statements

May include an impersonal evaluative comment.

Organisational Frameworks

The information above is included in most texts used to describe; however, the organisational framework used to construct each text will vary, depending on the form and topic.

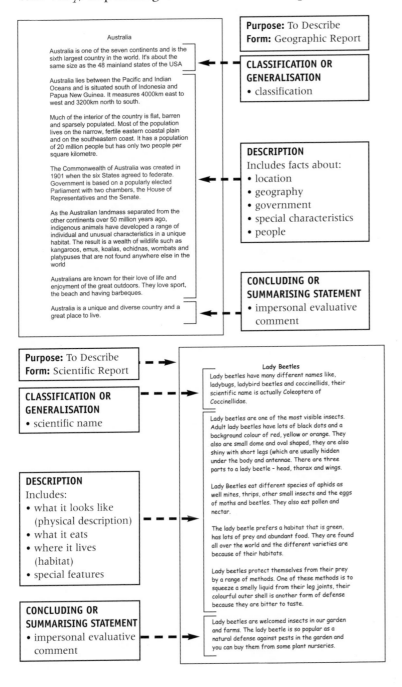

Purpose: To Describe
Form: Geographic Report

CLASSIFICATION OR GENERALISATION
• classification

DESCRIPTION
Includes facts about:
• location
• geography
• government
• special characteristics
• people

CONCLUDING OR SUMMARISING STATEMENT
• impersonal evaluative comment

Australia

Australia is one of the seven continents and is the sixth largest country in the world. It's about the same size as the 48 mainland states of the USA

Australia lies between the Pacific and Indian Oceans and is situated south of Indonesia and Papua New Guinea. It measures 4000km east to west and 3200km north to south.

Much of the interior of the country is flat, barren and sparsely populated. Most of the population lives on the narrow, fertile eastern coastal plain and on the southeastern coast. It has a population of 20 million people but has only two people per square kilometre.

The Commonwealth of Australia was created in 1901 when the six States agreed to federate. Government is based on a popularly elected Parliament with two chambers, the House of Representatives and the Senate.

As the Australian landmass separated from the other continents over 50 million years ago, indigenous animals have developed a range of individual and unusual characteristics in a unique habitat. The result is a wealth of wildlife such as kangaroos, emus, koalas, echidnas, wombats and platypuses that are not found anywhere else in the world

Australians are known for their love of life and enjoyment of the great outdoors. They love sport, the beach and having barbeques.

Australia is a unique and diverse country and a great place to live.

Purpose: To Describe
Form: Scientific Report

CLASSIFICATION OR GENERALISATION
• scientific name

DESCRIPTION
Includes:
• what it looks like (physical description)
• what it eats
• where it lives (habitat)
• special features

CONCLUDING OR SUMMARISING STATEMENT
• impersonal evaluative comment

Lady Beetles

Lady beetles have many different names like, ladybugs, ladybird beetles and coccinellids, their scientific name is actually Coleoptera of Coccinellidae.

Lady beetles are one of the most visible insects. Adult lady beetles have lots of black dots and a background colour of red, yellow or orange. They also are small dome and oval shaped, they are also shiny with short legs (which are usually hidden under the body and antennae. There are three parts to a lady beetle – head, thorax and wings.

Lady Beetles eat different species of aphids as well mites, thrips, other small insects and the eggs of moths and beetles. They also eat pollen and nectar.

The lady beetle prefers a habitat that is green, has lots of prey and abundant food. They are found all over the world and the different varieties are because of their habitats.

Lady beetles protect themselves from their prey by a range of methods. One of these methods is to squeeze a smelly liquid from their leg joints, their colourful outer shell is another form of defense because they are bitter to taste.

Lady beetles are welcomed insects in our garden and farms. The lady beetle is so popular as a natural defense against pests in the garden and you can buy them from some plant nurseries.

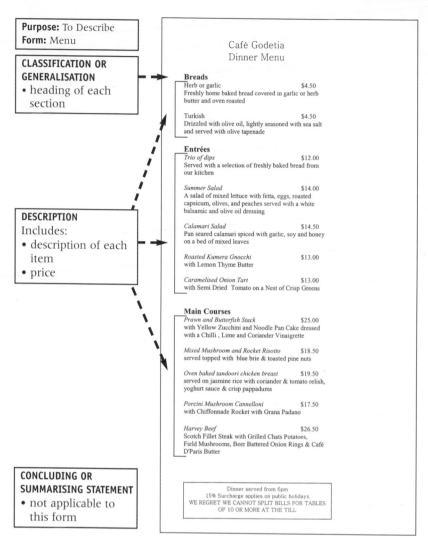

Figure 1.18 Framework Samples from Texts Used to Describe

Language Features

Texts used to describe usually include these language features:

- Nouns and pronouns that refer to generalised participants, e.g. lions, computers, they, it.
- Timeless present tense, e.g. are, have, exists, grows.
- Action verbs (behaviours), e.g. runs, hunts, erupts.
- Adjectives that are factual and precise, e.g. 5.6 megabytes, sandy coloured.
- Technical vocabulary, e.g. marsupials, monotremes, information processing system.
- Formal objective style, i.e. first-person pronouns and the writer's opinions are not generally appropriate.
- Signal words for classifying, defining, comparing and contrasting, e.g. are called, belong to, are similar to, are more powerful than.

Adapted from Derewianka, B. (1990)

Assessing Writing to Describe

Students are in the stage where they display most of the bulleted points.

Beginning Stage	Developing Stage	Consolidating Stage	Extending Stage
Can state the purpose and audience of texts to be composed and includes basic organisational features of simple forms used to describe.	Is aware of the purpose and audience when composing texts and uses a partial organisational framework of a small range of forms used to describe.	Considers the purpose and audience to select specific vocabulary and uses appropriate organisational frameworks to compose a variety of forms used to describe.	Crafts forms used to describe by selecting vocabulary and manipulating organisational frameworks to suit the context of the writing event.
The writer: • shares information about a known topic • writes an observation and comment • focuses on a specific part of a whole class of things, e.g. 'My cat eats meat' not 'Cats eat meat'. • describes features that are not necessarily important or relevant • groups similar information together • writes a concluding statement that is a personal comment rather than a summary, e.g. I like cats. • uses personal or subjective language, e.g. 'I really like. . .' • uses simple vocabulary. e.g. big, little • uses a limited range of signal words, e.g. and	The writer: • provides limited factual information about a given topic • uses a limited range of forms and formats, e.g. report, chart • introduces the topic by providing a classification that may lack precision, e.g. Dogs are animals. • gives limited general information, e.g. size, colour, habitat • includes information under headings • writes a concluding statement with some attempt to summarise what has been written • is beginning to use objective language • uses some technical or subject-specific vocabulary • is beginning to use timeless present tense e.g. are, hunt • uses simple words to signal compare and contrast, e.g. like, as big as…	The writer: • provides detailed factual information about a given topic • uses a variety of forms and formats, e.g. description, slide show, encyclopaedia entry • introduces the topic by providing a precise classification or generalisation • includes details that are clearly related to the topic and elaborates on special features • groups related information into paragraphs introduced by a topic sentence • writes a summary or concluding paragraph that reiterates the key points and may include an evaluative comment, e.g. This invention will change the course of history. • maintains objective language throughout • uses technical and subject-specific vocabulary appropriately • uses timeless present tense, e.g. fly, live, suckle • uses appropriate signal words to compare, contrast, define and classify, e.g. are similar to, belong to	The writer: • provides information that is selected, sorted and synthesised • adapts forms and formats for a target audience • writes an introduction that successfully classifies or generalises information essential to the subject or topic • includes detailed information selected because of its relevance to the subject or topic • organises information into paragraphs that link cohesively to compose a coherent text • writes a concluding paragraph that accurately summarises the main points • uses formal objective style to suit purpose and audience, e.g. humanity faces increasing. . ., the family is. . . • chooses precise technical and subject specific language to suit purpose and audience, e.g. carnivorous, mammals, pollutants • maintains consistent use of tense throughout • writes cohesively using a wide range of signal words to compare, contrast, define and classify. e.g. more powerful than, nevertheless
Familiarising, Analysing, Modelling, Sharing, Guiding and Applying See pages 30–37 and 43–45		Familiarising, Analysing, Modelling, Sharing, Guiding and Applying See pages 30–37 and 46–47	

Focus on Assessing

Focus on Teaching

Figure 1.19 Assessment Guide for Writing to Describe

Supporting Students at the Tuning-In Stage

This section provides ideas for supporting students who have not yet reached the Beginning stage on the Writing to Describe Assessment Guide (Figure 1.19).

Focus on building students' awareness of the language features and organisational frameworks of the form being introduced. The following familiarising activities are suited to any form associated with writing to describe.

1 Sample Displays see page 31

2 Reading with and Reading to Students see page 31

3 Literacy Activities

- Provide plenty of oral language activities. Give students opportunities to focus on the language used to describe the attributes of objects, e.g. Show and Tell, Barrier Games, picture talks. Encourage students to consider questions such as:

— What is it called?   — What does it do?
— What kind of thing is it?   — What special features does it have?
— What does it look like?   — What is it similar to?
— What noise does it make?   — What is it different from?
— Where is it found?

- Work together to build descriptive Word Webs around familiar topics, e.g. **chickens**.

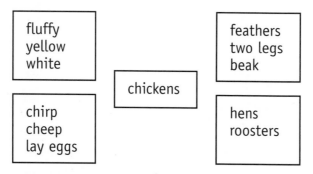

Figure 1.20 Sample Word Web

- Play oral games, such as Who Am I?, What Am I?, I Spy, True or False. Each game involves one student orally describing a person or object, while other students try to guess who or what is being described.
- Focus students' attention on the language used to describe people, characters, objects and places when the class is reading literary and informational texts. Discuss words that indicate who or what is being described. Record the descriptive words on a chart for future reference.

- Create meaningful contexts for displaying models of texts used to describe, e.g. a science table with labelled exhibits, labels on storage cupboards, descriptions of each student in the classroom.
- Play Definition Games where students are challenged to match technical and subject-specific vocabulary to definitions, e.g. an animal that suckles its young — mammal.

Supporting Students at the Beginning and Developing Stages

The main focus for these students is to help them understand the purpose, organisation, structure and language features of the text form being introduced.

Modelling and Sharing

The following modelling and sharing suggestions are separated into two stages; the first is specific to the Beginning Stage, and the second is more relevant to students in the Developing Stage. However, the suggestions should be seen as cumulative. When selecting a focus for the Developing Stage, teachers should also consider what is listed in the previous stage.

Beginning Stage	Developing Stage
Focus on understandings of text organisation, structure and language features. During Modelled, Shared and Interactive writing sessions demonstrate how to:	
• collect information about a chosen topic	• select information appropriate to the audience
• decide on appropriate headings to organise the text	• include details that are relevant to the topic and audience
• sort information under headings, e.g. food, habitat, appearance, offspring	• select special features and elaborate on them
• introduce the topic	• introduce the topic by providing a precise classification or generalisation
• write a concluding statement that summarises the key points	• list references used
• use objective language	• choose language that is objective
• use subject specific and technical vocabulary to provide more specific information, e.g. A kangaroo is a marsupial.	• include illustrations and diagrams to enhance the writing, e.g. tables, graphs, charts, maps
• use signal words that compare and contrast	• use signal words that compare, contrast, define and classify
• use timeless present tense, e.g. The Dall Porpoise has small flippers.	• combine paragraphs to build a description of the topic.

Figure 1.21 Suggested Focus for Modelling and Sharing Sessions

Guiding

The following guided-practice activities are suitable for students in the Beginning and Developing Stages, allowing them to build their understandings about texts used to describe. Each activity should be used in a meaningful context across different learning areas.

Word Webs

Have students construct Word Webs when they are collating facts or key words about a topic. Provide opportunities for students to take related facts and make them into one or more sentences.

Building Vocabulary

Have students brainstorm adjectives, technical terms and subject-specific vocabulary related to the current topic. Display these words in the classroom so that students can use them as a reference.

What Do You Want to Know?

Have students list everything they want to know about a specific topic, leaving a line between each item on their list. Invite them to share their list with a partner or small group to gather further suggestions. Have students cut their lists into strips, organise them into categories, then create a suitable heading for each category, e.g. habitat, lifestyle, what it looks like. Students can then use their personalised frameworks as a springboard for writing.

Guess What?

Students write several sentences to describe a common object, e.g. This object was invented by Alexander Graham Bell as a means of communication. In recent times they have become multimedia tools, allowing photos to be taken. Encourage them to use detailed descriptions and subject-specific language. Students then swap with a partner who attempts to identify the object described.

Ask the Expert

Invite an expert to visit your classroom and speak on a topic that is being studied, e.g. the zoo keeper in charge of orang-utans. Have students prepare their questions prior to the talk to ensure that the expert provides the information they want to know. This activity could also be used with individual students acting as the 'expert' in an area of interest.

Fact and Opinion

Provide small groups of students with a list of facts and opinions about a specific topic. Have students discuss whether each written statement is a fact or an opinion. Encourage students to identify the vocabulary that indicates the difference.

Reporting the Essentials

Read students a text that describes facts about a topic being studied. Have students record the key facts in diagrammatic form, e.g. Venn diagram, tree diagram, mapping. Students can then use their diagrams as springboards for writing, or as a stimulus for further investigation of the topic.

Technical Terms

Students brainstorm a list of technical terms and subject-specific words related to a chosen topic, then find definitions for any words they don't know. Encourage them to use the list-words in their writing.

Referencing

Have students reference any texts they refer to in researching their topic. Listing the author and the text title may be sufficient at the Beginning and Developing Stages.

Glossary

Have students choose subject-specific words or technical terms related to the current topic of study and use them to construct a class glossary. Have students write their definitions of the terms, then use references to find out if their definition is correct or needs amending. Correct words and definitions can then be added to the class glossary for future reference.

Across Learning Areas

Provide across learning areas opportunities for students to compose texts used to describe, e.g.

Health and Physical Education	Menu of healthy foods.
Society and Environment	Report about a country.
Technology and Enterprise	Labelled diagram of a model.
Science	Scientific report about animals.
The Arts	Contents page for a text on musical instruments.

Supporting Students at the Consolidating and Extending Stages

The main focus for these students is to help them to enhance their control over the text form, including their ability to adapt and manipulate the text.

Modelling and Sharing

When selecting a focus for the Consolidating and Extending Stages, teachers should also consider what is listed in previous stages.

Focus on continuing to build students' understandings of text organisation, structure and language features, by demonstrating how to:
- organise information to form a coherent text
- write a concluding paragraph that accurately summarises the main points
- include references when appropriate
- include texts such as a table of contents, index or glossary within other texts
- maintain consistent use of tense
- add illustrations, photographs, diagrams and labels that match and enhance the writing
- select technical and subject-specific language appropriate to the audience
- use objective language appropriate to the audience.

Guiding

The following guided-practice activities are suitable for students in the Consolidating and Extending Stages, to further develop their understandings about texts used to describe. Each activity should be used in a meaningful context across different learning areas.

Vocabulary Development

Have students brainstorm vocabulary related to a specific topic. Provide time for students to separate their words into subject-specific language, e.g. **primrose**, and everyday language, e.g. **flower**. Encourage them to research technical terms for selected words, e.g. **genus Primula**.

A Picture is Worth 1000 Words

Have students look at a range of texts used to describe. Discuss how photographs, illustrations, diagrams and maps have been included to enhance the text. Encourage students to refine their own writing by adding illustrations, photographs, maps or diagrams.

Rapid Research

Invite small groups of students to select a topic of interest, e.g. Sydney Harbour Bridge, mountain bikes. Encourage groups to gather as many facts as they can in an allotted time, then have each group report their findings to the class. Later, have students use the assembled facts as the basis for writing texts that describe.

Who is the Audience?

Provide students with a text used to describe, e.g. a report. Ask students to read the text and discuss who is the intended audience. Jointly highlight those words that indicate the intended audience. Allocate a new audience to each small group and provide time for them to make necessary changes, e.g. add more details, simplify the language. Have each group share their new audience and their new text with the class.

Add the Missing Piece

Select an appropriate text used to describe, then delete the conclusion or introduction. Have students work in small groups to compose the missing piece. Provide time for students to compare the piece they have written with other students' 'missing pieces' and with the original text.

Citing References

Provide opportunities for students to discover how various information sources are referenced in different ways e.g. website, journal article, book. Encourage students to cite their references when they create texts.

Across Learning Areas

Provide opportunities across learning areas for students to compose texts used to describe, e.g.

Society and Environment	Description of a landform.
Technology and Enterprise	Index for a report about robots.
Mathematics	Glossary to describe mathematical terms.
Science	Description of a specific plant.
The Arts	Report on a period in art history.

Social Purpose: Writing to Entertain — Poetry

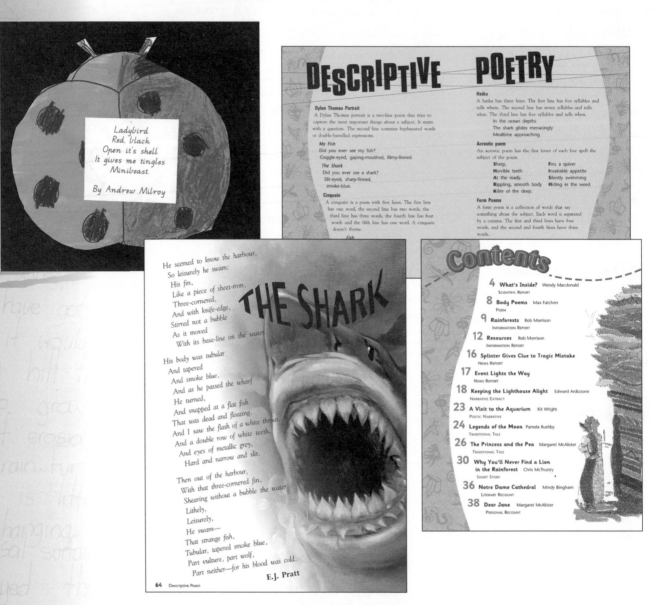

Figure 1.22 Samples of Poetry Texts Used to Entertain

Understanding Texts That Entertain — Poetry

Fiction is a generic term given to a range of texts that seek to entertain the reader, and includes poetry and prose. Poetry is a way of manipulating and arranging words to create unique perspectives of the world. The writer (or poet) combines words and images in order to share personal thoughts and feelings about a subject.

Lines of poetry are usually short and concise. Writing poetry requires the writer to be selective in choosing words that capture their intended meaning.

Poetry, in its broadest sense, cannot be described in generic terms, even though some poems conform to specific structures, such as haiku, limericks, cinquains and sonnets. The variation possible in the organisation and structure of a poem is part of the essence of poetry.

Organisational Frameworks

There are many different forms of poetry, and each form has its own distinctive organisational framework. The following examples provide a snapshot of some of the most common forms.

Haiku

A Haiku is a form of Japanese poetry consisting of three lines. Each line has a specific number of syllables.

1st line: 5 syllables, and tells *where*

2nd line: 7 syllables, and tells *what*

3rd line: 5 syllables, and tells *when*

Lantern Poem

This five-line poem is written in the shape of a Japanese lantern. Each line is limited by a specific number of syllables.

1st line: 1 syllable

2nd line: 2 syllables

3rd line: 3 syllables

4th line: 4 syllables

5th line: 1 syllable

Cinquain

A cinquain is a poem derived from the haiku and tanka forms. It consists of five lines, each with a specific number of words. A cinquain doesn't rhyme.

1st line: one word (title)

2nd line: two adjectives

3rd line: three verbs

4th line: 4 words to describe a feeling

5th line: one word (refers to the title)

List Poem

As the name suggests, a list poem is a list of items written down the page. These can be lists of single items, lists of phrases or a combination of both. These poems can be rhymed or unrhymed.

Acrostic Poems

In this form of poetry, the letters of the topic are written vertically. Each letter of the topic word therefore forms the first letter of the word beginning each line. Some acrostic poems use only single words for each line while others use a phrase. Acrostic poems can be rhymed or unrhymed.

Figure 1.23 A Sample of Poetry Frameworks

Diamantes

A diamond poem usually consists of seven lines. Lines one and seven are antonyms.

1st line: a one-word noun

2nd line: two adjectives to describe the noun

3rd line: three verbs that the noun does

4th line: four nouns that are things that the noun in line 1 and the noun in line 7 both have

5th line: three verbs that the noun in line 7 does

6th line: two adjectives that describe the noun in line 7

7th line: a one-word noun that is the opposite of line 1.

Limerick

A limerick is a humorous poem of five lines. The poem is constrained by both the rhythm and the rhyme.

In a limerick, the first and second lines rhyme. The third and fourth lines (which are shorter than the first two) rhyme, and the fifth line rhymes with lines one and two. This is called an AABBA rhyming pattern.

Most limericks are also constrained by syllabic structures. For example:

1st line: 9 syllables

2nd line: 9 syllables

3rd line: 5 syllables

4th line: 5 syllables

5th line: 9 syllables

Sonnet

A sonnet is a poem of fourteen lines. The English or Shakespearean sonnet begins with three quatrains and finishes with a couplet. The rhyming pattern is usually ABABCDCDEFEFGG.

Most sonnets have a definite rhythm.

Free Verse

Free verse has no set conventions for punctuation or structure. These poems need not rhyme or have a distinctive rhythm. The lines need not scan or conform to any pattern. Words used should be those that evoke strong images, moods and emotions.

Couplets and Triplets

Couplets and triplets are, respectively, two- and three-line poems. In this type of poetry, the lines rhyme and contain the same number of syllables, or have the same metre.

Tanka

A tanka is a form of Japanese poetry that consists of five lines, each line constrained by a specific number of syllables.

1st line: 5 syllables

2nd line: 7 syllables

3rd line: 5 syllables

4th line: 7 syllables

5th line: 7 syllables

Concrete (Shape) Poems

These poems use words and the physical formation of those words to convey meaning. This may be done with colour, the shape of the letters or the arrangement of the words. The meaning of the poem can be enhanced by manipulating the size, direction and placement of words and lines.

Villanelle	Clerihew
A Villanelle is a French poem that consists of 19 lines, arranged in six stanzas. The first five stanzas contain three lines and rhyme in the pattern ABA. The sixth stanza consists of a quatrain with a rhyming pattern of ABAA. In addition to the rhyming pattern, the first and third lines alternatively repeat throughout the poem, and are repeated as the last two lines of the final quatrain.	Named after the British writer, Edmund Clerihew Bentley, these short humorous verses consist of two rhyming couplets. Clerihews are written about people and the person's name generally serves as one of the rhymes. The first line usually ends with the person's name. The second line ends with a word that rhymes with the name.

Quatrain

A quatrain is a poem of four lines that rhymes in one of four ways. The rhyming patterns for a quatrain are: AABB, ABAB, ABCB or ABBA.

Figure 1.23 Samples of Poetry Frameworks

Language Features

Texts used to entertain through poetry usually include the following language features:

- Nouns and verbs that refer to specific objects, events, emotions, things or actions.
- Adjectives and adverbs that are more imaginative than factual and precise, e.g. glistening, harmonious, rebelliously.
- Literary devices such as:
— alliteration: the repetition of consonant sounds, usually at the beginning of words, to create effect
— assonance: the repetition of vowel sounds, e.g. Ousted from the house …
— onomatopoeia: words that sound like the item being described
— imagery: the creation of likenesses through order and word choice
— simile: comparison of two items, made explicit by using 'as' or 'like'
— metaphor: an implicit comparison between two items that are not normally connected
— personification: using human characteristics to describe abstract concepts and natural phenomena
— hyperbole: an obvious exaggeration used for effect
— symbolism: symbols used to represent feelings or objects
— rhetorical question: a question to which an answer is not expected
— rhyme: words that match in sound
— rhythm: the beat represented by stressed and unstressed syllables
— repetition: repeating words and phrases for effect.

Assessing Writing to Entertain—Poetry

Students are in the stage where they display most of the bulleted points.

Beginning Stage	Developing Stage	Consolidating Stage	Extending Stage
Can state the purpose and audience of texts to be composed and includes basic organisational features of simple forms used to entertain through poetry.	Is aware of the purpose and audience when composing texts and uses a partial organisational framework of a small range of forms used to entertain through poetry.	Considers the purpose and audience to select specific vocabulary and uses appropriate organisational frameworks to compose a variety of forms used to entertain through poetry.	Crafts forms used to entertain through poetry by selecting vocabulary and manipulating organisational frameworks to suit the context of the writing event.
The writer:	The writer:	The writer:	The writer:
• writes simple poems that innovate on a given structure	• writes simple rhyming and non-rhyming poems often choosing inappropriate words for the context	• writes using structure of poetry without regard for personal voice	• writes a range of poetic forms expressing complex concepts in creative ways
• innovates on a given pattern, e.g. I like…, I like…, I like.	• experiments with a range of known poetry forms, e.g. rhyming couplets, free verse	• writes poetry in a range of forms, e.g. haiku, cinquains, shape poems, limerick, rap	• writes poetry in a range of complex forms, e.g. ballads, sonnets, odes
• chooses words based on personal choice	• is beginning to observe structural constraints of different types of poetry, e.g. rhyming couplets have two lines	• knows and adheres to structural constraints when necessary, e.g. syllable patterns in cinquains, haiku	• chooses whether to conform or manipulate structure for effect and impact
• attempts to use simple literary devices, such as alliteration	• is beginning to select appropriate words to convey meaning	• selects specific words to enhance meaning, e.g. specific nouns, appropriate adjectives and adverbs	• selects words that vividly and precisely convey images, feelings, mood and tone
• gives missing rhyming word to complete a simple rhyme, e.g. I saw a fish, sitting on a	• begins to use some literary devices, although they may not be appropriate for the context	• uses literary devices although they may seem contrived	• chooses to use a wide range of literary devices, e.g. metaphor, simile
	• when appropriate, uses a simple rhyming pattern, e.g. rhyming couplets, ABAB pattern	• when appropriate, uses an explicit rhyming pattern that has been explored, e.g. limerick	• writes using complex rhyming patterns but chooses to be freed from the constraints of rhyme when necessary
	• is unable to maintain rhythmic pattern in own poetry	• chooses known rhythmic patterns to compose own poetry	• creates rhythmic patterns for effect, e.g. words sounding like a horse galloping

Focus on Assessing

Focus on Teaching

Familiarising, Analysing, Modelling, Sharing, Guiding and Applying
See pages 30–37 and 54–57

Familiarising, Analysing, Modelling, Sharing, Guiding and Applying
See pages 30–37 and 58–60

Figure 1.24 Assessment Guide for Assessing Writing to Entertain — Poetry

Supporting Students at the Tuning-In Stage

This section provides ideas to support students who have not yet reached the Beginning stage on the Writing to Entertain — Poetry Assessment Guide (Figure 1.24).

Focus on building students' awareness of the language features and organisational frameworks of the form being introduced. The following familiarising activities are suited to any form associated with writing to entertain—poetry.

1 Sample Displays see page 31

2 Reading to and Reading with Students see page 31

3 Literacy Activities
- Provide opportunities for students to read and recite rhymes, poems, raps and chants.
- Encourage students to create actions to accompany familiar rhymes.
- Encourage students to retell or recite favourite poems for a variety of audiences.
- Encourage students to join in with familiar parts or repetitive refrains from known poems.
- Provide opportunities for students to reconstruct poems that have been cut into individual stanzas. Invite them to share their reasoning behind the final order.
- Talk about the purpose of writing poetry.
- Display charts of poems in the classroom. Model how to use these charts as a resource, and provide opportunities to read the poem charts on a regular basis.
- Provide opportunities for students to prepare Readers' Theatre for a familiar poem.
- Have a class poetry festival. Invite students to display or recite their favourite poems.
- Encourage students to explore patterns of rhyme and rhythm by reading poetry aloud. Discuss the difference between rhyme and rhythm.
- Invite a poet to visit the classroom and read their poetry.
- Listen to poems on tape, CD or Internet sites.
- Highlight some of the literary devices used by poets.
- Involve students in brainstorming and charting descriptive words to describe unique characteristics of objects, events, people or feelings.
- Introduce students to the terminology of poetry. This could include generic terms such as rhyme, rhythm and alliteration, or specific terms such as haiku, limerick and cinquain.

- Have students create word association webs, e.g. sky: planes, clouds, rain, wind, flight, azure, clear, up and away
- Jointly create and display collections of interesting words, such as:
  — words starting with the same sound
  — words ending with the same sound
  — words that describe the senses
  — words that sound interesting, e.g. shemozzle, murmur, smidgin
  — words for special purposes, e.g. people words, country words, happy words
  — words that are various parts of speech.
- Write a familiar poem or rhyme on a chart. Invite students to identify words in the poem that could be replaced, then work together to brainstorm a list of 'replacement' words. Write the replacement words on cards and store them in a container near the chart. Provide time for students to compose new poems by placing replacement word cards over some of the poem's original words. Read the new poem aloud.
- Play word games and activities that use rhyme, e.g. Snap, Bingo, Fish, Concentration.
- Involve students in activities to develop an awareness of rhythm, such as:
  — using students' names to clap out syllables
  — using percussion instruments to tap out the rhythm when singing or reciting familiar rhymes
  — using physical responses to demonstrate the rhythm, e.g. snapping fingers, clapping, stomping feet.
- Involve students in text innovations involving familiar or favourite poems.
- Compile students' favourite rhymes to make a class big book; encourage students to read the book for pleasure.

Supporting Students at the Beginning and Developing Stages

The main focus for these students is to help them understand the purpose, organisation, structure and language features of the text form being introduced.

Modelling and Sharing

The following modelling and sharing suggestions are separated into two stages; the first is specific to the Beginning Stage, and the second is more relevant to students in the Developing Stage. However, the suggestions should be seen as cumulative. When selecting a focus for the Developing Stage, teachers should also consider what is listed in the previous stage.

Beginning Stage	Developing Stage
Focus on understandings of text organisation, structure and language features. During Modelled, Shared and Interactive writing sessions, demonstrate how to:	
• write structured poetry, e.g. cinquain, acrostic	• write a range of poetry, e.g. tanka, haiku
• write rhyming patterns, e.g. couplets	• use more sophisticated rhyming patterns, e.g. limerick, quatrains
• write free verse	• apply the structural constraints when writing different forms of poetry, e.g. lantern poems have five lines
• create the 'message' or meaning of the poem rather than the mechanics	• choose specific words to enhance meaning
• generate rhyming words	• use literary devices, e.g. onomatopoeia
• select appropriate words to convey meaning	• write rhythmic patterns

Figure 1.25 Suggested Focus for Modelling and Sharing Sessions

Guiding

The following guided-practice activities are suitable for students in the Beginning and Developing Stages, allowing them to build their understandings about texts used to entertain through poetry. Each activity should be used in a meaningful context across different learning areas.

The Minister's Cat

During this game, each player repeats a sentence stem, '*The minister's cat is a … cat and his/her name is …*'. The first student begins with the letter A, adding an adjective to the first space in the sentence and adding a name for the cat to the second space, e.g. 'The Minister's cat is an angry cat and his name is Anthony'. The next student repeats the sentence stem but adds words that begin with the letter B, e.g. 'The Minister's cat is a beautiful cat and her name is Bonny'. (This is not a memorisation game, so there's no need for students to repeat the previous sentence.) The game continues until either a student is unable to add a word beginning with their letter, or all the letters of the alphabet have been used. Allow some creativity when students are adding words beginning with X, e.g. EX-ceptional, EX-traordinary.

Alphabet Books

Write each letter of the alphabet on a separate slip of paper, then put the slips into a container. Have students work in pairs. Each pair selects a letter, then composes a sentence for 'their' letter. For example, D is a dandelion wavering in the gentle breeze. Or a sentence for R: Red roses ramble over the roof. Collate the sentences to form a class alphabet book. As a variation, change the audience, e.g. an alphabet book for younger students, car enthusiasts or football fanatics.

Secret Sentences

Provide students with a sentence pattern that lists only the parts of speech, e.g. adjective, adjective, noun, verb, adverb, adjective, noun. Give out recording sheets that have a column for each part of speech (i.e. six parts of speech = six columns). Students work in small groups to brainstorm four or five words for the first part of speech, and write these in the first column of the recording sheet. They then fold back the paper to hide the words they've written in the first column and brainstorm words for the second column. Students continue in this way until they have filled all the columns. Students then unfold the entire recording sheet and read out the sentences, reading across the page. Allow some minor modifications at this stage, to ensure that the sentences are properly constructed. Leave sentences with wacky content, as these usually appeal to the students.

Sensory Experiences

Provide students with a sensory stimulus, e.g. piece of music, different smells, and have students list all the thoughts that come into their mind during that sensory experience. Emphasise that certain words students list may trigger other word associations, and this is quite acceptable. After a specified time, have students stop writing and read back over their list of words. They could use their listed words to compose a poem using free verse or a known structure.

First Liners

Students often have difficulty in starting to write a poem. Provide several first lines and have students complete the line by providing the action and elaborating on the details. Make sure that students have a choice of opening lines, as they will inevitably be inspired to go in different directions. Encourage students to add other thoughts so that the finished writing looks more like a poem and less like a single sentence.

Possible opening lines:

A willy-wagtail darted …	Did you ever see … ?
When I came home …	I am me, and I …
Have you ever tasted … ?	The wind blew …
The dog growled …	My favourite …

Alliteration

Students often enjoy making up tongue twisters. However, there are other forms of alliterative verse they might enjoy writing. Give students a first line (see above) and have them complete the line by adding alliterative words. Have students brainstorm a list of alliterative words before they start writing; this frees them to concentrate on choosing the best combination of words, e.g.

Have you ever seen
green grasshoppers making the most of summer?
beautiful butterflies hovering?

Text Innovation

Many poems lend themselves to text innovation. Provide time for students to innovate on poems by replacing words but keeping a given structure or rhythmic pattern.

Across Learning Areas

Provide opportunities across learning areas for students to compose texts used to entertain through poetry, e.g.

English	Limerick about a character.
Society and Environment	Free verse about an historical event.
Physical Education	Diamante about a sporting hero.
The Arts	Acrostic about a painter.

Supporting Students at the Consolidating and Extending Stages

The main focus for these students is to help them to enhance their control over the text form, including their ability to adapt and manipulate the text.

Modelling and Sharing

When selecting a focus for the Consolidating and Extending Stages, teachers should also consider what is listed in previous stages.

Focus on continuing to build students' understandings of text organisation, structure and language features, by demonstrating how to:

• write more complex rhyming poetry. e.g. villanelle
• write structured poetry, e.g. sonnets
• write free verse
• write alternative rhymes, e.g. end rhyme, internal rhyme
• use vocabulary to convey images, feelings, mood and tone
• use rhythmic patterns for effect
• refine poetry by choosing the most effective words
• use literary devices to create specific effects, e.g. metaphor, simile, alliteration, assonance, personification, onomatopoeia.

Guiding

The following guided-practice activities are suitable for students in the Consolidating and Extending Stages, to further develop their understandings about texts used to entertain through poetry. Each activity should be used in a meaningful context across different learning areas.

Text Innovation

Continue providing opportunities for students to innovate on familiar poetic forms. Innovating on a known text allows students to concentrate on the selection of words, without also having to think about poetic structure.

Concrete Concepts

Poetry often deals with abstract concepts, such as nature, devotion and beauty. These are concepts that are difficult for students to write about without becoming vague and ambiguous. Instead, have students write a paragraph that focuses on the concrete details associated with the concept. For example, if students were writing about nature they could describe the sunset, the size of a tree, the colour of the tree's leaves, and any noises heard. Later, they could take some of their written images and arrange them to form a poem.

Something Different

This activity involves finding different ways to look at a familiar item. Choose something familiar, such as a rock, then have students think about different ways of describing it, e.g.

The Rock
a glass breaker
a crystal holder
a rainbow of colours
a hefty weight
worn to a grain of sand.

Prepositional Poetry *(Brownjohn 1994)*

Discuss prepositions. Have students brainstorm and record a list of prepositions, e.g. **behind, outside, around, up, down**. Choose an object in the class, e.g. **the window**. Ask each student to write a line about that object, beginning with a preposition. Provide time for each student to read their line, thus creating an instant poem.

Alphabetical Verbs *(Brownjohn 1994)*

This activity is a form of text innovation. Provide students with a framework and a topic. The framework is a list created by using the letters of the alphabet. Each line begins with a noun and a verb starting with that letter of the alphabet. For example,

The School Excursion
Anthony ate his lunch on the bus
Bethany bought the picnic rug
Chang caught a frog by the pond
Dorian danced on her toes
Evan emptied his water bottle on the road
Felicia fell in the pond.

My Favourite Words *(Mansutti 2004)*

To improve students' poetry writing, encourage them to 'fall in love with words'. Collect interesting words, then print each word on a strip of card, e.g. **pernickety, phenomenon, oozing, guffaw, joyousness**. Distribute a card to each student at random. Have students research 'their' word, e.g. **meaning, derivation**, and use it in their next poem. Encourage students to begin making their own collection of words; set aside a space in the classroom for displaying these favourite words.

Torn Apart *(Mansutti 2004)*

Collect several poems and make one copy of each. In front of the class, tear the poems into several pieces and distribute the pieces randomly around the room. Ask students to collect a piece of torn poem and locate those students who have the other pieces of the same poem. Make a chart for each poem, listing its title, e.g. WANTED: A Poem Called .... When students are satisfied they have all the pieces of their poem, they can glue their poem onto the chart. Have students read through their poem as a group to check that the pieces do actually fit together. As a whole class, discuss how students decided which pieces of poem fitted together. To make the task more challenging, retain two or three pieces of the torn poems.

Whole-Class Poem

Revise the literary devices of onomatopoeia, personification and alliteration. Brainstorm words or phrases on a selected topic that use the devices, e.g. **storm**. Piece the words and phrases together and revise for careful word selection, rhythm, rhyme and repetition.

Across Learning Areas

Provide opportunities across learning areas for students to compose texts used to entertain through poetry, e.g.

English	Haiku about a text read.
Society and Environment	Ballad about an historical event.
Maths	Concrete (or shape) poem about a mathematical shape.
The Arts	Cinquain to accompany a piece of music.

Social Purpose: Writing to Entertain — Prose

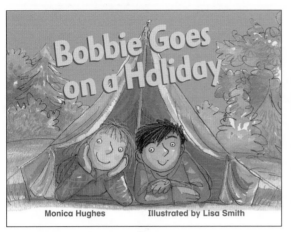

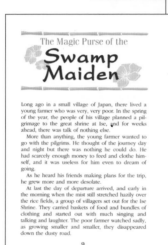

Figure 1.26 Samples of Prose Texts Used to Entertain

Understanding Texts that Entertain — Prose

Fiction is a generic term given to a range of texts that seek to entertain the reader, and includes poetry and prose. Prose takes many forms: narratives, cartoons, song lyrics and jokes are all texts designed to entertain through prose, and they can be presented on paper, live or on screen. These texts are usually imaginative or creative in nature, and provoke an emotional response through the development of character, setting and plot.

The narrative form contains several different types. Students may compose narratives such as fairytales, fables, legends, adventure stories and historical or realistic fiction accounts.

The following information is usually included in texts used to entertain through prose.

1 Orientation

This part of the text introduces the setting, time, main character — and possibly some minor characters. The orientation also sets the mood and tone, and invites the reader to continue reading. Details that will be important later are often introduced in this part of the text.

2 Event or Series of Events

This usually involves the main character and leads to a 'complication' in which the character is engaged in some conflict. There are often minor conflicts that serve to frustrate or hamper the main character from reaching their ambition or wish. These conflicts serve to hold the reader's interest and build the tension as they lead to a major problem or climax.

3 Resolution

The complication is generally resolved and loose ends are tied up. Some texts leave the reader to decide on the ending or resolution, while others fill in all details.

Organisational Frameworks

There are many different forms of prose. Each form has its own organisational framework that will vary depending on the form, the text type and the topic.

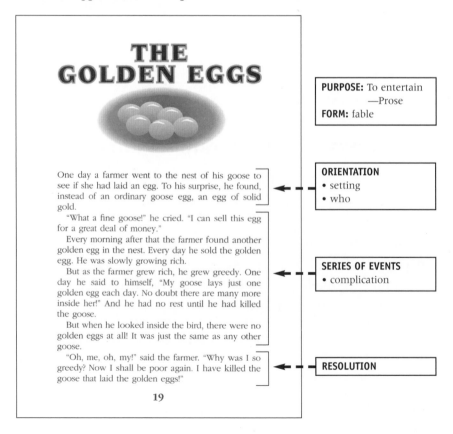

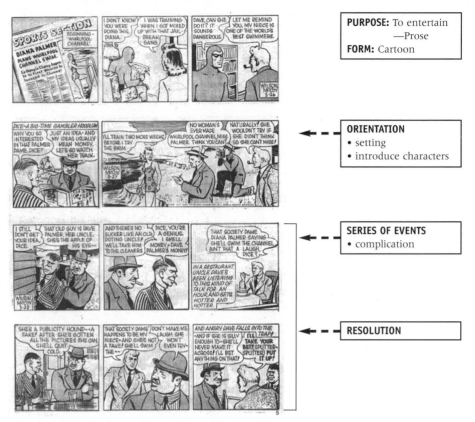

PURPOSE: To entertain
—Prose
FORM: Cartoon

ORIENTATION
- setting
- introduce characters

SERIES OF EVENTS
- complication

RESOLUTION

Figure 1.27 Framework Examples of Prose Written to Entertain

Language Features

Texts used to entertain through prose usually include the following language features:

- Nouns and pronouns that refer to specific participants, e.g. Harry Potter, the farmer, he, she, they.
- Often written in past tense.
- Action verbs (behaviours), e.g. ran, runs, will run.
- Verbs that reveal what was said, felt or thought, e.g. replied, empathised, contemplated.
- Imaginative adjectives used to create images, e.g. shimmering, lustreless.
- Usually written in the first person, e.g. I, we or third person, e.g. he, she, they.
- Linking words to indicate time, e.g. afterwards, the next day, much later.
- Dialogue.
- Use of devices to create imagery, e.g. similes, metaphors, onomatopoeia, personification.

Assessing Writing to Entertain—Prose

Students are in the stage where they display most of the bulleted points.

Beginning Stage	Developing Stage	Consolidating Stage	Extending Stage
Can state the purpose and audience of texts to be composed and includes basic organisational features of simple forms used to entertain through prose.	Is aware of the purpose and audience when composing texts and uses a partial organisational framework of a small range of forms used to entertain through prose.	Considers the purpose and audience to select specific vocabulary and uses appropriate organisational frameworks to compose a variety of forms used to entertain through prose.	Crafts forms used to entertain through prose by selecting vocabulary and manipulating organisational frameworks to suit the context of the writing event.
The writer: • writes a series of loosely connected events or actions concluding with a simple ending • attempts to orient the reader with some details of setting • writes a sequence of events that do not seem to be leading to a complication • focuses on one or two characters with no elaboration or description • includes characters that only perform actions but generally gives no details of reactions • writes a simple ending, e.g. I woke up. • uses limited descriptive vocabulary • rarely uses direct speech • uses simple linking words, e.g. and, then • has some difficulty in maintaining consistent tense	The writer: • introduces stereotypical characters and settings and focuses on a series of actions that lead to a complication and simple resolution • includes essentials of time, place and characters with little elaboration or description • includes initiating event leading to limited development of complication • copies complications from well-known texts, either visual or printed • introduces characters without indicating where they came from or why they have appeared • relies almost entirely on actions of the characters to develop plot • attempts resolution of a story; ending is often predictable and not very successful, e.g. They got married. • uses some descriptive vocabulary, focusing on stereotypical characteristics, e.g. handsome prince, beautiful princess • writes conversation, but the reader has difficulty in deciding who said what • uses linking words to do with time, e.g. afterwards, the following day • uses simple past tense	The writer: • selects details to enhance the development of characters, setting, complication and resolution • includes details of time, place and characters with elaboration to establish the context for the reader • includes initiating event developed into a complication • extends the plot by including more than one complication • develops characters and gives them substance according to their importance to the theme or plot • withholds some information to build or maintain tension • attempts to tie elements together to draw the story towards a conclusion • uses similes, adjectival and adverbial clauses and phrases to provide elaborate descriptions • uses direct speech to enhance meaning and create atmosphere • uses linking words to do with time and cause and effect, e.g. subsequently, consequently • maintains consistent tense	The writer: • chooses to use and manipulate conventional frameworks to achieve impact • provides appropriate detail to establish relationships between setting, and major and minor characters • develops a story line that is cohesive and coherent and elaborates and resolves each complication in episodes • manipulates the audience by the use of suspense, selectively disclosing information • fully develops characters, providing insight into characters' feelings and actions • ties elements together to draw the story towards a conclusion, showing interplay between characters and conflicts and resolving conflicts • carefully selects vocabulary and writing style to elicit emotional responses • uses devices such as imagery, metaphor and symbolism • makes effective use of dialogue to give insights into characters and their actions, and to establish the context for the reader • writes cohesively using a wide range of linking words • maintains consistent tense or manipulates tense for effect

Focus on Assessing

Focus on Teaching

Familiarising, Analysing, Modelling, Sharing, Guiding and Applying
See pages 30–37 and 66–70

Familiarising, Analysing, Modelling, Sharing, Guiding and Applying
See pages 30–37 and 71–73

Figure 1.28 Assessment Guide for Writing to Entertain — Prose

Supporting Students at the Tuning-In Stage

This section provides ideas to support students who have not yet reached the Beginning stage on the Writing to Entertain — Prose Assessment Guide (Figure 1.28).

Focus on building students' awareness of the language features and organisational frameworks of the form or text type being introduced. The following familiarising activities are suited to any form associated with writing to entertain—prose.

1 Sample Displays see page 31

2 Reading with and Reading to Students see page 31

3 Literacy Activities

- Discuss terminology related to texts that are used to entertain, e.g. **characters, setting, dialogue, problem.**
- Cut prose texts into individual paragraphs, then have students reconstruct the texts; invite students to share the reasoning behind their final order.
- Prepare and participate in Readers' Theatre sessions.
- Compare two or three texts by the same author, noting similarities and differences.
- Invite an author to visit your classroom and read their texts.
- Listen to a range of texts that are used to entertain through prose, e.g. **tapes, CDs, Internet sites.**
- Use puppets or props to dramatise familiar texts.
- Jointly retell familiar texts used to entertain through prose.
- Discuss the problem in a text and how it is solved.
- Discuss the use of language features.
- Have students collect and make class collections of interesting words, such as:
  — words to describe the senses
  — words that sound interesting, e.g. **shemozzle, murmur, smidgen**
  — words for special purposes, e.g. **people words, country words, happy words**
  — words that are various parts of speech, e.g. **adjectives, adverbs, verbs, prepositions.**
- Involve students in cloze activities. Identify words in a text that could be replaced, e.g. **nouns.** Have students brainstorm a selection of replacement nouns. Write the replacement words on cards or sticky notes and have students compose a text by placing the cards over selected original words.
- Involve students in brainstorming and playing word games and activities that build vocabulary used in narratives.

- Involve students in text innovations using familiar or favourite texts.
- Select some unfamiliar texts and read out the descriptions of characters from them, then ask students to draw the character they heard described. Students could draw a picture of a setting using the same method. Compare students' drawings with those in the text.
- Provide pictures of people, places or objects, then have students prepare an oral description of their picture.
- Have students work in pairs to play a matching game. Provide students with descriptive sentences on strips of paper and pictures of characters (or settings). Have students read the sentences, then choose the matching picture. Make sure there are more sentence strips than pictures. Invite students to discuss how they found the matching pairs.
- Provide students with a picture and a set of labels that describe different parts of the picture. Have students match the labels with the appropriate parts of the picture.
- Use story props to model how to compose a story, e.g. **people, cars, houses.** Invite students to offer suggestions, and use these to help compose the story. Have selected students retell the story. Keep the props available in the classroom for free-play activities.
- Provide multiple sets of picture sequences from familiar texts. Organise students into small groups, with as many students as there are pictures in the sequence. Each group sits in a circle, with each student assigned a number. Place the pictures in the middle of the circle. Student 1 selects and describes the picture that shows the first part of the story. If the group agrees, student 2 has a turn. If the group does not agree, they discuss the order of the story until they decide which is the correct picture. The game continues, with students taking turns until all the pictures are in a logical sequence. The group can then retell the story around the circle, with each student telling their part.

Supporting Students at the Beginning and Developing Stages

The main focus for these students is to help them understand the purpose, organisation, structure and language features of the text form being introduced.

Modelling and Sharing

The following modelling and sharing suggestions are separated into two stages; the first is specific to the Beginning Stage, and the second is more relevant to students in the Developing Stage. However, the suggestions should be seen as cumulative. When selecting a focus for the Developing Stage, teachers should also consider what is listed in the previous stage.

Beginning Stage	Developing Stage
Focus on understandings of text organisation, structure and language features. During Modelled, Shared and Interactive writing sessions, demonstrate how to:	
• sequence a series of events so that they lead to a complication	• write a variety of prose forms that entertain, e.g. science fiction, adventure, song lyrics
• write a complication and a resolution	• include relevant information to set the scene and develop characters
• include information about when, where, who	• include details of when, where, and who in the orientation to familiarise the reader
• introduce characters and their purpose	• initiate an event and develop it into a complication
• use descriptive vocabulary to enhance characters	• include multiple complications to extend plot
• use linking words associated with time, e.g. afterwards, the following day	• develop characters that are important to the plot
• use simple past tense, e.g. long time ago, he left	• build tension by withholding information
	• write a conclusion tying elements together
	• write a wide variety of sentences to enhance descriptions
	• use literary devices
	• include dialogue, giving indications as to which character is speaking
	• use a variety of linking words, e.g. time order, cause and effect
	• maintain correct tense

Figure 1.29 Suggested Focus for Modelling and Sharing Sessions

Guiding

The following guided-practice activities are suitable for students in the Beginning and Developing Stages, allowing them to build their understandings about texts used to entertain through prose. Each activity should be used in a meaningful context across different learning areas.

Character Interviews

After sharing a narrative text with students, ask them to choose their favourite part. Select a student to retell the event and to describe the characters involved. Invite students to brainstorm possible questions that they could ask one of the characters. Then select a student to role-play that character, while other students take turns to question the 'character'. Character Interviews allow students to discuss how authors construct their characters, and allow them to infer certain details about the characters.

Map a Story

Model how to draw a map that captures the events in a story. The map should show the important events and different settings of a narrative text. After several demonstrations of story mapping, ask students to make a map of a text that they have read. Provide time for students to retell the text using their map.

Plot Profiles

After reading a narrative text several times, have students brainstorm the main events. Record these events in order, then rate each event on a scale from calm to exciting and graph the results. Involve the students in a discussion about the plot profile and any patterns they may see, e.g. **Where does the climax of the story take place?**

Picture Story Books

Share a Picture Story Book with the students — but show only the pictures. Discuss the storyline as it is told through the pictures. Have students work in pairs or small groups to tell the story orally, as they perceive it from the pictures. Alternatively, read the text without showing the pictures then have students draw pictures to accompany the text.

Guiding Questions

Brainstorm and list questions that would be useful to consider when planning a narrative text. Demonstrate how to use the list. Have students plan their text by talking through their ideas with others. For example:

Orientation
• How will you start your story in a way that makes the reader want to keep reading?
• What will your first sentence be?
• When and where will your story begin?
• What will the setting look like?
• What words will you use to describe the setting?
• How can you help the reader paint a mind picture of the setting?
Characters
• Who are the most important characters in the story?

- What are the characters like? What do they look like?
- What personalities do the characters have? How do they talk?

Complication

- What problems does the main character need to overcome?

Story Organisation

- What events happen first, next and last?
- What does the main character do?
- How will you describe the actions?

Resolution

- How will things work out?
- What loose ends will need to be tidied up?
- How will your story end?

Character Profiles

Help students develop multi-dimensional characters by constructing character profiles. To construct a profile, they need to think broadly about their character, e.g. **What will the characters look like? What are their interests? How will they act? What will they do when something goes wrong? What sort of a person are they? How will the character interact with other characters? What might they say?** Encourage students to keep adding to their profiles.

Pass it on

Have students sit in small groups. Ask them to write the first sentence of a story to set the scene, and name two characters (one male and one female), e.g. **Once, long ago in a small country town, Jessie and Tom were hiding in the shed near the farmhouse.** Have students fold back the section they have written on, hiding their writing, and pass their paper to the next person in the group, who writes a sentence that begins with 'Suddenly', e.g. **Suddenly a large brown snake slithered by.** Have students repeat the procedure, folding, passing and adding sentences. Begin subsequent sentences with 'She said', 'After that' and 'In the end'. Students then unfold the paper and read the text to the group.

Picture This

Provide assorted pictures of people, places and objects. Have students compose a written description of one of the pictures, then collect the descriptions and pictures and redistribute them at random. Challenge students to find the picture that matches the text (and vice versa).

Understanding Dialogue

Students often overuse dialogue to such an extent that their written texts become hard to follow. Highlight passages of direct speech during Shared Reading sessions and encourage students to discuss the reasons for the inclusion of that dialogue, e.g. move the story along, tell the reader more about a character. Allow students to investigate the use of dialogue in different narrative text forms, and to formulate some guidelines for its inclusion. Encourage them to apply the guidelines when they are creating texts of their own.

Developing Dialogue

Select a narrative text that has several characters, but little or no dialogue. During the reading of the text, stop and ask students what the characters might say at this point. Record students' dialogue and add it to the text. Reread the entire text and include the new dialogue.

Substitutions

Many writers need practice at writing in first or third person, and in maintaining the use of correct tense. Delete one particular part of speech from a text, e.g. pronouns, words associated with tense, then ask students to fill the blanks with words that would make sense. Students then determine the types of words that are used when writing in first or third person, and those used when writing in past or present tense.

Change the Narrator

Provide opportunities for students to write texts from both first and third person stance. Find a simple piece of connected text written in either first or third person, then have students change the stance. As a class, discuss the words that needed to be changed and why, e.g.
He was running away from the savage beast when his foot caught in a tangled branch.
I was running away from the savage beast when my foot caught in a tangled branch.

Across Learning Areas

Provide opportunities across learning areas for students to compose texts used to entertain through prose, e.g.

English	Fairytale of personal choice.
Society and Environment	A play script about an historical event.
Health and Physical Education	A joke about healthy eating.
Mathematics	A cartoon about a mathematical concept.

Supporting Students at the Consolidating and Extending Stages

The main focus for these students is to help them to enhance their control over the text form, including their ability to adapt and manipulate the text.

Modelling and Sharing

When selecting a focus for the Consolidating and Extending Stages, teachers should also consider what is listed in previous stages.

Focus on continuing to build students' understandings of text organisation, structure and language features, by demonstrating how to:

- write a variety of forms used to entertain through prose, e.g. science fiction, adventure, song lyrics
- manipulate frameworks to achieve the greatest impact on the audience
- create effective complications and resolutions in narratives to build relationships between setting, characters and plot
- create cohesion and coherence within a text
- make use of words and literary devices to evoke the reader's emotions
- manipulate tense for effect
- include dialogue that develops the characters or moves the plot along
- refine texts choosing the vocabulary and style that best suits the audience.

Guiding

The following guided-practice activities are suitable for students in the Consolidating and Extending Stages, to further develop their understandings about texts used to entertain through prose. Each activity should be used in a meaningful context across different learning areas.

My World

Students' real-life experiences are a rich source of ideas for texts that entertain through prose. Have students bring an object or photo of personal significance from home. The photograph could be of a special person, place or event. Provide time for students to describe their object or photograph, including the memories or feelings that it evokes. Then encourage them to use their oral description as the basis of a prose text.

Borrowed Blurbs

Support students as they develop their notion of 'complication' in prose texts. Ask students to visit the library and collect several prose texts they have not read, but which appeal to them. Have them read the blurbs in search of a complication that could be used to create their own text. The idea is to borrow only the complication — not the supporting detail.

Five Alive

Teach students to heighten the use of their senses when creating settings. Have students visualise being in a particular environment and accurately record what they hear, see, smell, feel and taste, e.g. in the school yard, in their bedroom. Students should also record their reactions to the sensations. Provide time for students to write about this setting, emphasising word choice and word order.

Get Real

This activity will help students to develop characters that seem to be 'real' people. Collect photos of a range of people from magazines, newspapers and the Internet. Give a photo to each pair of students, then have them study the photo and create a profile for that character. Students can then include 'their' character in a prose text of their own.

Name:
Age:
Appearance:
Job:
Strengths:
Weaknesses:
Likes:
Dislikes:
Family:
Friends:
Personality Features:
Fears:
Hopes:

Figure 1.30 'Get Real' Sample

Creating Characters

Have students select a character from a familiar text and write a description of that character from two different points of view. Or they could write a description intended to create a different impression of that character.

Change the Point of View

Discuss a text with students and ask them to identify the point of view it was written from. Then ask them to consider how the text would change if it was written from a different point of view, focusing discussion on possible alternative actions, behaviours and events. After several discussions of this nature, have students take an existing text and rewrite it from the perspective of a different character.

Across Learning Areas

Provide opportunities across learning areas for students to compose texts used to entertain through prose, e.g.

English	Fable on a chosen topic.
Society and Environment	Myth based on a local event.
Health and Physical Education	Song lyrics about a health topic.
Science	Word puzzle using topic words.

Social Purpose: Writing to Explain

Memo

To: Ellie Sheridan
From: Will Girdler
Date: April 6 2005
Subject: Preparation for your trip to the UK

For your upcoming visit to the UK I have jotted down some information to assist in your travel preparation.

Ring Susan at Travel Plus (08 567 1234) and get her to organise your tickets for you. You will need to let her know the dates. She should give you a couple of options and you can choose which is the best for your given dates, times and prices.

Once you've confirmed your flights you will need to fill in the appropriate forms. For this trip you will need:
- Travel Authorisation Form
- Insurance Form
- Cash Advance Form

They are all stored on the B drive. Once you have filled them in pass them onto Patrick. He will give you some pounds before you leave which is very helpful when you first arrive in London.

I suggest that you take a special folder to store all receipts from any purchases you make, as you will need these to reconcile your expenses. Ensure you always ask for a receipt, even when just buying a sandwich or a coffee. It's amazing how quickly it can all add up. We can go through how to reconcile your expenses on your return.

Let me know if you have any problems.

Lost Pet Information

What to do if you find a lost pet
- Never touch a lost animal. It might be mean or sick.
- Have a grown-up call the police or an animal shelter. They will take the animal to a safe place.
- Put up signs in shops and on lamp posts.
- The signs should describe the lost animal, where you found it, and where it is now.

What to do if your pet is lost
- Check all the animal shelters in your area.
- Call the police. Ask them to watch out for your pet.
- Put up signs in shops and on lamp posts.
- The signs should have a picture of your pet and a phone number someone can call.

Figure 1.31 Samples of Texts Used to Explain

Understanding Texts That Explain

Texts used to explain set out the stages involved in a process, rather than a 'thing', e.g. how things work, how things come to be the way they are. Information is usually presented in a sequential and logical order; this requires the writer to analyse the process in order to show the relationship between the parts. Text forms used to explain include memos, rules, explanations, timetables, affidavits, complaints and policy statements.

The following information is usually included in texts used to explain.

1 Heading Statement

This can be a definition written as a statement or question (*an explanation*), the purpose (*a policy*) or details of the writer and the subject (*a memo*).

2 Sequence of How, and Reasons Why

This can describe the components (or parts) and their application, proposals, recommendations for further actions or conditions of operation.

3 Summary

This section can state special features of the phenomenon, reiterate main points — or simply be a signature.

Organisational Frameworks

There are many different forms of texts used to explain. Each text has its own organisational framework that will vary depending on the form and the topic.

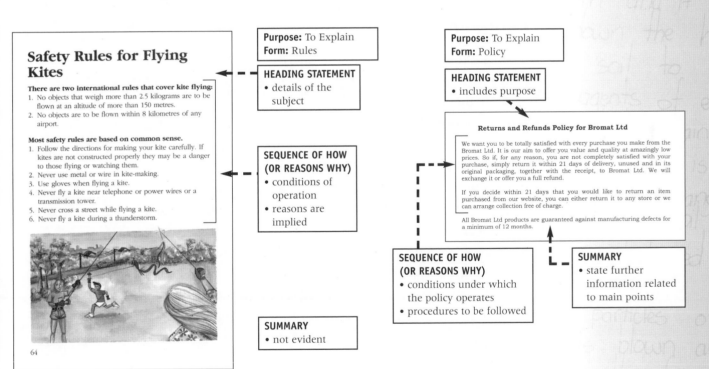

Safety Rules for Flying Kites

There are two international rules that cover kite flying:
1. No objects that weigh more than 2.5 kilograms are to be flown at an altitude of more than 150 metres.
2. No objects are to be flown within 8 kilometres of any airport.

Most safety rules are based on common sense.
1. Follow the directions for making your kite carefully. If kites are not constructed properly they may be a danger to those flying or watching them.
2. Never use metal or wire in kite-making.
3. Use gloves when flying a kite.
4. Never fly a kite near telephone or power wires or a transmission tower.
5. Never cross a street while flying a kite.
6. Never fly a kite during a thunderstorm.

64

Purpose: To Explain
Form: Rules

HEADING STATEMENT
• details of the subject

SEQUENCE OF HOW (OR REASONS WHY)
• conditions of operation
• reasons are implied

SUMMARY
• not evident

Purpose: To Explain
Form: Policy

HEADING STATEMENT
• includes purpose

Returns and Refunds Policy for Bromat Ltd

We want you to be totally satisfied with every purchase you make from the Bromat Ltd. It is our aim to offer you value and quality at amazingly low prices. So if, for any reason, you are not completely satisfied with your purchase, simply return it within 21 days of delivery, unused and in its original packaging, together with the receipt, to Bromat Ltd. We will exchange it or offer you a full refund.

If you decide within 21 days that you would like to return an item purchased from our website, you can either return it to any store or we can arrange collection free of charge.

All Bromat Ltd products are guaranteed against manufacturing defects for a minimum of 12 months.

SEQUENCE OF HOW (OR REASONS WHY)
• conditions under which the policy operates
• procedures to be followed

SUMMARY
• state further information related to main points

Purpose: To Explain
Form: Explanation

HEADING STATEMENT ➤

SEQUENCE OF HOW
AND REASONS WHY
• description of the
 parts
• how and why it
 works

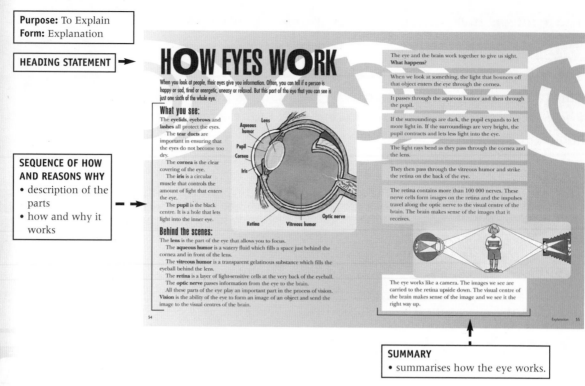

SUMMARY
• summarises how the eye works.

Figure 1.32 Sample Text Form and Framework for Text Written to Explain

Language Features

Texts used to explain usually include the following language features:

- Nouns and pronouns that refer to generalised participants, e.g. erosion, the water cycle, it.
- Linking words to indicate time, e.g. first, then, following, finally.
- Signal words to indicate cause and effect, e.g. if, then, because, consequently, as a result.
- Action verbs, e.g. evaporates, increases, changes.
- Adjectives that are precise and factual, e.g. sedimentary, cellular, atmospheric.
- Formal objective style, i.e. first-person pronouns and the writer's opinions are not generally appropriate.
- Technical terms, e.g. condensation, evaporation.
- Some passive verbs, e.g. are saturated, are changed.
- Timeless present tense, e.g. are, happens, turns.

Adapted from Derewianka, B. (1990)

Assessing Writing to Explain

Students are in the stage where they display most of the bulleted points.

	Beginning Stage	Developing Stage	Consolidating Stage	Extending Stage
Focus on Assessing	Can state the purpose and audience of texts to be composed and includes basic organisational features of simple forms used to explain.	Is aware of the purpose and audience when composing texts and uses a partial organisational framework of a small range of forms used to explain.	Considers the purpose and audience to select specific vocabulary and uses appropriate organisational frameworks to compose a variety of forms used to explain.	Crafts forms used to explain by selecting vocabulary and manipulating organisational frameworks to suit the context of the writing event.
	The writer: • writes a simple observation and comment, e.g. Snow is made from water and it's cold. • draws simple pictures or diagrams • writes an opening statement that is personal e.g. I am going to tell how … • includes information, but not necessarily in sequence • uses subjective language, e.g. It makes me feel cold instead of It lowers body temperature • may include inappropriate vocabulary, e.g. It goes as fast as a rocket • uses simple present tense, e.g. makes, goes • uses common signal words to show cause and effect, e.g. and …then….	The writer: • uses a limited range of forms and formats e.g. charts, explanations, to explain how or why something works • writes labels related to pictures and diagrams • writes an introductory question or title, e.g. How the Water Cycle Works • groups related information together • begins to use objective language • uses some subject-specific terms, e.g. evaporation • uses simple present tense consistently, e.g. falls, evaporates • uses signal words to show cause and effect, e.g. if … , then …, because	The writer: • uses a variety of forms and formats e.g. explanations, slide show, to explain the way things are or how things work, and to give reasons • creates diagrams, pictures and flowcharts with accurate labels and captions • writes an introductory definition or statement, e.g. Igneous rock is formed when molten rock cools and solidifies • includes information in a logical sequence • uses objective language that includes some use of passive verbs • uses subject-specific terms that are precise and factual, e.g. Acid rain is precipitation containing harmful nitric and sulphuric acids • uses appropriate tense to suit the text, e.g. The explanation of the application may be written using past tense • uses more complex signal words that indicate cause and effect, e.g. consequently, as a result	The writer: • uses the most appropriate form and format to clearly explain processes • provides detailed reasons to support the processes explained • creates accurate diagrams, pictures cross-sections and magnified diagrams to enhance understanding of content • writes a clear, precise opening paragraph that introduces the topic to be explained • sequences information to form a cohesive and coherent text to suit the purpose and audience • maintains formal objective language style that includes appropriate use of passive verbs • uses appropriate subject-specific terms and technical vocabulary and includes definitions of terms as required • chooses appropriate signal words and tense to develop a coherent text • effectively links information to clearly demonstrate cause and effect
Focus on Teaching	Familiarising, Analysing, Modelling, Sharing, Guiding and Applying See pages 30–37 and 79–81		Familiarising, Analysing, Modelling, Sharing, Guiding and Applying See pages 30–37 and 81–82	

Figure 1.33 Assessment Guide for Writing to Explain

Supporting Students at the Tuning-In Stage

This section provides ideas to support students who have not yet reached the Beginning stage on the Writing to Explain Assessment Guide (Figure 1.33).

Focus on building students' awareness of the language features and organisational frameworks of the form being introduced. These familiarising activities are suited to any form associated with writing to explain.

1 Sample Displays see page 31

2 Reading with and Reading to Students see page 31

3 Literacy Activities
- Ask students informal questions that require oral explanations:
  — How does your invention work?
  — Why did the block tower fall down?
  — Why did your boat float?
  — How can you design a boat that floats?
  — Why didn't the wolf eat the third pig?
- Model questions for students to use as a guide when they are sharing how something has been made and how it works:
  — What is it called?
  — What did you need to make it?
  — How did you make it?
  — How does it work? Why does it work?
  — Did you have any problems? What did you do?
- Work together to build concept maps about selected topics. Introduce additional technical language and record these words on a class chart for future reference.
- Discuss signal words that indicate cause and effect, e.g. **because, so, as a result, consequently, due to.** Encourage students to look for signal words when they are reading; record the words on a class chart for future reference.
- Display an object and have a student give an oral explanation of how the object works. Encourage them to use specific vocabulary rather than general terms. Record the explanation onto a cassette. Remove the object from display and replay the explanation; this time, invite students to decide whether or not the explanation is clear.
- Provide each group of students with a graphic, e.g. **diagram, picture, flowchart,** and the associated labels or captions. Ask students to match the labels or captions to the relevant sections

of the graphic. Discuss the decisions students had to make when they were adding the labels.

- Give each student a diagram or picture sequence. Have students work in pairs and take turns to explain the text to their partner verbally, e.g. how erosion occurs, how the water cycle occurs.
- Work together to label diagrams, pictures and flowcharts using the appropriate terms.

Supporting Students at the Beginning and Developing Stages

The main focus for these students is to help them understand the purpose, organisation, structure and language features of the text form being introduced.

Modelling and Sharing

The following modelling and sharing suggestions are separated into two stages; the first is specific to the Beginning Stage, and the second is more relevant to students in the Developing Stage. However, the suggestions should be seen as cumulative. When selecting a focus for the Developing Stage, teachers should also consider what is listed in the previous stage.

Beginning Stage	Developing Stage
Focus on understandings of text organisation, structure and language features. During Modelled, Shared and Interactive writing sessions, demonstrate how to:	
• write the title as either a statement or a question, e.g. The Cause of Weather or What Causes Weather?	• write an introductory definition or statement
• sequence the explanation of how or why something occurs	• include reasons that explain why or how
• write labels for pictures and diagrams	• create pictures, diagrams and flowcharts with labels and captions
• use subject-specific terms	• use precise and factual subject specific-terms, e.g. igneous, volcanic
• use linking words to indicate time, e.g. first, then	• create a glossary when necessary
• use objective language	• use objective language that includes some passive verbs, e.g. is collected, was harvested
• use different signal words to show cause and effect	• use the appropriate tense

Figure 1.34 Suggested Focus for Modelling and Sharing Sessions

Guiding

The following guided-practice activities are suitable for students in the Beginning and Developing Stages, allowing them to build their understandings about texts used to explain. Each activity should be used in a meaningful context across different learning areas.

Defining Terms

Provide opportunities for students to practise writing definitions and explanations of technical terms, e.g.

Term: microwave oven
Meaning: a household appliance used for cooking food
Features: has a turntable, digital display, found in the kitchen
Example: fan-forced microwave
Explanatory Sentence: A microwave oven is a household appliance that cooks food and is usually found in the kitchen. An example is a fan-forced microwave.

Developing Subject-Specific Vocabulary

Provide small groups of students with a general noun related to a selected topic. Have students build lists of suitable adjectives and adjectival phrases to accompany the word, e.g. **gales: forceful, north-easterly, on-shore.** Compile a cumulative record of collected words for later use.

Glossary

Allocate each student a subject-specific word or technical term related to a current topic. Ask students to write their definition of the word, then research to find whether their definition is correct or needs changing. When the definitions are correct, use them to create a class glossary.

Enhancing Texts

Diagrams, flow charts and pictures often accompany texts used to explain. Give each small group of students a graphic and ask them to write an explanation to accompany it. Alternatively, give students a written explanation and ask them to draw the associated graphic.

Gleaning the Essentials

Read students an explanatory text. Ask them to identify key words in the text, then use those words to create a pictorial representation of the explanation. Compare students' representations with the original text.

Cloze

Create a cloze activity by deleting the signal words from an explanatory text, e.g. **as a result of, because.** Then have students try to fill in the missing words or phrases. Discuss and compare students' word choices.

Cause and Effect

Write assorted Causes and Effects on separate cards. Ask students to find the matching cause and effect. Alternatively, give students a Cause card and have them state the effect, e.g. **It didn't rain for many months so ….** Or give students an Effect card and ask them to state the cause, e.g. **The sun was blacked out because ….**

Across Learning Areas

Provide opportunities across learning areas for students to compose texts used to explain, e.g.

Health and Physical Education	Rules for playing a sport.
English	Timetable for use of the computer.
Science	Explanation of 'The Life Cycle of a Frog'.
Society and Environment	Classroom policy for school excursions.

Supporting Students at the Consolidating and Extending Stages

The main focus for these students is to help them enhance their control over the text form, including their ability to adapt and manipulate the text.

Modelling and Sharing

When selecting focuses for the Consolidating and Extending Stages, teachers should also consider what is listed in previous stages.

Focus on continuing to build students' understandings of text organisation, structure and language features, by demonstrating how to:
- build personal knowledge as the topics become more technical
- write an opening that clearly and precisely introduces the topic
- sequence the explanation, and explain the relationships between the parts
- write a summary appropriate to the form
- express cause and effect by using words other than conjunctions, e.g. **the effect (noun), this causes (verb)**
- include definitions of technical vocabulary to enhance the reader's understanding

- create magnified diagrams and cross-sections
- change verbs into nouns, e.g. **Then the water begins to evaporate. Evaporation begins ...**
- select the most appropriate signal words.

Guiding

The following guided-practice activities are suitable for students in the Consolidating and Extending Stages, to further develop their understandings about texts used to explain. Each activity should be used in a meaningful context across different learning areas.

Glossary

Have students work individually to compose a glossary of the technical terms used in a text. Discuss the completed glossaries, emphasising how they help the reader to understand the content.

Organisation

Have students experiment with different ways of organising the written and visual parts of texts. Compare the students' layouts and discuss which layout best assists the reader. Ideally, use word processors for this activity.

Explaining What

Have students work in pairs. One student reads an explanation to their partner, but omits the title. The partner then tries to work out the explanation's topic as quickly as possible. Discuss the results, inviting students to identify the key words that helped them identify the topic.

Restating

Provide a series of statements that have a related cause and effect. Have students restate the initial relationship using an alternative signal word, e.g. **Attempts were made to cross the mountains because there was limited fertile land.** This could be restated using 'so', e.g. **There was limited fertile land so attempts were made to cross the mountains.**

Across Learning Areas

Provide opportunities across learning areas for students to compose texts used to explain, e.g.

Society and Environment	Complaint to local government.
Health and Physical Education	Policy for playing outside.
Mathematics	Rules to explain a mathematical concept.
Science	Explanation of a phenomenon, e.g. Why Volcanoes Erupt.

Social Purpose: Writing to Inquire

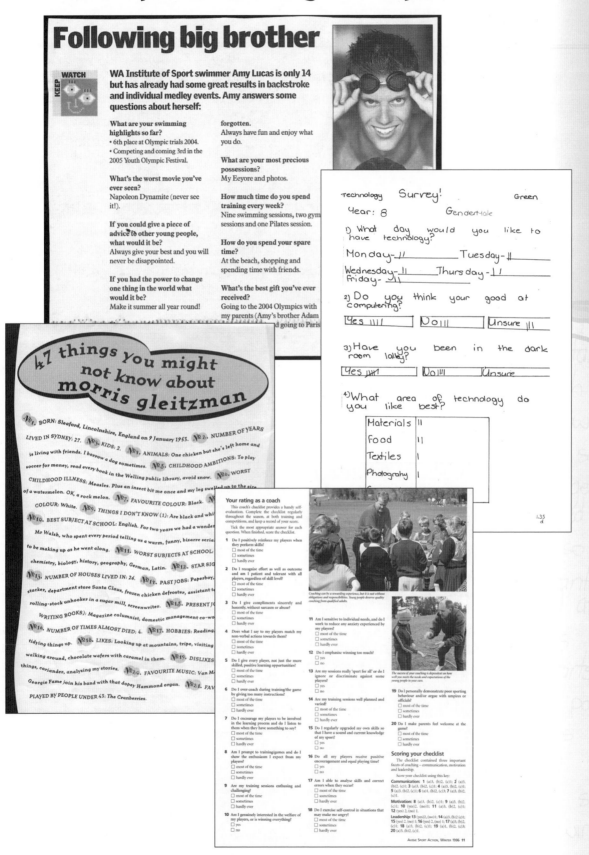

Figure 1.35 Samples of Texts Used to Inquire

Understanding Texts That Inquire

Texts that inquire often focus on information gathering or data collection. A question, in its simplest form, is a text designed to inquire. Interviews, questionnaires and surveys are more substantial examples of text forms that inquire. Each of these text forms varies in the nature of the questions, how they are grouped and how they are arranged.

The following information is usually included in texts used to inquire.

1 Orientation

The orientation creates a context for the reader by establishing the time, place and purpose of the text. The context is sometimes inferred, but should always give enough background information to orient the reader and encourage them to keep reading.

2 Body

This section of the text consists of a question or a series of questions. It is usually organised in a cohesive way, often in chronological order or a logical sequence.

3 Prompt

The prompt is a call to action. It contains instructions about what to do with the survey, questionnaire or form, and stresses the importance of its correct completion. In some cases the prompt is optional or implied.

Organisational Frameworks

The information outlined above is usually included in texts used to inquire; however, the organisational framework used to construct each text will vary depending on the form and topic.

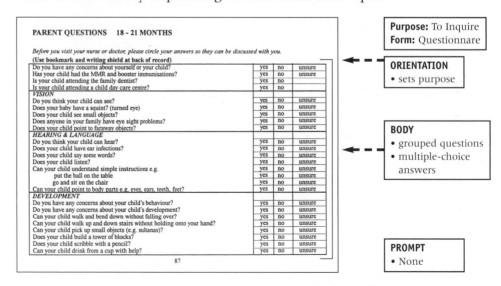

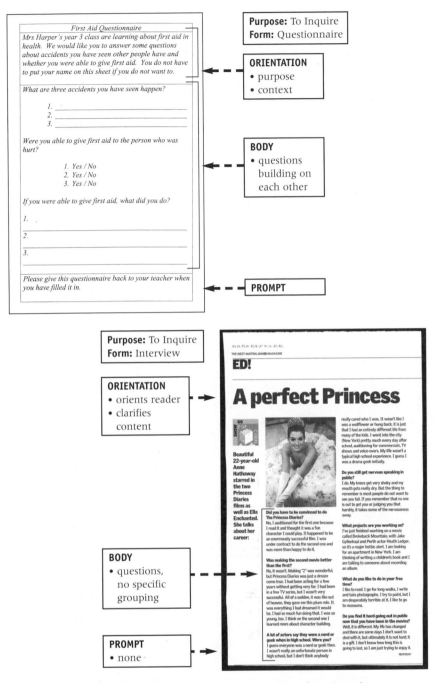

Figure 1.36 Framework Samples from Texts Used to Inquire

Language Features

Texts used to inquire usually include the following language features:
- Second person pronouns, e.g. Have you ...?
- Action verbs, e.g. use, circle, check, describe.
- Space for the reader to write a response.
- Concise language.
- Signal words that indicate questions or statements of inquiry, e.g. who, where, when, analyse, discuss.
- Questions or statements of inquiry, e.g. Are you happy with the current level of service from your library?

Assessing Writing to Inquire

Students are in the stage where they display most of the bulleted points.

Focus on Assessing

Beginning Stage	Developing Stage	Consolidating Stage	Extending Stage
Can state the purpose and audience of texts to be composed and includes basic organisational features of simple forms used to inquire.	Is aware of the purpose and audience when composing texts and uses a partial organisational framework of a small range of forms used to inquire.	Considers the purpose and audience to select specific vocabulary and uses appropriate organisational frameworks to compose a variety of forms used to inquire.	Crafts forms used to inquire by selecting vocabulary and manipulating organisational frameworks to suit the context of the writing event.
The writer: • attempts to write simple questions, but sometimes writes statements • includes minimal information about purpose of the inquiry, expecting that the reader shares background • writes questions about established information • writes questions that are closed, learned or highly predictable • needs teacher support to generate a clarifying question • needs teacher support to write a prompt, e.g. *RSVP in invitation* • experiments with question marks • relies heavily on simple stems, such as *what* and *who*	The writer: • writes simple questions, invitations and surveys that relate to the information required • attempts to orient the reader, giving some details of purpose, with little elaboration or description • writes questions that relate to information required • writes questions that require thought, inference or investigation • generates a simple clarifying question • writes a simple prompt where appropriate • uses question marks, sometimes inconsistently • uses an expanded range of question stems: who, when, where, what, why, how	The writer: • writes questions, surveys and questionnaires that elicit the different kinds of information required from local audiences • orients the reader by including details that fully explain the purpose of the inquiry • attempts to 'hook' the reader, sometimes in a contrived way • writes questions that demonstrate a sound knowledge of the information required • writes questions that elicit a range of responses: literal, inferential • writes a small range of different question types for different purposes • writes a prompt that is appropriate for purpose and audience • uses question marks consistently • uses a range of question stems strategically: who, when, where, what, why, how	The writer: • writes questions, surveys, forms, interviews, debates and questionnaires that elicit optimal and strategic information from extended audiences • writes a cohesive orientation that orients and engages the reader • provides a compelling reason to respond to the inquiry • writes questions that are comprehensive, clear and concise in requesting the information required • writes questions to serve multiple purposes, e.g. database • writes a variety of questions for a range of purposes • writes a prompt that restates the importance of responding • uses question marks consistently • writes questions as statements when necessary • uses a range of question stems strategically with question types: who, when, where, what, why, how

Focus on Teaching

Familiarising, Analysing, Modelling, Sharing, Guiding and Applying See pages 30–37 and 88–90		Familiarising, Analysing, Modelling, Sharing, Guiding and Applying See pages 30–37 and 90–92	

Figure 1.37 Assessment Guide for Writing to Inquire

Supporting Students at the Tuning-In Stage

This section provides ideas to support students who have not yet reached the Beginning stage on the Writing to Inquire Assessment Guide (Figure 1.37).

Focus on building students' awareness of the language features and organisational frameworks of the form being introduced. These familiarising activities are suited to any form associated with writing to inquire.

1 Sample Displays see page 31

2 Reading to and Reading with Students see page 31

3 Literacy Activities

- Invite selected students to wear headbands that have the name of a person, place or object written on them. Make sure the headband titles are not seen by the wearers. Each selected student takes turns to ask the class a question in order to discover the name on their headband. The class can only answer 'yes' or 'no' to the questions.
- Play 'Twenty Questions'. Invite one student to think of a person, place or object. The class can then ask that student 20 questions to find out what they're thinking, with the aim of discovering the object in less than 20 questions. The student can only answer 'yes' or 'no' to the questions.
- Place a mystery object in a bag, then have students ask questions in order to identify the object.
- Have the class choose a character from a familiar text, then select a student to take on the role of that character. The class then ask questions of the character. Encourage questions that go beyond the literal level, e.g. for Little Red Riding Hood: 'Why did you walk through the forest to go to Grandma's house?'
- Invite a guest to visit your classroom. Before the guest's arrival, work with the class to create a list of questions to ask them. Record the questions on a class chart, then discuss how the questions could be altered to become more open ended. Conduct the interview with the guest, and have students ask the questions.
- Provide a table or an area in the classroom for displaying new or unusual items. Take advantage of occasions when students bring items to school, using the items to stimulate questions and responses. Then invite students to compose and record questions about the displayed items.
- Have students work in pairs. One student talks about themselves or someone they know who has a 'claim to fame'. The 'claim to

fame' should be a significant real-life event. The partner then sustains the conversation by asking questions and seeking clarification.

- Set up a situation where students conduct a 'conversation' without asking any questions. When the 'conversations' have taken place, discuss the difficulties of maintaining a conversation without questions.

Supporting Students at the Beginning and Developing Stages

The main focus for these students is to help them understand the purpose, organisation, structure and language features of the text form being introduced.

Modelling and Sharing

The modelling and sharing suggestions in Figure 1.38 are separated into two stages; the first is specific to the Beginning Stage, and the second is more relevant to students in the Developing Stage. However, the suggestions should be seen as cumulative. When selecting a focus for the Developing Stage, teachers should also consider what is listed in the previous stage.

Beginning Stage	Developing Stage
Focus on understandings of text organisation, structure and language features. During Modelled, Shared and Interactive writing sessions, demonstrate how to:	
• write open and closed questions	• include information to set the context for the reader
• create a user-friendly format	• write 'hooks' to gain reader's interest
• identify the difference between questions and statements	• write different types of questions that elicit different levels of answers
• use second person pronouns, e.g. Have you …?	• select the most appropriate questions to ask
• write different types of questions	• group questions depending on the information to be collected
• include various signal words that indicate questions or statements of inquiry, e.g. who, where, when, analyse, discuss	• use the most appropriate question stem that achieves the desired outcome, e.g. who, where, when, analyse, discuss
• write clarifying questions or statements	• write prompts that encourage a person to respond
• use question marks and other relevant punctuation	• write questions or statements of inquiry, e.g. Are you happy with the current level of service from your bank?

Figure 1.38 Suggested Focus for Modelling and Sharing Sessions

Guiding

The following guided-practice activities are suitable for students in the Beginning and Developing Stages, allowing them to build their understandings about texts used to inquire. Each activity should be used in a meaningful context across different learning areas.

Trivia Extravaganza

After playing several trivia games, analyse the questions used. Divide students into groups of four and have each group select a topic, e.g. whales, seals. Provide time for students to find interesting facts about their topic, then have them turn each fact into a trivia question. Collect all the questions and use them to play a game of Trivia Extravaganza.

Key Words

Display the key words: who, what, when, where, why, how. Emphasise that these are the key words used to compose questions. Invite one student to introduce a topic of their choice, e.g. my cat. Then have the other students in the class ask questions, using the key words. Discuss the questions that were asked and the type of information they elicited.

Picture Investigator

Provide a range of magazines, books, catalogues and brochures. Ask each student to select a picture or photograph, then write three questions about what is not shown in the picture. Have students share their picture and their questions with a partner, and discuss other possible questions.

Interview Questions

Organise a guest speaker to be interviewed by the class, e.g. a nurse. Prior to the interview, have students brainstorm general categories that they want information about, e.g. workplace, hours, qualifications. Allocate a category to each small group of students, then have them compose both open and closed questions; emphasise the use of the key words in the questions: who, what, where, why, when and how. Have an adult sit in as the 'guest speaker' and give students time to practise asking their questions. As a class, evaluate the responses given and refine the questions if needed. Use the refined questions when the guest speaker visits.

Open Versus Closed

Provide opportunities for students to transform open questions into closed questions, and, conversely, closed questions into open questions. For example, open: What did you do on your holidays?; closed: Did you go away on your holidays? Discuss which questions are more effective in different situations.

Buzz

This game will help students to develop an understanding of the difference between open and closed questions. Select a student to answer the questions asked by the class. The aim for the class is to compose questions that are easily answered by saying 'yes' or 'no'. The aim for the student answering is to answer without using the words 'yes' or 'no'. If the student answers 'yes' or 'no' they are buzzed out of the game and a new player is elected.

Across Learning Areas

Provide opportunities across learning areas for students to compose texts used to inquire, e.g.

English	Interview questions for an author.
Health and Physical Education	Survey of dietary and exercise habits.
Society and Environment	Questionnaire about a local issue.
Technology and Enterprise	Survey to ascertain needs before designing a system.

Supporting Students at the Consolidating and Extending Stages

The main focus for these students is to help them enhance their control over the text form, including their ability to adapt and manipulate the text.

Modelling and Sharing

When selecting focuses for the Consolidating and Extending Stages, teachers should also consider what is listed in previous stages.

Focus on continuing to build students' understandings of text organisation, structure and language features, by demonstrating how to:
• format various texts to gain the best information
• write a variety of questions for a range of purposes
• write an orientation that motivates the reader to respond
• write a title that arouses the reader's interest
• determine what information will be essential to know, and what information will be useful
• group questions or statements from general to specific

- reword the same question to elicit a more detailed response
- use concise language that is easily understood by all respondents
- use and refine questions or statements of inquiry, e.g. **Courage, cowardice, good and evil: what do these words mean to you?**
- compose questions that use multiple-choice responses.

Guiding

The following guided-practice activities are suitable for students in the Consolidating and Extending Stages, to further develop their understandings about texts used to inquire. Each activity should be used in a meaningful context across different learning areas.

Grouping Questions

Have students work in small groups. Give each group several questions about the same topic, with each question written on a separate card. Ask each group to cluster the questions according to the type of information they will collect, e.g. **tigers: physical features, diet, habitat.** Then have students order the questions within each cluster. Invite students to place the clusters of questions in the order they could occur in an interview.

Rating Scales

Provide opportunities for students to compose multiple-choice rating scales for characters from familiar literary texts, e.g. **Goldilocks was perfect / good / bad.** Rating scales could also be composed for people from familiar informational texts, e.g. **Anne Frank was heroic / brave / cowardly.**

Interviewing Characters

Select a particular event from a familiar text, then have students brainstorm a list of questions they could ask the characters involved in the event. Nominate students to take on the role of each character and have them answer the questions from the point of view of their character. Discuss how the same question can elicit different responses.

Analysing Responses

Analyse a range of simple surveys or questionnaires related to topics of interest e.g. **horse riding, television programs watched, mode of transport, favourite books.** Have students work in small groups to reword the questions so that they elicit more information. Students could then answer the newly worded questions and discuss their responses.

Across Learning Areas

Provide opportunities across learning areas for students to compose texts used to inquire, e.g.

The Arts	Interview questions for an artist.
Health and Physical Education	Survey of sports played by students.
Society and Environment	A questionnaire to improve community activities.
Science	Interview questions for a local conservationist.

Social Purpose: Writing to Instruct

Figure 1.39 Samples of Texts Used to Instruct

Understanding Texts That Instruct

Texts that instruct are often multi-modal. They can be used to guide behaviour or to tell how something is done. For example, a STOP sign is a simple text designed to instruct; a repair manual is a more complex, extended series of steps written for the same purpose. Other text forms that are used to instruct include recipes, experiments, directions, manuals, timetables and blueprints.

The following information is usually included in texts used to instruct.

1 Goal or Aim

This part of the text states what is to be done, or it may outline the situation that has arisen, e.g. **How to change the batteries.** Sometimes the goal or the aim may form the title of the text, e.g. **Chocolate Chip Muffins.**

2 Materials or Requirements

This part usually lists what is needed to complete the task. It can include tools, instruments, utensils, ingredients, materials, parts or data.

3 Method

This is often presented as a series of ordered steps. The steps might be preceded by numbers, letters or bullets, or they might be written as connected sentences or paragraphs. Headings, subheadings, diagrams, and photographs are often used to help clarify this part of the text.

4 Evaluation

This states how the success of the steps can be tested or evaluated. Sometimes the evaluation is presented as a photograph or a drawing of the completed item.

Organisational Frameworks

The information outlined above is usually included in texts used to instruct; however, the organisational framework used to construct each text will vary depending on the form and topic.

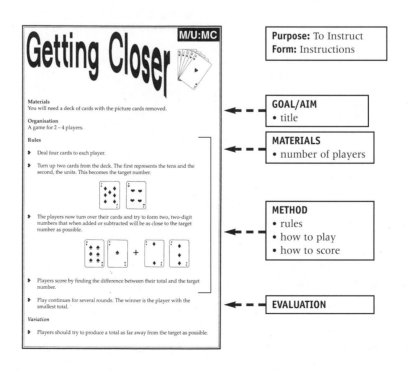

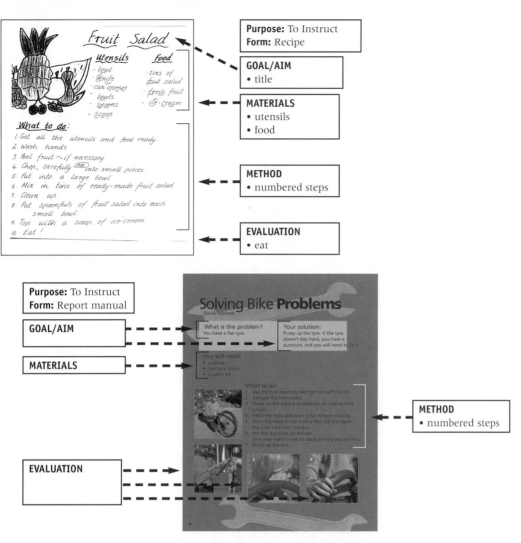

Figure 1.40 Framework Samples from Texts Used to Instruct

Language Features

Texts used to instruct usually include the use of the following language features:

- Nouns and pronouns that refer to generalised and specific participants, e.g. ingredients, utensils, the eggs, the rotor, it.
- The reader following the instructions is referred to in a general way, e.g. each player, you. Sometimes the reader is not even mentioned at all, e.g. Draw a 10 cm line.
- Signal words to do with time, e.g. first, then, when.
- Mainly action verbs, e.g. put, twist, hold, take.
- Simple present tense, often written as a 'command', e.g. stir, cut, mix.
- Adjectives that are detailed and factual, e.g. square, 6 cm, Phillips-head screwdriver, 400 g.
- Adverbs that give detailed information on how, where and when each action is completed, e.g. slowly, lightly, after you have folded the serviette.

Adapted from Derewianka, B. (1990)

Assessing Writing to Instruct

Students are in the stage where they display most of the bulleted points.

Beginning Stage	Developing Stage	Consolidating Stage	Extending Stage
Can state the purpose and audience of texts to be composed and includes basic organisational features of simple forms used to instruct.	Is aware of the purpose and audience when composing texts and uses a partial organisational framework of a small range of forms used to instruct.	Considers the purpose and audience to select specific vocabulary and uses appropriate organisational frameworks to compose a variety of forms used to instruct.	Crafts forms used to instruct by selecting vocabulary and manipulating organisational frameworks to suit the context of the writing event.
The writer:	The writer:	The writer:	The writer:
• writes simple text forms that instruct, e.g. lists	• uses a limited range of forms and formats used to instruct, e.g. science experiment, rules, recipes	• uses a variety of forms and formats to compose texts used to instruct, e.g. directions	• selects, sorts and synthesises information to precisely instruct a target audience, using a form that is appropriate to the subject and topic
• writes an introductory statement which may mention the goal, e.g. This is how you make a cake	• writes an introductory statement or title that includes the goal	• states goal precisely in an appropriate way, e.g. title, statement	• where appropriate, states goal using precise terminology suitable to the form and audience
• lists some materials	• lists all the materials required	• lists all materials and quantities required, with some order	• lists all materials and precise quantities in the order of use
• includes main steps	• includes most of the necessary steps in sequence	• lists instructions with adequate detail and in the correct sequence	• writes explicit instructions for each step in the sequence
• may illustrate or number some steps	• uses simple visual aids to support the reader, e.g. illustrations, headings, numbered steps	• uses appropriate visual aids to elaborate and support the text, e.g. subheadings, diagrams, photographs, cross-sections	• chooses the most appropriate visual aids to elaborate, support and enhance the text
• has difficulty maintaining present tense	• uses simple present tense and action verbs, e.g. Stir the mixture until it boils	• maintains simple present tense and action verbs throughout	• maintains simple present tense and action verbs throughout
• uses generalised 'you', e.g. You put some bananas in, then you mash them	• omits 'you' and starts sentences with a verb or adverb, e.g. Stir, Add, Cut, Carefully glue	• refers to the reader in an objective way or not at all, e.g. each player, turn the handle, add the water	• refers to the reader in a general way or not at all
• uses simple linking words, e.g. and, then	• uses linking words to signal time or order, e.g. first, when, then, after	• uses linking words to precisely signal time or order, e.g. after ten minutes, subsequently, finally	• ensures cohesion and coherence through use of appropriate linking words
• uses language close to speech, e.g. The first thing you do is put an egg in.	• includes vocabulary appropriate to the topic, e.g. plastic drinking straw, nylon string	• uses subject-specific vocabulary, e.g. Phillips-head screwdriver, basmati rice	• guides reader accurately by use of subject-specific vocabulary and precise adverbs or adjectives, e.g. slowly unwind the larger spool, carefully cut a 10 cm wide strip from the left side

Focus on Assessing

Familiarising, Analysing, Modelling, Sharing, Guiding and Applying
See pages 30–37 and 98–100

Familiarising, Analysing, Modelling, Sharing, Guiding and Applying
See pages 30–37 and 100–102

Focus on Teaching

Figure 1.41 Assessment Guide for Writing to Instruct

Supporting Students at the Tuning-In Stage

This section provides ideas to support students who have not yet reached the Beginning stage on the Writing to Instruct Assessment Guide (Figure 1.41).

Focus on building students' awareness of the language features and organisational frameworks of the form being introduced. These familiarising activities are suited to any form associated with writing to instruct.

1 Sample Displays see page 31

2 Reading to and Reading with Students see page 31

3 Literacy Activities
- Provide opportunities for students to make or do things, then share the process with the class. Guide students' oral presentations by asking a range of questions:
  — What did you use to make it?
  — What was the first thing you had to do?
  — What did you do after that?
  — If you had to tell someone who hadn't done this before, what is the main thing that you would tell them to remember?
- Provide opportunities for students to give oral directions on how to play familiar games, e.g. computer games, board games, playground games.
- Play games where students have to give or follow directions, e.g. Simon Says, Snakes and Ladders, Barrier Games. Focus students' attention on the key words in the directions.
- Select a student. Send that student away for a moment while the class decides on a 'secret' object or picture. Invite the student back and have them draw the object, following the verbal directions given by the class. Compare the drawing with the original object, then discuss which directions were helpful and which were misleading. Discuss the type of vocabulary used.
- Provide opportunities for students to take part in Language Experience activities that lend themselves to writing to instruct, e.g. baking a cake, planting seeds, building sandcastles. After the experience students can:
  — sequence photographs of the actions
  — draw pictures to illustrate the steps
  — match a set of directions with illustrations
  — follow simple directions by reading a set of sequenced pictures with labels

— compile a class list of words related to the topic, e.g. **flour, eggs, stir, beat.**

- Model writing directions, focusing on drawing and labelling the steps involved. For example, if the class is going to plant seeds, draw a pot, soil, packet of seeds and a watering can — and label them 'materials'. Draw and label each step required, then have students follow the steps to plant their seeds.

- Make simple drawings of a procedure carried out in the class, e.g. **things to do in the morning when you arrive at school.** Work together to write the instructions that accompany each drawing. Distribute the procedure as a jumbled text, keep drawing and text together, then have students sequence the instructions correctly.

- Discuss how gestures add meaning when giving oral instructions. Talk about words that could be used to replace the gestures when writing the instructions down, e.g. **quickly, slowly.** Record these words on a chart and have students use them when they are writing forms used to instruct.

Supporting Students at the Beginning and Developing Stages

The main focus for these students is to help them understand the purpose, organisation, structure and language features of the text form being introduced.

Modelling and Sharing

The modelling and sharing suggestions in Figure 1.42 are separated into two stages; the first is specific to the Beginning Stage, and the second is more relevant to students in the Developing Stage. However, the suggestions should be seen as cumulative. When selecting a focus for the Developing Stage, teachers should also consider what is listed in the previous stage.

Beginning Stage	Developing Stage
Focus on understandings of text organisation, structure and language features. During Modelled, Shared and Interactive writing sessions, demonstrate how to:	
• write a title that describes or sets a goal	• write a succinct title or statement that states the goal
• list all materials required	• include specific information, e.g. quickly mix, 2-litre bottle
• include the necessary steps in sequence	• sequence steps using various formatting devices, e.g. numbers, bullets, dashes
• include labels, diagrams and illustrations to assist the reader	• include visual aids that elaborate and support the text, e.g. subheadings, photographs
• use action verbs to start each new step, e.g. mix, add, stir	• include accurate measurement, utensils and materials in list form
• use vocabulary appropriate to the topic	• use subject-specific words, e.g. blanch, sauté, conductor
• use signal words that indicate time or order, e.g. firstly, then, finally	• use abbreviations, e.g. tbsp, SW
	• use signal words that detail time, place and manner, e.g. bake in a hot oven for ten minutes, half-fill a container, gently stir.

Figure 1.42 Suggested Focus for Modelling and Sharing Sessions

Guiding

The following guided-practice activities are suitable for students in the Beginning and Developing Stages, allowing them to build their understandings about texts used to instruct. Each activity should be used in a meaningful context across different learning areas.

Jumbled Directions

Write directions for an appropriate task, e.g. a craft activity, with each step on a separate sentence strip. Give the strips out to students and have them place the strips in sequence. Read through the sequence as a whole class, then have students carry out the task.

Finish the Directions

Give students a sequence of directions for a common task, e.g. making a phone call. Omit one step — either the first or the last — then have students write the missing step in the same style as the other steps.

Direction Cloze

Write out the directions for a familiar classroom task, but omit selected words. Then have students supply appropriate words so that the directions still make sense. Discuss the words students suggest.

Finding the Way

Give students a simple map of the classroom, the school or the local area. Have them write directions on how to get from point A to point B, e.g. How to get from our classroom to the library. Have students follow the directions, then discuss which directions were the easiest to follow, and why.

Changing the Form

Once students are familiar with the purpose and organisation of writing forms used to instruct, have small groups change a retell into a text used to instruct, e.g. change When I Made a Sandcastle into How to Make a Sandcastle. Discuss the changes students needed to make.

Supporting the Reader

Have students re-read a text that they have written and identify where a visual aid would help the reader. Provide time for students to add visual aids, e.g. headings, illustrations, numbered steps.

Across Learning Areas

Provide opportunities across learning areas for students to compose texts used to instruct, e.g.

Studies of Society and Environment	Directions to visit the local cinema.
Science	Experiments undertaken.
Mathematics	Directions to play a game.
Health and Physical Education	Recipes for favourite dishes.

Supporting Students at the Consolidating and Extending Stages

The main focus for these students is to help them enhance their control over the text form, including their ability to adapt and manipulate the text.

Modelling and Sharing

When selecting focuses for the Consolidating and Extending Stages, teachers should also consider what is listed in previous stages.

Focus on continuing to build students' understandings of text organisation, structure and language features, by demonstrating how to:

- state a goal using precise terminology
- write steps that are explicit, but have sufficient detail
- include exact details such as weight, size, quantities, types of tools
- include cautions to warn readers of difficult or dangerous steps
- include reasons for doing things e.g. **The fly on the tent must be secure otherwise it might blow away**
- make commands active or passive, e.g. Active: **Add the sugar to the cup**; Passive: **The sugar is added to the cup**
- use adverbial clauses to indicate reason, e.g. **so that, in order to**
- use adverbial clauses to indicate time, e.g. **until, when.**

Guiding

The following guided-practice activities are suitable for students in the Consolidating and Extending Stages, to further develop their understandings about texts used to instruct. Each activity should be used in a meaningful context across different learning areas.

Instructions for Games

Have students create board games that include written directions. Provide headings that will help students to write the directions, e.g. **Numbers of Players, Equipment Needed, How to Score.** Students could create Snakes and Ladders games based on a literary or informational text they have read, e.g. **Bridge to Terabithia.** They would need to identify several good events and several bad events in the text, then decide on a suitable reward or punishment for each event.

User-Friendly Directions

Have students work in groups of three or four. Ask each group to write a set of directions for the same activity — but give each group a different audience, e.g. **How to Use the Photocopier: instructions for parents, students and teachers.** Invite students to share their completed directions with the class and discuss the differences they had to make for each audience.

Effective Visuals

Provide students with a variety of texts composed to instruct and have them evaluate the effectiveness of the visuals in the texts. Then provide texts that lack visuals and have students create suitable visuals to enhance the clarity of the text.

Comparisons

Provide opportunities for students to view different formats of texts that instruct, e.g. a cooking show on TV and a recipe book. Have students compare the televised directions with the written instructions. Discuss similarities and differences between both formats, as well as the prior knowledge required of the reader or the viewer. Have students compose instructions on the same topic but using different media, e.g. printed, live, electronic.

Manipulations

Provide students with a text that instructs that has active commands, e.g. Break the eggs into a bowl. Discuss the commands, then have students rewrite the text so that the instructions are passive, e.g. The eggs are broken into a bowl. Discuss how the text change affects the reader.

Across Learning Areas

Provide opportunities across learning areas for students to compose texts used to instruct, e.g.

Science	Directions for handling chemicals.
The Arts	Manual for operating the kiln.
Mathematics	Directions for a mathematical game or task.
Health and Physical Education	Directions for administering first aid.

Social Purpose: Writing to Persuade

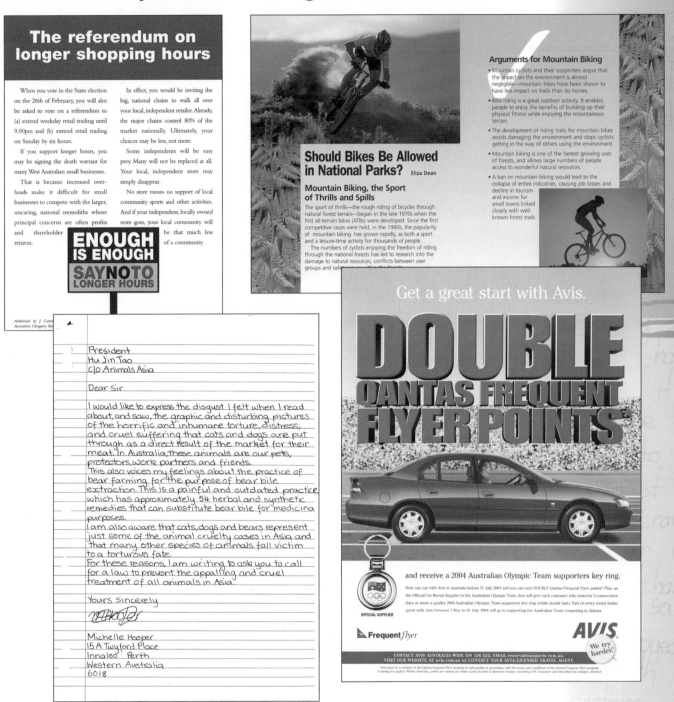

Figure 1.43 Samples of Texts Used to Persuade

Understanding Texts That Persuade

A text written to persuade expresses an opinion about a topic.
Writing to persuade involves the critical evaluation of ideas, and
can include discussion, argument, persuasion or debate. All texts
that persuade contain arguments and assertions, although these
may be presented in different ways:

- A single perspective, in order to persuade readers to agree with a particular point of view.
- A compare and contrast perspective, developing a case that aims to persuade the reader that the writer's premise is correct.
- An analysis of a topic perspective, where all points of view are presented and a logical conclusion is stated. The writer's aim is that the reader, having read the information provided, will form the same conclusion.

Different forms of texts that persuade include expositions, discussion papers, job applications, editorials and advertisements.

The following information is usually included in texts used to persuade.

1 Thesis

This part of the text generally provides an overview of the topic or question and a statement of the basic position to be taken.

2 Arguments or Assertions

The subsequent paragraphs of the text contain arguments or assertions. Generally, the arguments 'for' are stated first and the arguments 'against' are stated last. Supporting evidence is usually provided for each argument or assertion.

3 Conclusion or Summary

This may be in the form of an evaluation, a reiteration of the position or a re-defining of the arguments or assertions.

Organisational Frameworks

The information outlined above is usually included in texts used to persuade; however, the organisational framework used to construct each text will vary depending on the form and topic.

Should Dolphins Be Held in Captivity?

Dolphins are a part of nature and should not be caught and put into aquariums. I believe that they have the right to stay in their natural environment and should not be held in captivity.

Keeping dolphins in captivity can cause many health problems. Water that contains chemicals and bacteria causes numerous health problems such as pneumonia, ulcers, skin problems and stress related diseases.

Dolphins often have very high infant death rates when born in captivity. When baby dolphins are born they are sometimes kept away from their mother until it is sure they will survive.

Another reason for not keeping dolphins in captivity is that they often suffer from boredom. This may cause them to swim around in repetitive patterns and bang their heads against the walls.

Some people believe that keeping dolphins in captivity helps with research but it is better to learn about dolphins in their natural habitat.

Some people believe that keeping dolphins in captivity increases their life span but are they happy? Dolphins in the wild can live for up to forty years but this is not the case in captivity.

In conclusion I believe dolphins should be allowed to remain in their natural environment otherwise they will become extinct in the future.

Written By Kerry
Age: 13

Purpose: To persuade
Form: Exposition

THESIS
• overview of the basic position to be taken

ARGUMENTS/ASSERTIONS
• arguments for, and supporting evidence
• arguments against

CONCLUSION
• reiteration of position

Purpose: To Persuade
Form: Advertisement

THESIS
• statement

Sought-after Scarborough

Set on 420 sq m of land in Scarborough, this new two-storey home is spacious and stylish.

A staircase with a large feature window leads from the impressive entry hall, while sliding doors open to a large home theatre.

The living area consists of a kitchen and a large meals area/family room that opens onto a covered patio overlooking the pool. The kitchen has solid granite benchtops, stainless-steel appliances and a walk-in pantry.

Three bedrooms (all with walk-in robes) and two bathrooms are located down a long hallway.

The master bedroom has a large walk-in robe, television socket and a phone jack. The en-suite has floor to ceiling tiles, a spa bath, a big shower recess and two basins set in a granite vanity bench.

For a viewing opportunity, call Grant Hoskins on Harcourt Real Estate on 0423 214356.

ASSERTIONS
• supporting evidence

CONCLUSION
• request for action

fFigure 1.44 Framework Samples from Texts Used to Persuade

Language Features

Texts used to persuade usually include the following language features:

- Nouns and pronouns that refer to generalised participants; these are sometimes human, but are often abstract ideas, e.g. smoking, pollution.
- Technical terms, e.g. carcinogens, contamination, algal bloom.
- Generally use timeless present tense when presenting their position and points in the argument, but might change according to the stage of the text, e.g. if historical background is being given, the tense will change to the past; if predictions are being made, the tense might change to the future.
- Frequent use of passives, e.g. are polluted by, is caused by, is a result of.
- Verbs are often changed into nouns to make the argument sound more objective, e.g. to pollute becomes pollution.
- Signal words to indicate cause and effect, problem and solution, compare and contrast, conclusions, e.g. as a result of, one reason for this, on the other hand, in conclusion.
- Formal objective styles, i.e. first-person pronouns are not generally appropriate, personal opinions are disguised as facts. Emotive but impersonal language, e.g. It must surely be a catastrophe, endangering civilisation as we know it.

Adapted from Derewianka, B. (1990)

Assessing Writing to Persuade

Students are in the stage where they display most of the bulleted points.

Beginning Stage	Developing Stage	Consolidating Stage	Extending Stage
Can state the purpose and audience of texts to be composed and includes basic organisational features of simple forms used to persuade.	Is aware of the purpose and audience when composing texts and uses a partial organisational framework of a small range of forms used to persuade.	Considers the purpose and audience to select specific vocabulary and uses appropriate organisational frameworks to compose a variety of forms used to persuade.	Crafts forms used to persuade by selecting vocabulary and manipulating organisational frameworks to suit the context of the writing event.
The writer: • writes an opening sentence that states a personal position • presents information that may not maintain the stated position • provides little or no justification for viewpoint, e.g. I don't think they should chop down trees • includes information that is more personal opinion than evidence • writes a final statement that may not refer to the position taken • uses language close to speech, e.g. I reckon it's not fair ... • uses vague vocabulary, e.g. good, bad, nice • uses a limited variety of linking words, e.g. and, then, but	The writer: • writes an introduction that states a position • includes arguments in an arbitrary manner providing some supporting evidence, e.g. I don't think they should chop down trees because ... • attempts to generalise; however includes some personal statements • concludes with a personal statement, e.g. Therefore I don't think it is fair because ... • uses personal or subjective language • begins to choose vocabulary for effect • uses a limited range of linking words to do with problem and solution or cause and effect, e.g. however, although, on the other hand	The writer: • writes an introduction that clearly states the position to be taken • presents reasoned arguments in some planned or systematic way, but with limited supporting evidence for each assertion made • attempts to conceal a subjective viewpoint • is able to generalise information • attempts to summarise with a paragraph that substantiates the position adopted • uses an impersonal style, e.g. Trees should not be chopped down. Trees provide.... • chooses vocabulary for impact, e.g. remarkable, evil • uses a range of linking words to indicate cause and effect; problem and solution; compare and contrast	The writer: • writes a clear, precise thesis that states the position taken and previews the arguments that will follow • presents a well-researched argument selecting assertions and evidence in an attempt to influence the reader • generalises to authenticate the argument, e.g. Vehicles pollute the air • writes a final paragraph that reiterates the main points with an evaluative conclusion • uses formal objective style to suit purpose and audience, e.g. uses nominalisation to make argument seem more objective • selects vocabulary to influence the reader • writes cohesively using appropriate linking words

Focus on Assessing

Focus on Teaching

Familiarising, Analysing, Modelling, Sharing, Guiding and Applying See pages 30–37 and 109–112	Familiarising, Analysing, Modelling, Sharing, Guiding and Applying See pages 30–37 and 113–115

Figure 1.45 Assessment Guide for Writing to Persuade

Supporting Students at the Tuning-In Stage

This section provides ideas to support students who have not yet reached the Beginning stage on the Writing to Persuade Assessment Guide (Figure 1.45).

Focus on building students' awareness of the language features and organisational frameworks of the form being introduced. These familiarising activities are suited to any form associated with writing to explain.

1 Sample Displays see page 31

2 Reading to and Reading with Students see page 31

3 Literacy Activities

- Have students create a display or poster of their likes and dislikes. Then have them use the display to give an oral presentation expressing their likes and dislikes, e.g. **I like … because … ; I don't like … because … .**

- Create a line on the floor; label one end 'Yes' and the other end 'No'. Pose a question or statement that requires an affirmative or negative response. Have students stand along the line in a position that matches their opinion. Encourage them to explain why they are standing in that position, e.g. **I'm standing at the 'Yes' end because …; I'm standing in the middle because ….**

- Invite students to discuss local, national or international issues, and to share their opinions. Write an issue on the board, draw up columns on the board marked 'for' and 'against', then scribe students' oral responses in the columns.

- Have students work in groups of four. Present each group with a topic or issue for discussion. One pair works on arguments 'for' the issue, while the other pair focuses on arguments 'against'. Have each pair present their case. Finally, as a group of four, have the students summarise the discussion.

- Have students role-play situations where they need to take on different points of view. For example, a child has gone into a shop and accidentally broken an expensive item. Have students explain the situation, and what they feel should be the outcome, from different points of view, e.g. **child, parent, shop owner.**

- Provide time for students to conduct a weekly class meeting where they discuss class or school issues. Encourage them to use questions that invite responses, e.g. **Who else thinks …? Who doesn't agree with …? Who has a different thought about …?**

- Teach students how to conduct interviews as a means of obtaining information and varying opinions about an issue or a topic.
- Have class debates on issues from literary texts, e.g. **Was Goldilocks an innocent child or a burglar?** Encourage students to provide supporting evidence for their opinions.
- Provide opportunities for students to participate in informal debates. Arrange students into small groups. Have them discuss the debate topic, decide on their position (affirmative or negative), then generate reasons for choosing that position. Have students present their case to the whole group, substantiating their opinions and evaluating the arguments that have been presented by other groups.
- Invite a guest speaker to talk to students about a current issue. At the conclusion of the presentation, have students review the topic and summarise the speaker's arguments.
- Provide a range of catalogues. Have students review the catalogues and select what they would like to buy. Then have them identify the text features and any devices used to persuade the reader.
- Have students select a character or person from a text they have heard. Explain that the author needs to delete one of the characters from the text, then have students prepare a justification as to why 'their' character should be retained. Invite students to give an oral presentation of their case.

Supporting Students at the Beginning and Developing Stages

The main focus for these students is to help them understand the purpose, organisation, structure and language features of the text form being introduced.

Modelling and Sharing

The following modelling and sharing suggestions are separated into two stages; the first is specific to the Beginning Stage, and the second is more relevant to students in the Developing Stage. However, the suggestions should be seen as cumulative. When selecting a focus for the Developing Stage, teachers should also consider what is listed in the previous stage.

Beginning Stage	Developing Stage
Focus on understandings of text organisation, structure and language features. During Modelled, Shared and Interactive writing sessions, demonstrate how to:	
• develop a definite point of view before attempting to write the text	• order arguments for effect, e.g. positioning the strongest first
• write an introduction that states the position to be taken	• write a summary that substantiates the position adopted
• locate and collate evidence to support an argument	• make a point and effectively elaborate on it
• structure sentences that include justification of opinions, e.g. I think …, because…	• use general rather than personal statements of opinion to develop credibility
• select vocabulary to create a particular effect	• write positive and negative statements
• use linking words about problem and solution or cause and effect	• use the language of opinion in a more neutral tone, e.g. many argue that …., it seems that …
• use language that represents fact and opinion, e.g. It is reported rather than I think	

Figure 1.46 Suggested Focus for Modelling and Sharing Sessions

Guiding

The following guided-practice activities are suitable for students in the Beginning and Developing Stages, allowing them to build their understandings about texts used to persuade. Each activity should be used in a meaningful context across different learning areas.

Thumbs Up or Thumbs Down

Have students read texts that provide arguments for and against an issue. As a class, discuss the issue and the case for and against. Re-read the text to the students and have them put their thumbs up when they hear a statement that supports the thesis, or thumbs down if the statement refutes the thesis. Use sticky notes to mark each statement in the text; at the conclusion of the reading, identify how the information was organised, e.g. the information for each argument was grouped together.

Sorting Activity

Provide students with an envelope that contains a discussion topic, e.g. Homework should be abolished. Also provide a series of strips containing arguments for and against that topic. Have students read the strips and sort them into the affirmative and negative points. Encourage students to form an opinion based on the arguments presented, then have them share their opinion.

Flip Side

Provide students with an issue and one side of the argument. Have them use the information provided to compose a list of arguments representing the other point of view.

Text Response

Have students write opinions about characters, actions or events in a literary text, then have them provide justification for their opinion. Students' opinions should be based on evidence in the text, as well as on their personal experience.

Rate It

Invite students to use a rating scale to rank their level of reaction to an issue, e.g. **strongly agree, agree, undecided, disagree, strongly disagree.** Then have them read a text on that issue; when they finish, have them review their rating to see if it needs to be changed. Discuss the information that caused students to change their opinions, and have them cite examples from the text.

Word Cline

Select a word, then have students generate synonyms for that word, e.g. **some: several, various, countless, innumerable.** Then select a criterion to apply to the word (such as size: most to least), and have students arrange the words in rising intensity. Discuss the word range, and emphasise how the language the writer chooses has an impact on the text.

Cloze Activity

Have students complete cloze activities where particular words have been deleted, e.g. **linking words.** Allow time for students to discuss their word choice and its effect on the text.

Finish This

Provide a series of sentence stems for students to complete, e.g. **We should be allowed to wear casual clothes to school because … ; Another reason for casual clothes at school is ….** Have students provide a reason or justification to complete each sentence.

Behaviour Posters

Have students create posters that present desired school behaviours in a positive way, e.g. **Place all rubbish in the bin so that our school remains pest free and pleasant to look at.**

From Questions to Statements

Provide a series of questions, then have students turn the questions into statements and justifications, e.g. Question: Should logging be allowed in old-growth forests? Response: Logging of old-growth forests should never be allowed because …

Make it Stronger

Give students a piece of text that has several statements in it. Ask them to replace selected words to make the statements even stronger, e.g. change 'could' to 'should' or 'must'; change 'a few' to 'many'; change 'some' to 'most'.

Ranking

Provide students with a series of arguments in support of a specific issue. (Or have students generate the arguments.) Then have students rank the arguments in order from strongest to weakest, providing justification for their ranking. Invite students to reflect on how the order could change if the audience changed.

Fact or Opinion

Provide students with a series of statements, then have them sort the statements into two categories: those that are facts, and those that are opinions. Have students justify their sorting. Discuss what would be required to turn the opinions into factual statements.

Picture This

Have students collect the words used in advertisements to describe certain product lines, e.g. diet soft drinks, cars, holidays, mobile phones. Have student work in pairs to analyse and discuss the images the advertisers are trying to create. Students can then consider the audience to which the advertisers are trying to appeal.

Across Learning Areas

Provide opportunities across learning areas for students to compose texts used to persuade, e.g.

English	A job application for school or class council.
Society and Environment	A slogan about a local issue.
Health and Physical Education	An exposition about drug use.
Science	An advertisement to promote recycling.

Supporting Students at the Consolidating and Extending Stages

The main focus for these students is to help them enhance their control over the text form, including their ability to adapt and manipulate the text.

Modelling and Sharing

When selecting focuses for the Consolidating and Extending Stages, teachers should also consider what is listed in previous stages.

Focus on continuing to build students' understandings of text organisation, structure and language features, by demonstrating how to:

- capitalise on the background knowledge and possible opinions of the target audience when constructing text
- present a case by appealing to emotions while still sounding objective
- reinforce arguments by including diagrams, tables and statistical data
- present an argument that includes a number of perspectives, e.g. fishermen, conservationists, local shop owners
- generalise information to substantiate an argument, e.g. Smoking is dangerous
- influence the reader to take a particular point of view, e.g. present more arguments for one side than the other, quote authorities, use technical language, include data and statistical analysis
- conclude the text in an appropriate way, e.g. with a recommendation, a summary, a final or overall argument, reiteration of writer's belief
- use signal words to guide the reader through the reasoning behind the argument, e.g. firstly, however, on the other hand
- engage the reader by using devices such as rhetorical questions, preview of arguments or an appeal for reader response
- select words specifically for their nuance of meaning, e.g. 'criminal' or 'felon' rather than 'thief'.

Guiding

The following guided-practice activities are suitable for students in the Consolidating and Extending Stages, to further develop their understandings about texts used to persuade. Each activity should be used in a meaningful context across different learning areas.

Who's the Audience?

Provide several texts written to persuade; have students review the texts, then ask them to identify the possible audience for each text. Have students highlight those words or phrases that alerted them to the possible target audience.

You Heard it Here

Have students listen to (or view) a debate, TV interview or documentary. Provide time for students to summarise the text by recording the issue, arguments for, arguments against and any recommendations that were given.

Buy, Buy, Buy!

Provide a range of catalogues. Have students select a catalogue item that they would like to own. Then have students design an advertisement for that item, aimed at persuading buyers that it is a 'must have' item.

Cartoons

Collect a range of cartoons that comment on current issues. Have students discuss the message being portrayed through the illustrations and through the text. Encourage speculation on why the cartoonist has presented the information in cartoon form, then go on to discuss different portrayals of the same issue.

Infomercials and Advertising

Collect a variety of advertisements and infomercials. Have students identify the persuasive devices used by the advertiser to get their message across. Discuss the effectiveness of different devices.

Character Home

Provide a variety of real-estate advertisements. Have students select an advertisement, read it, then rewrite it, stating what they think is implied, e.g. 'A real fixer-upper' might mean 'This house needs major renovation work'; 'Has old world charm' might mean 'It lacks modern conveniences'.

Elect Me

Invite students to write a nomination speech for certain elected positions to become available in the classroom or school, e.g. sports monitor, class-meeting chairperson. Each speech should include statements, and provide supporting evidence about why that student is the most suitable representative for the position.

Be the Expert

As a class, select a topic of interest, e.g. Mobile phone use at school. Brainstorm a list of parties (or stakeholders) who might have a vested interest in the topic, e.g. teachers, students, parents, mobile phone company representative. Allocate one stakeholder to each small group of students, and ask each group to prepare a position statement from their stakeholder's point of view. Re-form the groups so that each group contains a representative from every stakeholder. Have students take turns to present the case from their stakeholder's point of view. Provide time for students to ask questions after the presentations have taken place.

Alternatively, groups could design a poster representing their stakeholder's perspective. Display the posters, inviting students to discuss which information on the poster helps them to identify the stakeholder.

Across Learning Areas

Provide opportunities across learning areas for students to compose texts used to persuade, e.g.

English	An exposition on the worst character in a selected text.
The Arts	An advertisement promoting a forthcoming production.
Science	An editorial about land conservation.

Social Purpose: Writing to Recount

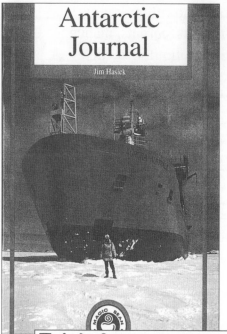

Antarctic Journal

Jim Hasick

movies

BY philip gore

KILLING ME SOFTLY

Joseph Fiennes and Heather Graham rip each other's gear off three times before the chocolate melts on your choc top. It's the only action that has any believable motive in this low-budget thriller. Enjoy, I say.
In brief: Video fodder.
Best/worst line: "I'll begin at the beginning ... it's usually the best place."

6/10

Trio's freeway bravery saved officer

DANIEL EMERSON

The only thing Bill Bennett and Ivan Routledge had in common on the morning of February 17 last year was that they were both travelling north on Mitchell Freeway, enjoying a clear run in post-rush hour traffic.

But their paths suddenly crossed in dramatic fashion when they found themselves furiously working with Const. Keith Tarver to free Const. Alicia Salvaris from a burning unmarked police car.

The car was hit by a light truck after the two officers stopped to clear debris from the freeway.

For their courage that day, Mr Bennett and Const. Tarver will get Bravery Medals and Mr Routledge a

Commendation. Mr Bennett, who stopped when he saw the police car become a spiralling ball of flames, and Mr Routledge, a bus driver who doused the flames, are both uncomfortable with the hero tag.

"I was just driving along and saw something that needed to be fixed and that's it," Mr Bennett, 50, of Darlington, said.

"We all think we know how we would react in a situation like that but the truth is we don't. We just go into automated response and what followed was just instinct."

Mr Routledge, 59, of Kingsley, said: "I don't think I'm a hero. I was just doing what I had to do at the time.

"But it does make life seem more

valuable. A few more seconds and it could have been disastrous."

Const. Tarver said the pair arrived at the critical time.

"These people just turned up out of the blue when everything was on fire and risked their lives without any formal training or responsibility to help out," he said.

"As we moved away from the wreckage the tyres were exploding and windows were smashing from the heat.

"I looked back at the car and when I saw how quickly it had just melted, I realised it had been pretty close."

Now a first-class constable with the traffic enforcement group, Const. Salvaris said the men's bravery gave her a second chance at life.

afterwards, fter seeing this. iscovery of love, s entertainment.

t but it's her a pile of metal."

9/10

a no-brainer, in the nicest sense. The characters from the popular Nickelodeon *Hey Arnold!* TV about wicked ity fight-back. time. but I love him!"

7/10

ustralian Table **15**

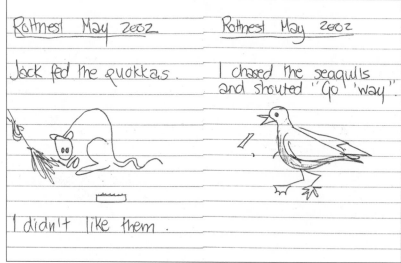

Rothnest May 2002

Jack fed the quokkas.

I didn't like them.

Rothnest May 2002

I chased the seagulls and shouted "Go 'way".

Figure 1.47 Samples of Texts Used to Recount

Understanding Texts That Recount

Texts that recount involve the writer retelling or recounting past experiences or events. The audience is given an insight into an experience, when it happened, who was involved, what happened and why. Writing to recount can be direct or indirect.

Direct Recounting: writers recount experiences in which they have been directly involved. Recounts are probably the most common form of this type of writing. Young students often write recount texts directly after being involved in oral Newstelling or Show and Tell.

Indirect Recounting: writers document events, incidents or particulars outside their direct experiences. Students are involved in this form of writing when they investigate historical people, for instance, to write a biography.

Different text forms used to recount include diary entries, journal entries, autobiographies, biographies, reviews, minutes of meetings and retells.

The following information is usually included in texts used to recount.

1 Setting or Orientation
Includes background information to assist the reader establish the context of the text. Details about who, where, when, what, why and how are described in this part of the text.

2 Events
Important events are usually arranged in chronological order, then elaborated upon.

3 Concluding Statement
The concluding statement depends on the purpose and audience of the text. It could include an evaluative comment; reflect the author's feelings, e.g. **We were all tired and very full**; or be an evaluation of the significance of the events described, e.g. **Captain Cook's voyage brought many benefits to the English government of the time.**

Organisational Frameworks

The information outlined above is usually included in texts used to recount; however, the organisational framework used to construct each text will vary depending on the form and topic.

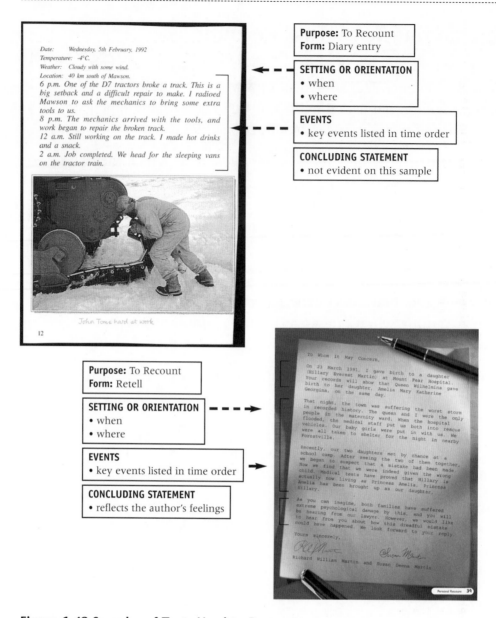

Figure 1.48 Samples of Texts Used to Recount

Language Features

Texts used to recount usually include the following language features:

- Nouns and pronouns that refer to specific participants, e.g. My family, Captain Cook, she, we, they.
- Simple past tense, e.g. went, swam, sailed.
- Mainly action verbs, e.g. went, discovered, led.
- Linking words to do with time or sequence, e.g. then, next, firstly, after that.
- Adverbs to indicate time and place, e.g. across the Pacific Ocean, down the street, in 1776.
- Reported and direct speech, e.g. The fire chief reported that the fire had been deliberately lit; Dad said, 'Here we go.'

Adapted from Derewianka, B. (1990)

Assessing Writing to Recount

Students are in the stage where they display most of the bulleted points.

Beginning Stage	Developing Stage	Consolidating Stage	Extending Stage
Can state the purpose and audience of texts to be composed and includes basic organisational features of simple forms used to recount.	Is aware of the purpose and audience when composing texts and uses a partial organisational framework of a small range of forms used to recount.	Considers the purpose and audience to select specific vocabulary and uses appropriate organisational frameworks to compose a variety of forms used to recount.	Crafts forms used to recount by selecting vocabulary and manipulating organisational frameworks to suit the context of the writing event.
The writer: • retells personal experiences	The writer: • reconstructs personal experiences or events using a limited range of forms and formats, e.g. recount, letter, email	The writer: • reconstructs personal and factual experiences and events using a variety of forms and formats, e.g. biographies, diaries, pamphlets	The writer: • recounts to suit purpose and target audience, choosing the most appropriate form and format
• provides little information about setting or the context in which the events happened, e.g. *tells who and where but not when*	• provides sufficient information to orient the reader, giving simple details about who, when, where, what, why and how	• provides an orientation that includes contextual and environmental details that impact on the way events unfold	• provides an orientation that both sets the scene and aims to interest the reader
• includes only those events that have personal significance • includes some events in sequence	• differentiates between events by including additional information about the more important events • lists all events in chronological order	• elaborates important events • elaborates substrands of participants that affect events, e.g. Helen Keller's perseverance in the face of adversity • gives credibility by the use of dialogue	• includes significant events chosen to add interest and impact • elaborates on events so that the reader can visualise the experience • chooses to include dialogue or reported speech for impact • manipulates time order of events for impact
• concludes with a personal comment, e.g. I had fun	• concludes with a personal evaluative comment, e.g. We arrived home, tired but happy	• concludes with an evaluative or summarising comment appropriate to the form	• concludes with a personal reflection, evaluative comment or summarises the text, appropriate to the form
• uses simple past tense • uses mainly simple action verbs, e.g. I went, I saw, I did • uses little variety of linking words, e.g. and, then	• uses simple past tense correctly • uses action verbs, e.g. *I played, we visited* • uses a limited number of linking words to do with time or sequence, e.g. after that, next	• maintains consistent tense • uses a variety of action verbs, e.g. I glimpsed, I travelled • uses linking words to indicate time, e.g. before, later in the day • uses both first and third person	• maintains consistent tense or manipulates tense for effect • writes cohesively using a large variety of action verbs and linking words • manipulates first and third person for impact

Focus on Assessing

Focus on Teaching

Familiarising, Analysing, Modelling, Sharing, Guiding and Applying See pages 30–37 and 121–124	Familiarising, Analysing, Modelling, Sharing, Guiding and Applying See pages 30–37 and 124–126

Figure 1.49 Assessment Guide for Writing to Recount

Supporting Students at the Tuning-In Stage

This section provides ideas to support students who have not yet reached the Beginning stage on the Writing to Recount Assessment Guide (Figure 1.49).

Focus on building students' awareness of the language features and organisational frameworks of the form being introduced. These familiarising activities are suited to any form associated with writing to recount.

1 Sample Displays see page 31

2 Reading to and Reading with Students see page 31

3 Literacy Activities
- Read students a variety of texts used to recount, including newspaper reports, letters, diaries, journals, retells, autobiographies and biographies. Discuss the following:
  Orientation: who, what, where, when, why, how
  Events: time sequence
  Ending: personal comment or evaluation
  Purpose: Why has this recount been written?
  Audience: Who is this recount written for?
- Newstelling is an ideal opportunity to familiarise students with the oral form of retelling. Provide opportunities for students to share personal or shared experiences with other class members, concentrating on the key components. Provide time for partner activities and small-group sessions as variations to whole-class sharing.
- Provide experiences that lend themselves to retelling:
  — Involve students in orally recalling information, e.g. from a language-experience activity, an art and craft activity, after playing a game.
  — Have students retell shared experiences with a partner, to a small group or onto a tape.
  — Encourage students to retell picture books.
  — Encourage students to use the class-writing bag to retell personal experiences.
  — Involve students in interviews with their peers or special guests.
  — Involve students in retelling a class experience or excursion to another class.
  — Record students' dramatic play on video and have them retell it to others.

- Provide experiences that encourage students to sequence events.
  — Provide pictures or photos of a shared experience, then have students put them in order.
  — Have students recall a class event and work in small groups to write each event onto a sentence strip, then have another group sequence the strips correctly.
  — Have students use pictures or sentence strips to reconstruct familiar stories that have obvious time-ordered events.
  — Provide opportunities for students to represent experiences or texts they have read or heard in different ways: pictorial timelines, flowcharts, story maps, acting out.

Supporting Students at the Beginning and Developing Stages

The main focus for these students is to help them understand the purpose, organisation, structure and language features of the text form being introduced.

Modelling and Sharing

The following modelling and sharing suggestions are separated into two stages; the first is specific to the Beginning Stage, and the second is more relevant to students in the Developing Stage. However, the suggestions should be seen as cumulative. When selecting a focus for the Developing Stage, teachers should also consider what is listed in the previous stage.

Beginning Stage	Developing Stage
Focus on understandings of text organisation, structure and language features. During Modelled, Shared and Interactive writing sessions, demonstrate how to:	
• include information in the orientation about who, what, where, when and why	• write a title that gives an insight into the text that follows
• sequence events in chronological order	• include sufficient background information in the orientation to familiarise the reader
• include information that relates to specific events or people, rather than general topics	• include specific details, e.g. At 5 pm on the corner of Myrtle and Collins Street ...
• select the events that require more detail	• include details about events or people that are important
• use action verbs, e.g. walked, discovered	• vary the action verbs used, e.g. instead of 'said' use 'shouted', 'whispered', 'yelled'
• use linking words that indicate time or sequence, e.g. before, after that	• use a variety of linking words that indicate time or sequence, e.g. secondly, later in the day
• use past tense correctly, e.g. I arrived, she explained	• use dialogue to give credibility
• write a personal evaluative comment as a conclusion	• write an evaluative or summarising comment as a conclusion
• use adjectives to build description	• use first person, e.g. I, we, when writing about personal experiences and third person at other times, e.g. Princess Mary, James Brown
• use words and phrases that indicate feelings and opinions	

Figure 1.50 Suggested Focus for Modelling and Sharing Sessions

Guiding

The following guided-practice activities are suitable for students in the Beginning and Developing Stages, allowing them to build their understandings about texts used to recount. Each activity should be used in a meaningful context across different learning areas.

Vocabulary Development

Work together to create class charts that focus on specific vocabulary used to write the orientation of texts used to recount:
When: yesterday, on the weekend, last night
Where: at the beach, in the playground
Who: Dad, my sister, the Premier.

News Plan

A News Plan can help students make the connections between what is spoken and what is written. Have students write key words under the headings of who, where, when, what, why. They can then use the information to help construct an oral or written recount of their news.

MY NEWS PLAN				
Who	Where	When	What	Why

Figure 1.51 Sample News Plan

Word Hunts

Have students read texts and search for specific words that indicate:
— the orientation, e.g. who, when, where, what, why, how.
— the time sequence, e.g. yesterday, today, tomorrow, first, next, after that, lastly.
— past events (time or content), e.g. A year ago, last night, horse and buggy, gramophone, telegram.
— the action, e.g. screamed, swam, chased.

Work together to collate and chart the groups of words. Encourage students to use the charts as a reference when writing.

Highlighting

Have students read texts that recount and underline or highlight where specific information has been included. This activity helps students focus on the key information in texts used to recount: who, where, when, what, why. Students can also use highlighting when they are refining their own writing, allowing them to add missing information, re-order information or add more detail.

when   *who*   *where*   *what*
Last week our family went to Margaret River for a holiday.
We wanted to spend time surfing and swimming.
                        why

Newshound

Provide students with a list of key words that cover the *who, where, when, what* and *why* of a news story. Challenge students to use the notes to construct a news report for the next edition of the newspaper.

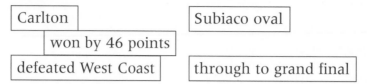

Carlton		Subiaco oval
	won by 46 points	
defeated West Coast		through to grand final

Adding Dialogue

Including dialogue in a personal retell will help students to add credibility to their writing. Have students re-read a personal retell they have previously composed. As students read the text, ask them to write anything that they can recall being said at the time of the event, e.g. **When the event was over, Mum said, 'Time to collect your gear and get in the car'**. Allow students to experiment with adding dialogue to their personal retells. Discuss how the dialogue helps to enhance the retell.

Across Learning Areas

Provide opportunities across learning areas for students to compose texts used to recount, e.g.

Society and Environment	A biography of a famous person.
Health and Physical Education	A personal recount of a sporting event.
Mathematics	A retell of a maths activity.
The Arts	A review of a play.

Supporting Students at the Consolidating and Extending Stages

The main focus for these students is to help them enhance their control over the text form, including their ability to adapt and manipulate the text.

Modelling and Sharing

When selecting focuses for the Consolidating and Extending Stages, teachers should also consider what is listed in previous stages.

Focus on continuing to build students' understandings of text organisation, structure and language features, by demonstrating how to:

- write an orientation that sets the scene and interests the reader
- manipulate the time order of events for impact, e.g. **flashback**
- select details to help the reader accurately reconstruct the event
- choose events that add interest and impact

- write appropriate conclusions, e.g. personal reflection, evaluative comment, summary
- manipulate the use of first and third person for impact
- include dialogue or reported speech
- use words and phrases that indicate time and location of events, e.g. Police radar indicated that the car was doing 146 kph on Ocean Highway at 10.16 p.m.

Guiding

The following guided-practice activities are suitable for students in the Consolidating and Extending Stages, to further develop their understandings about texts used to recount. Each activity should be used in a meaningful context across different learning areas.

Similarities and Differences

Provide retells of the same event, written by different authors. Have students read the retells, then work together to construct a list of their similarities and differences e.g. publication dates, audience, omissions, inclusions, use of language. Discuss the impact the differences could have on the reader of the retell.

Purpose and Audience

Discuss how texts that recount can be changed or modified according to their purpose and audience e.g. How would your retell change if you were going to present it at assembly rather than write it for the school newsletter? Focus on elements such as:
- use of language
- inclusion of details
- choice of format
- changing from first to third person
- changing from active to passive voice.

Have students work together to construct a modified retell that takes the elements above into consideration.

Changing Formats

Have students research and compose texts used to recount in different formats, e.g. a personal retell as a newspaper article; a biography as a pamphlet. Invite students to discuss what they need to consider when recounting in a different format.

Point of View

Provide opportunities for students to write factual recounts from different points of view, e.g. diary entries from Gallipoli for a Turkish soldier and an Australian soldier.

Sound Bite

Provide opportunities for students to research and report news from the school, local community or current world events. Have students organise and summarise their information into a thirty-second broadcast that could be put at the beginning or end of the news.

Recount Detective

Provide students with assorted samples of texts used to recount. Allocate different groups of students to search for words and phrases that indicate either time, location, action or dialogue. Have students create charts of the different language used, then use the charts as a reference when they are writing.

Joint Refining

Provide students with a text used to recount. Focus on improving different elements of the text by having students:
• manipulate the time order of events for effect
• add words or phrases that describe people, events or location in more detail
• write concluding paragraphs that summarise and evaluate events
• use different linking words.

Across Learning Areas

Provide opportunities across learning areas for students to compose texts used to recount, e.g.

English	Review of a book, film or theatre production.
Society and Environment	Diary of exploration.
Health and Physical Education	Retell of a sporting event.
Science	Journal of a science experiment.

Social Purpose: Writing to Socialise

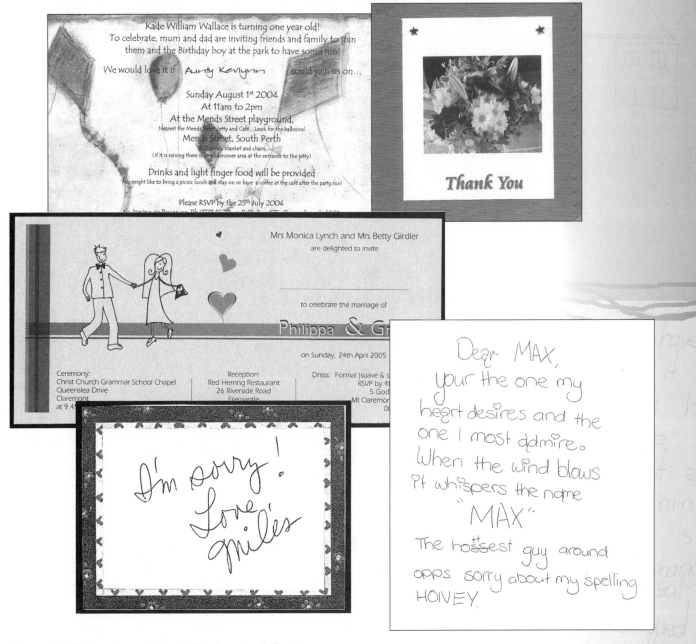

Figure 1.52 Samples of Texts Used to Socialise

Understanding Texts That Socialise

Texts used to socialise help writers to maintain or enhance relationships. These forms of writing can be formal or informal in tone, depending on the relationship between the writer and the audience. Different text forms used to socialise include apologies, thank you notes, invitations, greetings, notes and messages.

The following information is usually included in texts used to socialise.

1 Orientation

This part of the text establishes the purpose, and may include the time and place. These factors can also be inferred, especially if both the writer and the reader share the same context. The orientation may include a greeting.

2 Body

The body of the text consists of the 'message', stating the details of the communication.

3 Prompt

The prompt is often a call to action and involves instructions about what to do, e.g. **RSVP.** It may include how, by when and where that information is to be passed on. If the prompt is not a call to action, it is most likely to be a formal farewell, e.g. **Yours sincerely,** or an affectionate parting gesture, e.g. **Best wishes always.**

Organisational Frameworks

The information outlined above is usually included in texts used to socialise; however, the organisational framework used to construct each text will vary depending on the form and topic.

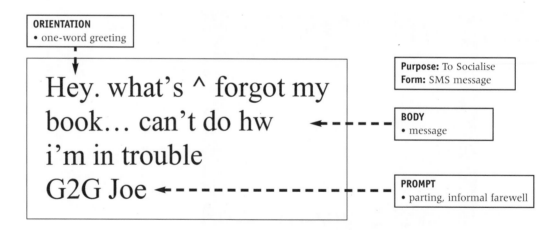

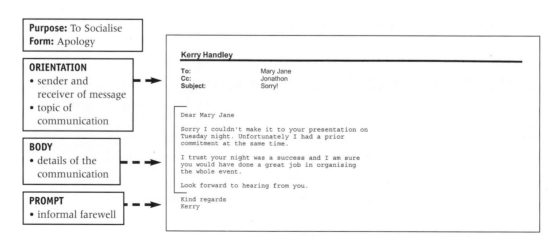

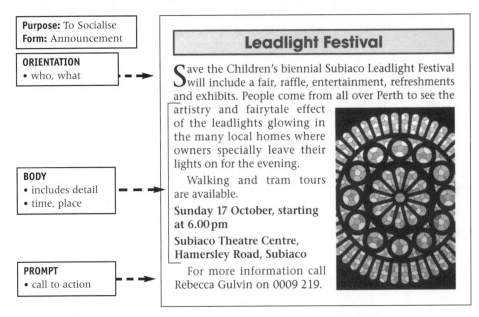

Purpose: To Socialise
Form: Announcement

ORIENTATION
• who, what

BODY
• includes detail
• time, place

PROMPT
• call to action

Leadlight Festival

Save the Children's biennial Subiaco Leadlight Festival will include a fair, raffle, entertainment, refreshments and exhibits. People come from all over Perth to see the artistry and fairytale effect of the leadlights glowing in the many local homes where owners specially leave their lights on for the evening.

Walking and tram tours are available.

Sunday 17 October, starting at 6.00 pm

Subiaco Theatre Centre, Hamersley Road, Subiaco

For more information call Rebecca Gulvin on 0009 219.

Figure 1.53 Framework Samples from Texts Used to Socialise

Language Features

Texts used to socialise usually include the following language features:

• First- and second-person pronouns, e.g. I, me, you, your.
• Specific participants, e.g. Mrs Smith, Li Chin, Grandma.
• Questions or statements of inquiry, e.g. Are you happy in your new house?
• Concise language.
• Simple past tense (although future tense for invitations).
• May contain a call to action, e.g. RSVP by 5th July.
• May include personal endearments, e.g. pet names.
• Action verbs.
• Signal words to show time.
• Formal or informal tone depending on the audience.
• May include statements of sentiment.
• May include abbreviations or pictograms, e.g. gr8, :).

Assessing Writing to Socialise

Students are in the stage where they display most of the bulleted points.

Beginning Stage	Developing Stage	Consolidating Stage	Extending Stage
Can state the purpose and audience of texts to be composed and includes basic organisational features of simple forms used to socialise.	Is aware of the purpose and audience when composing texts and uses a partial organisational framework of a small range of forms used to socialise.	Considers the purpose and audience to select specific vocabulary and uses appropriate organisational frameworks to compose a variety of forms used to socialise.	Crafts forms used to socialise by selecting vocabulary and manipulating organisational frameworks to suit the context of the writing event.
The writer: • writes to socialise with familiar audiences, e.g. family members • may leave the reader in doubt as to who the writer is • writes a simple message with no orientation or prompt, e.g. come to my party • omits many of the appropriate details regarding an event • uses the same few linking words, e.g. and, then • consistently uses an informal tone • begins to use vocabulary that reflects social conventions, e.g. thank you, dear	The writer: • writes to socialise with a limited audience, e.g. relations, peers • introduces self but gives no further details • uses a general orientation and prompt, e.g. to …, from … • states several of the details regarding an event, but not all • uses a limited number of signal words to do with time or sequence, e.g. firstly, after that, next • may use both informal and formal tones within a text • uses vocabulary that reflects social conventions, e.g. RSVP, Yours sincerely	The writer: • writes to socialise with unfamiliar audiences • introduces self and explains the group they represent but not their specific role • uses appropriate orientation and prompt to suit the audience • states all the appropriate details regarding an event, but may not include elaboration • uses signal words to indicate time and sequence, e.g. before, after that, later in the day • uses informal or formal tone appropriately • uses appropriate vocabulary to support or clarify the message, e.g. with deepest sympathy	The writer: • considers purpose and audience, most appropriate style, form and format when writing to socialise • introduces self and clearly outlines the group they represent and the role they play • opens and concludes with appropriate social conventions, e.g. in anticipation of your favourable response • clearly states all appropriate details, including any special considerations, in a succinct way • manipulates tense for effect • writes cohesively using a large variety of signal words to do with time and sequence • selects and manipulates tone appropriate to the audience and purpose • selects and adapts vocabulary to suit audience and purpose

Focus on Assessing

Focus on Teaching

Familiarising, Analysing, Modelling, Sharing, Guiding and Applying See pages 30–37 and 133–134	Familiarising, Analysing, Modelling, Sharing, Guiding and Applying See pages 30–37 and 135–136

Figure 1.54 Assessment Guide for Writing to Socialise

Supporting Students at the Tuning-In Stage

This section provides ideas to support students who have not yet reached the Beginning stage on the Writing to Socialise Assessment Guide (Figure 1.54).

Focus on building students' awareness of the language features and organisational frameworks of the form being introduced. These familiarising activities are suited to any form associated with writing to socialise.

1 Sample Displays see page 31

2 Reading to and Reading with Students see page 31

3 Literacy Activities
- Talk about the purpose of writing to socialise.
- Provide texts cut into individual paragraphs and have students reconstruct them. Invite students to share their reasoning behind the final text order.
- Provide authentic contexts for students to role-play writing to socialise, e.g. **Letterbox, message pads, notice boards, cards.**
- Share electronic postcards.
- Play 'Getting To Know You' to introduce the formal language of social courtesies. Have students stand in a circle and select one student to start. Have the 'game starter' walk around the outside of the circle, stop behind another student and say, 'Hi, I'm Peter. How do you do?' That student turns around and says, 'Hi, I'm Trudi. I'm very pleased to meet you.' They then shake hands. Each then runs in opposite directions around the circle. The first one back to the empty spot has the next turn to walk around the circle.
- Have students role-play conversations that would occur in classroom interest areas, e.g. **shopkeeper, home corner.** Reinforce the use of courteous language and behaviours, e.g. **greeting, thank you.** Work together to construct a class chart of the language used.
- Use puppets to model the language of socialising used during conversations. Provide opportunities for students to practise role-playing social conventions using the puppets.
- Provide opportunities for students to put themselves in someone else's position and speak and behave as they would. Ensure that students can relate the situation to their own experiences:
  — Answering the telephone (as Mum or Dad)
  — Giving messages (as an older sibling)
  — Thanking others for sharing (as the teacher).

Name			
Julie	✓		✓
Phuong		✓	✓

Figure 1.55 Sample Question Format

- Asking questions of other class members helps students to build relationships and develop the associated language. Give each student a recording format (see Figure 1.55) and a set of questions. Students write the name of each class member down the left-hand side and place the questions or pictures across the top. They then ask the questions, using stickers or check marks to record the answers.
  — Do you have a dog at home?
  — Do you have a cat at home?
  — Do you have a computer at home?
- Discuss how the audience determines the style of speaking and writing. Provide opportunities for students to interact with a variety of people, e.g. **peers, parents, older students, grandparents.** Discuss the type of language students used in each situation.
- Use classroom routines to reinforce the importance of social courtesies. Draw students' attention to correct behaviours and reinforce appropriate interactions. Provide time for students to role-play conversations related to appropriate and inappropriate behaviour:
  — Apologising for rudeness, forgetting, being late
  — Borrowing and returning items
  — Inviting and accepting invitations
  — Thanking and receiving compliments.
- Jointly construct written messages to send to other classes, teachers and other staff. Work together to construct a response when messages are received from other classes. Discuss the form and language used.
- Invite a guest speaker to visit the classroom. Before the visit, jointly construct invitations and introductions. Send out thank you cards after the event.

Supporting Students at the Beginning and Developing Stages

The main focus for these students is to help them understand the purpose, organisation, structure and language features of the text form being introduced.

Modelling and Sharing

The following modelling and sharing suggestions are separated into two stages; the first is specific to the Beginning Stage, and the second is more relevant to students in the Developing Stage. However, the suggestions should be seen as cumulative. When selecting a focus for the Developing Stage, teachers should also consider what is listed in the previous stage.

Beginning Stage	Developing Stage
Focus on understandings of text organisation, structure and language features. During Modelled, Shared and Interactive writing sessions, demonstrate how to:	
• use different prompts, e.g. personal endearments	• use the most appropriate orientation and closure to suit the audience
• write an orientation that introduces themselves	• write an orientation that introduces self and the group they represent
• include information when there is not a shared context, e.g. who, when, where, what	• include essential details needed to suit the audience, e.g. why
• use informal and formal language	• use concise language, e.g. date, time, place
• use different signal words to show time	• select appropriate vocabulary
• use abbreviations, e.g. RSVP, St	

Figure 1.56 Suggested Focus for Modelling and Sharing Sessions

Guiding

The following guided-practice activities are suitable for students in the Beginning and Developing Stages, allowing them to build their understandings about texts used to socialise. Each activity should be used in a meaningful context across different learning areas.

Literary Encounters

Have students select two characters from a familiar text and write a greeting, invitation or apology from one character to the other, then write the reply, e.g. an apology from Professor Snape to Harry Potter.

Paper Chain

Have each student randomly select the name of a class member, then write a positive note to that student on a strip of paper. Each student responds to their note on a different coloured strip of paper. Connect all the strips to make a paper chain.

Brown Bag ME

Place several items in a large paper bag prior to the class, with each item representing some substrand of yourself, e.g. picture of your dog, favourite CD, menu from your favourite restaurant. Take the items out of the bag one at a time and explain to the students the significance of each item. Then have each student compose their own Brown Bag ME, providing time for every student to share their brown bag. Use these sessions as a springboard to having students write notes and messages to each other.

Vocabulary Development

Jointly create class charts that focus on specific vocabulary used when using writing to socialise. For example:
When: yesterday, on the weekend, last night
Where: at the beach, in the playground
Who: Dad, my sister, the Premier.

Planning an Invite

Have students write key words under these headings: who, where, when, what, why. Then have them use the information to construct a written invitation. Once students are familiar with creating a plan, they can use it as a guide to write their own invitations.

Highlighting

Have students read texts used to socialise and underline or highlight where specific information has been included. This activity helps students focus on the key information in texts used to socialise: who, where, when, what, why. Students can also use highlighting when they are refining their own writing, allowing them to add missing information, re-order information or add more detail.

Across Learning Areas

Provide opportunities across learning areas for students to compose texts used to socialise, e.g.

Health and Physical Education	A thank–you note to a visitor.
Society and Environment	An invitation to view a display.
Science	A note of apology to the cleaner.
The Arts	An invitation to view an exhibition.

Supporting Students at the Consolidating and Extending Stages

The main focus for these students is to help them enhance their control over the text form, including their ability to adapt and manipulate the text.

Modelling and Sharing

When selecting focuses for the Consolidating and Extending Stages, teachers should also consider what is listed in previous stages.

Focus on continuing to build students' understandings of text organisation, structure and language features, by demonstrating how to:
- include information to establish the context
- select the form and format to suit the purpose and audience
- elaborate on details when necessary
- manipulate the tense for effect
- change from an informal to a formal tone when required (and vice versa)
- adapt vocabulary to suit the audience and purpose.

Guiding

The following guided-practice activities are suitable for students in the Consolidating and Extending Stages, to further develop their understandings about texts used to socialise. Each activity should be used in a meaningful context across different learning areas.

Greeting Cards

Provide opportunities for students to compose a greeting card from a selected character in a text to another character. Have students provide justification as to why the card would be sent, then discuss the receiver's possible reactions.

Conversational Journals

Provide a 'conversational journal' for each pair of students, who will become become 'conversation buddies'. Allow time for one student in each pair to write an introduction that ends with a question. The initial entry can be related to a literary experience, e.g. **When Lockie Leonard went surfing for the first time, he embarrassed himself greatly. I could certainly relate to Lockie as I have had many embarrassing moments. Can you tell me about one of your embarrassing moments?** Students pass on the journal to their 'conversation buddy' and wait for a response. Responses should always end with another question that will allow the written conversation to continue.

Consider the Audience

Discuss how texts used to socialise can be changed or modified according to the audience, e.g. How would your text change if you were going to invite the principal to the party, instead of your friend? Focus on elements such as:

• use of language
• inclusion of details
• choice of format
• changing from informal to formal tone.

Provide opportunities for students to jointly construct and compare texts for the different audiences, taking the above elements into consideration.

Joint Refining

Provide students with a text used to socialise. Focus on improving different elements of the text by having students:

• change from informal to formal tone
• manipulate order of information for effect
• add words or phrases that give more detail and clarify the message.

Excursions and Visiting Speakers

Excursions and visiting speakers give students authentic reasons to write texts used to socialise.

• Thank you notes to visiting speakers.
• Invitations to guests to visit the school or classroom.
• Requests to outside agencies for information.
• Messages or notes to other classes, principal, other staff members.

Message Board

Provide materials and an area in the classroom where students can communicate through notes and messages.

Across Learning Areas

Provide opportunities across learning areas for students to compose texts used to socialise, e.g.

English	A greeting card for a special event.
Health and Physical Education	A message to another class.
Technology and Enterprise	An invitation to attend awards night.
Mathematics	A note to parents for container collection.
The Arts	An apology for missing rehearsal.

CHAPTER 2
Contextual Understanding

Overview

This chapter focuses on how the interpretation, choice of language and the shaping of a text vary according to the context in which it is created — and the context in which it will be used.

When writers compose texts, several factors will influence their choice of language and the way they shape the text. It's important for writers to understand these factors. They include:
- the purpose of the communication
- the subject matter
- the mode of communication: spoken, written, visual
- the roles of, and relationships between, those communicating
- the physical situation in which the writing takes place
- socio-cultural beliefs, values and assumptions.

Students intuitively gain some understanding of situational and socio-cultural context by imitation, observation and repetition. However, it is important not to leave this to chance. Students need to be provided with explicit opportunities to reflect on how language varies — and how it needs to be amended according to purpose, subject, mode of communication and roles.

This chapter has one section:
- **Section 1 — Developing Contextual Understanding for Writing**

Figure 2.1

SECTION 1

Developing Contextual Understanding for Writing

Contextual Understanding and Writing

To become effective writers, students need to see writing as a social practice with a purpose and an intended audience. They need to understand how writers influence and affect their readers. They need to be aware of how their own socio-cultural context affects the way they use language, and that as writers they will often be making decisions for specific purposes.

Students also need to understand that the texts they write will be interpreted differently by various readers. Writers have the power to define, analyse and change the world (even in small ways) by influencing readers.

The ultimate goal is for students to use writing in real-life settings to communicate their ideas, share information, raise awareness, stimulate thinking, and influence and change social issues that concern them. The teacher's role is to introduce students to the idea that writing can be used as a way of interacting with others to bring about social change, and to set up situations in the classroom that allow this to happen.

All writing happens in a context. Context refers to the immediate situation, as well as the broader socio-cultural influences that influence all writing. Context influences what and how a text is written, and how the composed text is perceived. Writers need to be taught about situational context and socio-cultural context, to gain an understanding of how their own world view — and their social and cultural lives — impacts on the texts they write.

Situational Context

The decisions writers make about their writing vary according to the context of the writing event. These decisions are influenced by factors that guide the writer, and help them decide what to include and what to omit. These factors include:

- the situation or setting in which the writing takes place
- the writer's purpose for communicating
- the subject matter
- the language mode, i.e. more like spoken language, or more like written language
- the format of the communication, e.g. email, letter, brochure
- the roles and relationships between the writer and the audience, e.g. email from a company director to the employees, email from one friend to another
- the interactions with others while writing.

Changing any of these factors will impact on the choices a writer has to make. Similar factors influence how a reader uses and interprets a text.

Socio-cultural Context

Writers operate as members of a socio-cultural group, not as solitary individuals. All texts, to some extent, reflect the beliefs, views, expectations and values of the social and cultural groups of the time they were written. There are many factors that make up the socio-cultural context of a text:

- The choices that writers make reflect and shape their outlook.
- Writers are strongly influenced by their gender, ethnicity and status.
- Writers approach writing differently, according to their socio-cultural backgrounds.
- Writing is crafted, communicated and manipulated to influence others. This is often done to maintain or challenge existing power relationships between groups, such as employers and employees, businesses and consumers, governments and citizens.
- There are different varieties of English around the world, including varieties of standard English. Each variety reflects and shapes socio-cultural attitudes and assumptions.

What Students Need to Know

For students to write effectively and powerfully for various purposes and audiences, they need to be aware of the following:

- Writers make critical decisions when composing texts.
- Writers consciously choose to represent characters, people, events and ideas in different ways in literary and informational texts.
- Writers consciously select and use linguistic and print devices to enhance impact, or to influence particular audiences.
- Writers understand that their knowledge, experiences and perspectives influence the creation of texts.

• Writers use writing to influence change about social issues that concern them.

1 Writers make critical decisions when composing texts

Writers make informed choices about purpose, audience, form, content and language to meet specific situations. They evaluate the effectiveness of their writing by crafting and adjusting texts to suit the needs and expectations of their intended audience — and to influence them. Sometimes writers combine and subvert certain forms of texts, composing hybrid texts for specific effects.

Students need opportunities to examine a variety of texts, and to discuss some of the writing decisions authors have made and why they made them. Encourage students to reflect upon their own writing decisions, before, during and after writing.

Select and frame questions from the list in Figure 2.2 to stimulate discussion and reflection about the decisions that writers make.

Decisions Writers Make When Composing Texts

Questions about Purpose and Audience
• Why am I writing this text, rather than speaking or drawing?
• Who is the particular audience for this piece of writing?
• What does the audience already know?
• What do I know about my audience? e.g. age, gender, interests
• What does my audience want or need to know about my topic?
• What will my audience expect to see in this text?
• What will I do to appeal to my audience?
• How will I publish this text in a way that best suits my audience and purpose?

Questions about Form and Organisation
• What is the best way to get my message across?
• How will I organise my ideas?
• What text form will I choose?
• How will I set the text out? What organisational features will I use? e.g. headings, subheadings, diagrams
• How will the reader expect to see this set out?
• What is the best way to present or publish this information?

Questions about Content
• What do I want to tell them?
• What message do I want to give?
• What information needs to be included or left out?
• What points do I want to make?
• From what or whose point of view shall I write?
• What is the most appropriate language to use?
• Do I need to find further information?
• What resources could I use to find relevant information?
• What devices will I use to best suit my audience and purpose?

Figure 2.2 Decisions That Writers Make

2 Writers consciously choose to represent characters, people, events and ideas in different ways in literary and informational texts

Characters and events in literary texts are not real. They are constructed by writers as a means of presenting something and to invoke a particular response. When writers create informational texts they are presenting a particular view on a topic, selecting or rejecting facts and information to fit their view.

Students need opportunities to discuss how authors represent characters, people, events and ideas; this will allow students to transfer some of these understandings into their own writing.

Choose and frame questions from the list in Figure 2.3 to support students as they make decisions about how to represent characters, people, events and ideas.

How Will I Represent Characters and Events in Literary Texts?

- What words will I use to represent my characters?
- How will I describe the appearance of my characters?
- Will it matter what gender I choose for my characters?
- What names will I choose for my characters?
- Do I know any real people like the characters I am representing? How are they the same? How are they different?
- How do I want the reader to feel about my characters?
- What events will happen in this text?
- How will my text end?
- What special effects do I want to create in this text? e.g. humour, italics
- If I include illustrations, how will they support the text?

How Will I Represent People and Ideas in Informational Texts?

- What is the purpose of writing this text?
- Who is my audience for this text?
- What do I already know about the topic? What does my audience know?
- Where will I look for more information on this topic?
- What is my point of view on this topic?
- What do I want my audience to think and feel about this topic?
- What facts and ideas will I include in this text to support my view?
- What facts and ideas will I exclude to support my view?
- How will I represent the people or ideas?
- Will I include illustrations, photographs or diagrams to support my text? Where will I include them?

Figure 2.3 Making Decisions About Characters, Events, People and Ideas

3 Writers consciously select and use linguistic and print devices to enhance impact or to influence particular audiences

There are many different linguistic and print devices that writers can use to enhance their texts. Writers select from these devices depending on their purpose for writing and the needs of their audience. Writers evaluate the effectiveness of their choices and adjust their decisions throughout the writing process. Writers' use of devices often reflects their socio-cultural background.

Students need to become aware of how linguistic and print devices work when they are reading — this will allow them to use these devices to create impact in their own texts. Invite students to speculate on an author's reasons for choosing particular devices, and discuss their effectiveness.

Model the linguistic and print devices that writers use, and discuss their use. Encourage students to experiment with devices and reflect upon their effects. The main linguistic and print devices are outlined below.

Linguistic and Print Devices Used by Writers

Alliteration
Alliteration is the repetition of the initial letters or sounds in words that are close together, e.g. **the soft surge of the sea on the shore.**

Allusion
Allusion is an indirect reference to something outside the current literary work, e.g. **She was as mysterious as Mona Lisa.** The reference may be to a person, place or object in literature, history, modern culture, or another area. Allusion is often difficult for students to recognise and use, as they lack the necessary background knowledge.

Analogy
An analogy involves comparing one thing with another. It is often used to explain something unknown by comparing it to something known. Analogy can provide insights into similarities that would otherwise not be apparent, e.g. **The operations of a computer can be compared to the workings of the brain.**

Assonance
Assonance is the repetition of vowel sounds in words that are close together, e.g. **The owl swept out of the woods and howled around the house.**

Authorial Intrusion

Authorial intrusion occurs when the writer breaks into the text to directly address the reader, e.g. **As you can well imagine, dear reader …**

Bribery

Bribery is a persuasive device commonly used in advertising. Bonuses, free products, discounts and privileges are offered to the reader, e.g. **Buy one pair of shoes and get the second pair at 50% off.**

Choice of Language

The author can choose to use descriptive, technical or emotive language, e.g.
Descriptive: **The golden sun shone softly through the thin white clouds.**
Technical: **At the moment of solar eclipse, the Sun ….**
Emotive: **The blazing sun glowered down on the scorched earth.**

The author can also choose to use formal or informal language, e.g. **We had a most enjoyable excursion to the aquatic centre,** rather than, **It was wicked fun at the pool.**

Colloquialism

A colloquialism is a word used in everyday writing, but not in formal or literary texts. Colloquialisms are usually found in narrative texts. Slang words are colloquial and are usually culturally specific, e.g. **He was as crook as a dog.**

Connotation

Connotation is suggesting a meaning beyond a word's literal meaning. The suggestion can create positive or negative influences, e.g.
Professor Darcy Oliver had a reputation for being <u>wise</u>.
Professor Darcy Oliver had a reputation for being <u>shrewd</u>.
Professor Darcy Oliver had a reputation for being <u>judicious</u>.
Professor Darcy Oliver had a reputation for being a <u>smart alec</u>.

Consonance

Consonance is the repetition of consonant sounds in words that are close together, e.g. **A dark, deep dread crept into Derek's daydreams.**

Emoticon

An emoticon is a small icon composed of keyboard characters. It is a hybrid of the words *emotion* and *icon*. Emoticons are used in e-mails and instant messaging; they indicate the writer's mood and indicate to the reader how to interpret a message, e.g. **:-) = smile; :-(= sad.**

Figurative Language

Figurative language refers to using words in a non-literal way. The understanding of figurative language is often determined by a shared socio-cultural context. Figurative language is used by writers to express difficult ideas more clearly, by comparing them to something that the reader is already familiar with. Devices used figuratively include:

- **Euphemism** is the use of an expression that is a milder or less direct way of saying something, e.g. **The old lady passed away**, rather than, **The old lady died.**

- **Hyperbole** is an exaggerated statement, e.g. **He was scared out of his wits.** Hyperbole Understatement is the opposite, e.g. **She was a bit miffed when she found out she had lost her job.**

- An **Idiom** is a phrase with a meaning that has been established by common usage, but it is not evident from the actual words used, e.g. **It was a storm in a teacup.**

- **Imagery** is often used in literary texts to 'paint a picture' in the reader's mind. The image can be visual (creating a picture), auditory (creating a sound), tactile (how it would feel) or olfactory (how it would smell or taste).

- A **Metaphor** is an implied comparison between two things that are unlike, without using the words *like* or *as*. Rather than describing one thing as being like another, that thing becomes another. Words that indicate the metaphor are *is* and *are*, e.g. **Graham is a slimy toad.**

- **Metonymy** is substituting the name of something with the name of an attribute or object associated with it, e.g. **She gave him her heart (love).**

- **Personification** is giving human qualities to animals, non-human beings or inanimate objects and abstract ideas, e.g. **The fog crept over the sleeping village.**

- **Proverbs** are concise sayings that express a general truth, e.g. **A rolling stone gathers no moss.**

- **Rhetorical questions** are questions that are asked for effect, without expecting an answer, e.g. **Bank charges have gone up again. Don't you think they're making enough profits?**

- **Similes** are direct comparisons between two things to show their similarity. Words use to construct a simile are *like* or *as*, e.g. **That model is as skinny as a rake.**

Flashback

Flashbacks are commonly used in literary texts to explore events that occurred previously, explaining their impact on the current situation. They can be used to create a sense of nostalgia or to increase the reader's understanding. Flashbacks can be achieved using dream sequences, by a character reflecting on their memories, or by a character's narration.

Flattery

Flattery involves an appeal to the reader's self image, including the need to belong or the need for prestige, e.g. **Every good parent knows** …. Flattery also includes association, which is discrediting or enhancing a position by association with some other person, group or idea, e.g. **Leading scientists throughout the world agree on the importance of** ….

Foreshadowing

Foreshadowing is a device commonly used in literary texts to hint at what is to come, e.g. **As she sat watching television, there was a loud bang outside.**

Formatting

Writers make decisions about layout, text format and design. This is common with electronic texts, which can even involve using purpose-designed templates, e.g. **The use of a letter wizard in word processing software.** Writers use organisational units, such as headings, sub-headings, chapters, paragraphs and page breaks. These units add structure to the texts, signal important information and denote pauses and movements in plots and narratives.

Inclusion or Omission of Details

The author selects only those details that support their chosen perspective. Other details that contradict that perspective are omitted. In electronic texts, the author can choose to use hypermedia devices of symbols, images and sounds to focus and juxtapose views. Details can be added to texts by inserting hypertext to connect to other documents of any kind, including audio and film clips. The multi-modal text created is interactive, designed to enhance the reader's experience of the topic and to offer the reader some choice and control. However, the links used by the reader can modify or even disrupt the author's intended meaning.

Intertextual Devices

Kristeva (1984) describes intertexuality as the interdependence of texts, the relationship between two or more texts that quote from, refer to or connect to one another in some way. Intertextual devices are like 'in jokes', and are used by writers to attract and appeal to their readers. They will only be understood if the writer and the reader have a shared socio-cultural context. Intertextual devices are not always used consciously by writers; students, in particular, may not even be aware that they are using them. Some examples from Harris, McKenzie, Fitzsimmons and Turbill (2003) are:

- **Confirming or Disrupting Established Themes** The writer incorporates themes that support or contradict established archetypes, e.g. In Hutchins' *Rosie's Walk* (1968), Rosie and the fox appear at first to assume traditional roles as timid, defenceless prey and wily predator, but this is disrupted continually as Rosie outwits the hapless fox.
- **Parody** Parody is a humorous imitation of another text when an established text is 'sent up', e.g. Babette Cole's *Prince Cinders* (1987) is a parody of the original Cinderella fairy tale.
- **Pastiche** Pastiche is where elements of other texts are combined in writing a new text, e.g. Ahlberg's *The Jolly Postman* (1996) uses characters and events from nursery rhymes and fairy tales to create a new narrative. Anthony Browne's *Into the Forest* (2004) also makes references to fairy tale characters to add further depth to the story.
- **Versions of Earlier Texts With or Without a Twist** This might involve retelling a fairy tale from another point of view, e.g. Scieszka's *The True Story of the Three Pigs* (1989), told from the wolf's point of view, or creating contemporary versions of traditional tales to give texts a twist, e.g. Fiona French's *Snow White in New York* (1989).
- **Versions of Other Texts in Different Media** This often involves reworking books into movies, e.g. Making the movie *Shrek* from William Steig's picture book *Shrek!* (1990).

Irony, Wit, Humour

Irony, wit and humour rely heavily on a shared socio-cultural context to achieve the author's purpose.

- **Irony** contrasts the reality and the expectation, what is written and what is meant, e.g. While he watched the rain coming, Tim remarked, 'Lovely day for a picnic'.
- **Wit** refers to the perception and expression of a relationship between seemingly incompatible or different things in a cleverly amusing way.
- **Humour** is the perception, enjoyment or expression of something that is amusing, comical, incongruous or absurd.

Irrelevance

Irrelevance is including points or arguments that do not contribute to the main idea, with the aim of distracting the reader.

Jargon

Jargon (or technical language) is using words that are specific to a particular subject.

Neologism

Neologism is the creation of a new word or expression, e.g. 'brillig' in Lewis Carroll's *Jabberwocky*.

Onomatopoeia

Onomatopoeia is the use of words that sound like the action they represent, e.g. the swish of a skirt, the click of high heels.

Overgeneralisation

This is the use of a statement that encompasses a wide group of people or situations, and is not necessarily based on fact, e.g. Girls in kindergarten settings engage more in dramatic role-play than boys do.

Oversimplification

This occurs when a simple (and often single) statement is used to explain a situation that is the result of a number of complex and interwoven factors, e.g. He was unable to make a commitment in relationships because his parents had divorced when he was young.

Personalisation

Personalisation involves adopting a tone of intimacy through the use of first person or personal pronouns, e.g. We all know that what you said is just not true. It can include commands, e.g. Your country needs you! and rhetorical questions, e.g. Where have you been all my life?

Print Size, Colour and Font

Authors make decisions about print size, colour and font selection to suit their texts. Choosing specific words to be displayed in bold type, italics, underlined or in colour — or using a particular font size — can indicate what the author feels is important for the reader to notice. Different fonts can be used for different reasons. For instance, using a handwriting font to suggest a familiar or informal relationship between the author and reader. Certain fonts are deliberately selected by authors to match or enhance their texts, e.g. **A Funny Story**. A Chilling Tale.

Pun

A pun is a play on words where a word is used to suggest different meanings, e.g. Why did the teacher wear glasses? To control her pupils. Puns are generally found in humorous texts, such as jokes.

Quoting someone out of context

Authors often select a single part of a written or spoken text and use this part to present a different impression or point of view. Quoting someone out of context to mislead or influence the reader can create bias, and often appears in texts used to persuade.

Repetition

Repetition (or repeating words or phrases) puts emphasis on particular parts of a text; it can also be used to create dramatic tension, e.g. In the dark, dark house there was a dark, dark room.

Rhyme

Rhyme is repeating the same sound, and usually involves the final syllables, e.g. My little boy is now asleep. Into his room I softly creep. Each breath he takes is quiet and deep. Beside his bed, I kneel and weep.

Internal rhyme occurs when a sound is repeated within a line, e.g. Walking along, singing a song.

Rhythm

Rhythm is the recurring flow of strong and weak beats in a phrase, e.g. Chicka, chicka, boom, boom! Listen to the trombone.

Sarcasm and Satire

Sarcasm is scathing language that is intended to offend or ridicule. Satire ridicules human weaknesses, vices or follies with the intention of bringing about social reform. Sarcasm and satire rely heavily on a shared socio-cultural context to achieve the author's purpose.

Stream of Consciousness

This is a narrative method where the writer describes the continuous thoughts and feelings from 'inside' a character's mind. A classic example is *Ulysses* (1922), by James Joyce.

Symbolism

A symbol is a person, object, image, word or event that is used to represent or suggest something beyond its literal significance. Symbols are often used to add additional depth and meaning to writing, e.g. Using the season of spring as a narrative setting often suggests renewal. Many symbols are culturally specific and the reader needs to share a similar cultural background to the writer to understand them. The same symbolic meaning will not always transfer between cultures, e.g. The colour white is associated with weddings in Europe but with funerals in many parts of Asia.

Testimony

Testimony is the use of quotations from experts or people positively associated with a situation or product. It is used to state opinions disguised as facts. Testimony also includes the use of statistics, and is often found in advertising, e.g. Nine out of ten pharmacists recommend … .

Understatement

Understatement is used when trying to downplay the gravity of a situation or event, e.g. I only have a small lump in my lung.

Devices Used by Illustrators and Designers

Illustrators and designers use visual devices to influence the reader and to support and elaborate upon the text. Sometimes writers illustrate their own texts or collaborate with the illustrator of their text. But most of the time, the writer and the illustrator work separately. When students are publishing their writing, provide stimulus by having them examine and discuss picture books, informational books, magazines, advertisements, posters and other illustrated texts. Encourage students to experiment with the following illustrators' and designers' devices when they are publishing their own writing.

Amount of Detail

Illustrators include varying amounts of detail to enhance and complement the written text. Details can provide, in a single picture, an impression that would take the writer many sentences. Details may also give a more realistic feel to the illustrations.

Artistic Style

Artistic style refers to the way the illustrations are done, and it can tend towards realistic or representational. Subjects and objects are portrayed with detailed accuracy in realistic art, as they would be in real life. But the illustrator makes no attempt to make the art appear realistic in representational art. Each artistic style conveys a different message to the reader and is chosen to support the text.

Colour

Colours have symbolic meaning. Illustrators often choose colours to create certain effects or to support ideas in the text, e.g. **Red can indicate passion or violence, while green and blue suggest calm and tranquillity.**

Composition and Page Design

Placement is another device used by illustrators and designers. It refers to the use of visual elements on a page or within a text. Objects placed in the foreground have more prominence than objects in the background. Visual elements placed on the right-hand page of a text have greater prominence than those on the left-hand page. Illustrators and designers often include white space in a design to draw the reader's attention to certain substrands of the page.

Medium

Medium refers to the material or technique used by an illustrator, e.g. **collage, charcoal, watercolours, photographs.** An illustrator's choice of medium can provide readers with clues about the message or purpose of the text, e.g. **photographs suggest the text is realistic.**

Size

Writers and designers make choices about the relative size of each illustration, table, photograph and diagram. The relative size of visual elements can change at different places in a text to emphasise different points. Illustrators sometimes indicate the most important characters or people by making them larger than others.

4 Writers understand that their knowledge, experiences and perspectives influence the creation of texts

Writing is a social activity for most students; the interactions they have with each other as they write impact upon the texts they compose, by triggering and influencing ideas. Students need opportunities to discuss how their knowledge, experiences and perspectives influence the texts they compose. They need time to share and discuss their experiences before, during and after writing. Teachers need to consider how to bring students' home and community experiences into classroom writing experiences. The following examples describe how two teachers linked home and community.

A Circle in a Room Full of Squares

In the introduction to her student writing anthology *A Circle in a Room Full of Squares*, Suzanne Covich (2003, p.5) describes a project in which Years 8 and 9 students in a port city school in Western Australia were asked to 'write from the heart about what they knew well' about their lives and experiences at school and in the world. The students could use pseudonyms, fictionalise experience, remain anonymous or give their own names to their work. The resulting writing was edited by Suzanne and published professionally. Issues described included bullying, teasing, family relationships, ethnicity, sexuality, body image, difference, death, disability, illness, exclusion and being 'cool'.

In the foreword to the anthology, Wayne Martino explains how Suzanne created a 'public space' for students 'to write about what matters to them in terms and a language which is their own'. The result was writing that showed 'the power of student voices' with a 'capacity to inform our understanding and deep knowledge of these young people's lives or views of the world'. This sort of writing had the power to 'disrupt the stereotypes' and the 'capacity to transform dominant understandings' (Martino in Covich, 2003, p.4).

I would like to start by telling you a little about my mum, just because I need to. She is such a caring person and is always there for others and me. Though I know that her illness makes her tired she is never too tired to spend time with me, even if at times I am selfish. She understands. She loves me for who I am, not just the things I say, which can sometimes be hurtful. She's a great cook, a great listener, a great person and above all, a great mum.

When my grandfather died I understood that it was his time, and even when my young cousin, Travers, was killed in a car accident, I knew you had bigger plans for him. Many times I question why things happen on this earth, but do not get me wrong, I do not blame you. I just need to know that there is a purpose to all that happens. I struggle to find reasons and I get really frightened.

Why am I the circle in a room full of squares?

Why am I the face that gets the stares?

Why is the finger always pointed at me?

Why don't they understand and why can't they see,

That the difference I have is what makes me, me.

On Father and Son Kite Flying Day, way back when I was a kid, sometimes I'd have to sit in class while everyone else was out there with their dads. And sometimes I was out there too. It was my uncles who brought my kite.

I'm okay now. I've dealt with it and it's the least of my problems. I don't cry any more. I don't wonder anymore. I can't let you hurt me any more. When I say "you" it's my dad I am talking to. It's how I express my anger and sometimes it goes like this. I talk to him in my head.

Girl

I am a girl with no friends, nobody down here knows me, nobody really knows my name, where I am from and most of all who I am. I am a girl from Beagle Bay, now in Perth at boarding school.

I am a girl in a new world — a world of thousands of Gardias (white people) who are all so private and unfriendly. I am Aboriginal, born in Beagle Bay, lived in Beagle Bay . . . until now.

The first thirteen years of my life were the best thirteen years of my life. I knew everyone in the community and everyone knew me. Everyone was friendly, I could go into anyone's house because I knew them or they were family.

Figure 2.4 Samples of Students' Writing

Lives of Love and Hope

Students have a lot of expertise in 'home literacy'. Identifying language forms used and valued at home — such as storytelling, popular magazines and television programs — and giving them a place in a writing program is one way to give students more confidence and incentive to write.

Chris Searle in Knobel and Healy (1998) describes a writing project undertaken by 11-year-old students living on a housing estate in Sheffield, UK. The students interviewed their mothers, grandmothers and aunts in their own 'mother tongue', then translated the interviews into English. With the teacher's help, the interviews were written up as recounts. They were then edited and published as an anthology of stories documenting family and cultural histories, and stories of migration, racism and struggles in a new country. The recounts were published as *Lives of Love and Hope: A Sheffield Herstory*. Publication of the book gave crucial recognition to students' own languages, home experiences and validity in the school writing program, and became a powerful community resource.

Community Elders

A remote indigenous community in Western Australia invited community elders to come to school and record stories from their oral tradition in their community language. These stories were then transcribed by students and teachers into bilingual texts, illustrated by community artists and students and published professionally for use as school and community reading resources. The texts became community treasures and useful reading resources for other schools in the region.

Class Anthology

To engage students in writing tasks, it's important to provide them with opportunities to write in their own words as experts about topics of personal significance.

A Year 5 class in an inner city Perth school identified knowledge and skills they had as individuals that they felt comfortable sharing with the class — and which they thought their peers might find interesting. These included kite flying, making pizzas, spinning Tazos, making earrings, playing rugby, playing chess, dressing teddy bears, fishing and soap making. Students gave talks or demonstrations on their area of expertise to small groups of their peers, then wrote procedural texts. The texts were collated into a class anthology and shared with the school community.

The class later went on to compile a 'Yellow Pages' phone book (or class directory) advertising the skills and special knowledge of its members. This directory became a popular resource for students when researching topics or seeking assistance with projects.

The questions listed in Figure 2.5 relate to a writer's world view. They can be used to stimulate discussions before, during or after writing. Choose and frame the questions according to students' needs.

Discussing a Writer's World View

- What do you know about the topic?
- What do you need to research or further explore?
- What experiences have you drawn upon to compose this text?
- What texts have you read, heard or viewed which have influenced your text?
- What expertise or authority do you have for writing about this topic?
- Why did you choose to represent (a character, setting, event) in (a realistic, humorous, historical) way?
- From whose point of view have you written the text? Why?
- From what other point of view could the text have been written? How would the text change then?
- How do you think your background has affected the way you wrote the text?
- How might the reader's background, experience and perspective influence their reading of this text?
- What have you done that will assist your reader to understand and navigate the text?
- Which readers would find your text most appealing?
- Are there any groups of readers who would dislike or disagree with what you have written?

Reflecting on Your Writing Style

- Do you have a preferred writing style?
- What types of characters do you tend to create?
- What types of settings do you tend to use?
- Do you suggest certain values? e.g. It's okay to be different.

Figure 2.5 Discussing a Writer's World View

5 Writers use writing to influence change about social issues that concern them

The ultimate aim of any comprehensive approach to teaching writing is to produce confident, competent and independent writers who 'write for people … write to make a difference … write to do good work in the world' (Harwayne, 2000, p.55).

Bringing critical literacy practices into the writing process involves students in writing about social issues in their world from their perspective, and using their writing to have a real influence on the community.

Social-action writing begins when students share learning and ideas about 'issues' they see as relevant to their world. Home, family, neighbourhood, school and local community all offer relevant contexts. Such contexts allow students to identify and act on issues and problems that are important to them, and to collectively find solutions that bring about change in their own lives.

There is almost always some way students can make some contribution to change when topics are selected that are relevant to their lives, and to their local or global community (Murdoch, 1998). Even younger students can engage in this sort of writing collaboratively, using joint construction to develop an understanding that writing has the power to influence others – the pen *is* mightier than the sword!

There are numerous opportunities to use writing for social action in the classroom. The following examples have been collated from many teachers.

Social Action in the Classroom
- Using class-meeting times to identify issues the class is facing, then posting possible solutions in a suggestion box.
- Writing a note to the cleaner requesting the replacement of a flickering light bulb. Then writing a thank-you note when the light bulb was replaced.
- Using bulletin boards as a forum for students to post lost and found notes, or writing on class, local and global issues.
- Surveying students about their favourite books, then writing to the school librarian to request their purchase.
- Inviting a favourite author to talk to the class. Writing to an author with suggestions for future books.
- Creating posters and articles for the school newsletter to promote fundraising events, such as a cake stall to raise money for a school camp.

- Writing suggestions to the class and teacher for the best way to communicate with parents and the school community about learning projects.
- Writing captions, signs, posters and catalogues for class exhibitions that highlight learning projects.
- Writing invitations to parents and the community to attend class events.
- Creating a website to represent the class to the school community.
- Writing and self-publishing books and poems about social issues or scripting plays and performing them.

Social Action in the School

- Producing a catalogue of lost property items to send home.
- Writing a letter of complaint to the school council about the cleanliness of the school buildings.
- Devising questionnaires and surveys to evaluate the school PE program and making recommendations to the school council. Writing to the PE teacher to suggest new events or formats for the athletics carnival.
- Surveying students on ideas for a new canteen menu. Creating a petition and writing a protest letter to the canteen manager about the current menu, with recommendations for changes based on the survey.
- Devising a code of behaviour for playground areas. Designing posters to promote this code.
- Surveying other students to determine the play equipment they would most like. Writing to the P&C Association requesting new playground equipment based on the survey.
- Creating a website to promote the school and to share events with the school community. Providing protected spaces on the site for message boards, e-zines and blogs on school and community issues.
- Writing to the school radio station to request that they play students' favourite songs.
- Writing to the principal and school council to request changes to the school uniform. Creating a petition on the issue. Designing new uniforms. Writing a speech to present to the school council on the issue.
- Surveying students on experiences of bullying and writing suggestions to the principal and teachers for dealing with any issues.
- Analysing the school's use of renewable resources such as paper and water, and developing an action plan for recycling or conserving materials. Writing a news report for local newspapers describing the development of the action plan.

- Writing speeches and slogans, and producing posters, bumper stickers and badges during campaigns for student leadership.

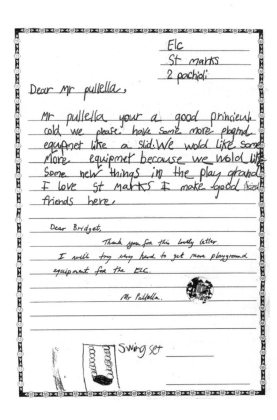

Figure 2.6 Social Action in the School

Social Action Beyond School

- Writing posters or banners or designing T-shirts with slogans for use in community events, such as street parades or festivals.
- Organising fundraising efforts to sponsor a child in a developing country or in response to a community, national or global disaster.
- Writing to or e-mailing local councillors to request improved community resources for young people, such as a new skatepark or playground. Devising surveys and petitions and compiling a report with suggestions.
- Creating surveys and petitions, then writing letters to companies involved in the pollution of local waterways. Writing to politicians, councillors and community organisations to highlight issues. Writing articles for newspapers. Making posters and banners for protests.
- Writing to TV stations to request coverage of particular sporting events.
- Writing letters to newspapers in support of (or against) local or global issues.

- Writing to toy manufacturers regarding stereotyping of particular toys and suggesting alternative representations.
- Using the Internet to engage in social-action projects around the world. Examples of such projects include collecting data on rare and endangered species, assisting schools in disadvantaged communities, adopting zoo animals, working with other indigenous students from around the world on collaborative projects, writing exchanges and various humanitarian efforts.
- Publishing personal work in e-zines in support of social action projects.

SNAPSHOT # 1   Conference on Sustainability

Seth Yeoman in Dougan and Gorman (2005) describes how a year 6/7 class at an inner-city port school in Western Australia worked with a local university to plan, organise and present a conference on Sustainability. This involved producing posters and pamphlets, devising a program and timetables, writing signs, writing letters, preparing oral and multimedia presentations, e-mailing university lecturers and other speakers, designing evaluation forms, writing reports for the local newspapers and writing reflections on their learning. The day was a huge success and generated an enormous amount of pride within the class.

Figure 2.7

Figure 2.8 Brochure from the Sustainability Conference

SNAPSHOT # 2   Recycling for the Local Community

The students in Sarah Cuthbertson's Years 1, 2 and 3 class in Victoria wondered why their community did not have recycling facilities (Murdoch and Wilson, 2004). After writing to their local council and receiving a response that the cost was too great, the students created a survey about waste and recycling, which they sent home to their families. The results were tallied and graphed, and solutions proposed. Letters were sent to relevant people and companies in the community summarising the data and the proposals. After a month, the general manager of Vincent Industries visited the students; he was so impressed with their work that he agreed to install a recycling station of six wheelie bins for glass, cans and plastics at the school by the end of the week. The students' learning had a great result for their community.

Figure 2.9

SNAPSHOT # 3   Toxic Waste

Barbara Lewis (1998) and her sixth-grade students from Utah found 50 000 corroded and leaking barrels in a dump near their school. After researching the importance of ground water and how easily it can be contaminated, they approached state health officials, who said nothing could be done. The class produced a neighbourhood survey, made a map of old wells in the community for testing, then wrote to the EPA, the site's owner and the mayor. They wrote public service announcements, created flyers, published articles in local and national papers and magazines, wrote and gave speeches to civic groups, and appeared on radio and TV.

They were finally successful in persuading the state to remove the barrels and conduct testing, which revealed a serious level of contamination by toxic waste. The students created a clean-up fund and lobbied successfully for the passing of a state Superfund clean-up law. Inspired by the power of their actions, they took on other projects involving writing for social action, such as pushing through a state law funding grants for kids to plant trees, organising a national kids' petition that resulted in a federal budget for youth neighbourhood improvement projects, hosting an anti-crime night for parents, lobbying police to have a nearby drug dealer's house bulldozed and replaced with a low-cost dwelling for a new family, creating a hotline for kids who had been abused or who wanted information about abuse, and designing an anti-abuse advertisement that was played on TV and displayed on billboards. These students had no doubt at all about the powerful effects of their writing.

Figure 2.10

> ### *SNAPSHOT # 4*   Behind the News
>
> Bronwyn Twining in Dougan and Gorman (2005) describes how her Year 6/7 class in Perth were avid viewers of the current affairs program *Behind the News (BTN)*, produced for schools by the ABC. They would regularly have intense discussions about the issues that arose each week. Hearing that the program was to be axed due to Government funding cuts, the students wrote to their local Federal member outlining their disappointment. Some weeks later, everybody received a reply from the Federal member outlining his own disappointment and explaining that he had spoken about it in Parliament and raised the issue with the ABC. There were many articles and letters in the newspapers about the demise of *BTN*, and although it was taken off air for a period, it has since been returned to the ABC schedule. The students felt very empowered by the effect their actions may have had on this decision.

Figure 2.11

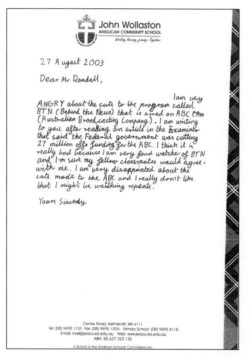

Figure 2.12 A student's letter, and the response

CHAPTER 3
Conventions

Overview

This chapter focuses on building students' knowledge and use of written conventions, such as spelling, grammar, punctuation, text structure and vocabulary. Students must be aware of the structures and features of Standard Australian English; this will allow them to communicate effectively through writing in a range of settings.

Knowledge of language structures and features enables students to make choices about the mode of communication, the type of text, the grammatical structures, the presentation style and the most appropriate words for a particular setting. They are able to talk about the choices they have made and the language structures and features they can recognise in their daily encounters with language. For example, students preparing a recount of a school event for a local newspaper might conclude, after reading several newspaper articles, that they need to use a particular text structure and its grammatical conventions to meet the expectations of the paper's readers.

This chapter includes information on developing students' knowledge and understandings of conventions. The two sections are as follows:
- **Section 1 — Connecting Spelling Instruction to Writing**
- **Section 2 — Developing Grammar.**

Figure 3.1

SECTION 1

Connecting Spelling Instruction to Writing

Spelling as Part of Writing

Learning to spell is part of learning to write. Writing provides the context for spelling development, as spelling is one of the tools a writer uses to communicate effectively. Writing gives spelling its context; without writing, spelling has no purpose and no audience. Conventional spelling helps writers express themselves to a range of audiences in a way that is clearly understood. It is vital that students see the connection between spelling and being able to communicate effectively through writing. Students need to understand that adults will sometimes judge other people's intelligence and level of literacy on the accuracy of their spelling — and this is why students need to use conventional spelling.

One of the best ways way to help students acquire spelling proficiency is to teach spelling within the context of everyday writing. Addressing individual spelling needs during writing tasks is an effective way to individualise instruction and teach at the point of need. However, a comprehensive approach to teaching spelling also needs to provide explicit teaching, frequent opportunities to investigate and analyse words, and daily opportunities for authentic writing. Authentic writing allows students to practise and apply their new understandings.

This section outlines six characteristics of effective spellers. These characteristics will help teachers consider what to teach those students who are less proficient at spelling. The section also explores how to support spelling development in the classroom, focusing on the organisation and management of a student-centred approach. This approach helps teachers support students' different needs in the classroom and connects spelling instruction to writing. Each student creates their own individualised list of words to learn each week. The list is based on the spelling errors they made in their writing, and on choices they have made about which words are important to learn.

Effective Spellers

It is important for students to build knowledge and understandings that enable them to become effective spellers. The following characteristics are typical of effective spellers, and can provide a focus for whole-class, small-group and individualised instruction at all phases of development.

Characteristics of Effective Spellers

Effective spellers:

- use a variety of spelling strategies to spell and learn new words
- automatically recall high-frequency words, personally significant words, and topic and signal words
- continually build their vocabulary
- understand the English orthographic system
- understand and apply spelling generalisations
- self monitor and generate alternative spellings for unknown words.

Effective Spellers Use a Variety of Spelling Strategies to Spell and Learn New Words

Effective spellers use a range of strategies interactively when they are spelling unknown words and learning new words. The explicit teaching of a range of spelling strategies is an important part of supporting students' spelling development. Strategies are most effectively introduced through teaching practices such as modelling, sharing and guiding, and through opportunities for students to apply their use in meaningful contexts. Having control of a wide range of spelling strategies is vital to successful writing, as it enables students to take control of their spelling.

The following spelling strategies are detailed in Chapter 4, pages 203 – 204:

- Sounding out
- Chunking
- Using spelling generalisations
- Using analogy
- Consulting an authority
- Using meaning
- Using memory aids
- Using visual memory.

Effective Spellers Automatically Recall High-Frequency Words, Personally Significant Words, Topic and Signal Words

Students copy, recall or have-a-go at spelling words during independent writing at all phases of development. Effective spellers continually add to the number of words they can spell automatically. The 'bank' of words that students can automatically spell and use can be made up of:

- high-frequency words: words that occur frequently in texts
- personally significant words: words that are significant to each student
- topic or theme words: words related to topics, themes or subject areas being studied
- signal words: words that are associated with text forms and text structures and signal the relationships between ideas in the text, e.g. therefore, before, although, because.

Once students explore and use these words in their own reading and writing, it will reinforce their ability to recognise, spell and use the words. Some students need ongoing systematic instruction to develop the ability to spell automatically. Other students develop the ability to automatically spell a bank of words from repeated reading and writing of texts. Being able to write a large bank of words quickly and correctly allows students to focus their attention on other substrands of writing.

Effective Spellers Continually Build Their Vocabulary

Effective spellers continually expand their vocabulary so they can express meaning precisely in their own writing by using rich and varied language. Invite students to use new and varied vocabulary in their writing, rather than only using words they know how to spell. Broaden students' vocabularies by having them read and discuss a wide variety of texts, focusing on interesting words, and participating in word studies and word games.

Before students can write across a range of learning areas, they need to have built up their vocabularies across a broad range of contexts and experiences. Explicitly teaching subject-specific vocabulary that students need to spell and use frequently will assist this process.

Effective Spellers Understand the English Orthographic System

Orthography refers to the system of assigning graphic symbols to the sounds of a language, i.e. spelling. The English language has approximately half a million words; these words are spelt using twenty-six letters that singularly or in combination make about forty-four sounds. However, due to the history of the language, many words are not spelt the way they sound. Learning to spell is a lifelong process of working out the systems and patterns of the English language, then applying this knowledge to new words.

To build understandings about the English orthographic system, students need to develop phonological awareness, graphophonic knowledge, morphemic and etymological knowledge.

Phonological Awareness

Phonological awareness is the ability to hear, recognise, combine and manipulate the different sound units of spoken words. The main understandings to be developed are:

- Word Awareness: Spoken language is made up of words.
- Syllable Awareness: Some words have a single syllable while other words have more than one.
- Onset and Rime Awareness: Single syllable words are made up of onsets and rimes, e.g. train: 'tr' is the onset, 'ain' is the rime. A list of common onsets and rimes is available on the *First Steps Writing* CD-ROM.
- Phonemic Awareness: Words are made up of individual sounds or phonemes.

There is no evidence to suggest that all students acquire phonological awareness in a particular developmental sequence. However, there seems to be agreement that some elements of phonological awareness appear to be more difficult than others (Stahl and Murray, 1994; Stanovich, Cunningham and Cramer 1984). Table 3.2 summarises the phonological elements and the levels of difficulty within each element.

Phonological Elements and Levels of Difficulty				
Element	**Easier** ➝			**More difficult**
Size of the Phonological Unit	word awareness	syllable awareness	onset and rime awareness	phonemic awareness
Phoneme Position	initial	final	medial	
Number of Phonemes	1–3 phonemes			More than 3 phonemes
Phonological Properties	continuants, e.g. /m/, /r/, /f/			stop sounds, e.g. /t/, /d/, /p/
Phonological Dimension	isolating	blending	segmenting	manipulating
Phonological Task (Illustrated with rhyming)	identifying *Does dog rhyme with log?*	matching *Which one rhymes with dog? (cat, log)*	oddity *Which one doesn't rhyme: toy, cat, boy?*	producing *Give me a word that rhymes with dog.*

Figure 3.2

Graphophonic Knowledge

Graphophonics is the study of how sound/symbol relationships apply to the alphabetic principle of written language. It is important for students to understand that letters have a name and represent sounds in words. Letters can represent a number of different sounds, depending on their position in a word and the surrounding letters. For example, the letter 'a' represents different sounds in the words 'apple', 'was', and 'lady'. Students will gradually discover the range of sounds and their representations as their experience of the written language increases.

Students need to develop the following graphophonic understandings:
- Letter names are constant, whereas sounds vary. Students need to know the names of the letters of the alphabet so that they can talk about which letters represent particular sounds, and vice versa.
- Letters can represent different sounds, e.g. **A**ndrew, **A**my, **A**udrey.
- Letters sometimes work alone and sometimes work in groups, e.g. m**e**, br**ea**d, sh**ee**t t**ea**m.
- The sound that a letter or group of letters represents in a word depends on where that letter is, and what other letters surround it, e.g. **c**at, **c**ity, **C**hristmas, **c**hop.
- The same sound can be represented by different letters, e.g. b**ea**ch, m**e**, k**ey**, sk**i**, th**ie**f.
- The same letter or letters can represent different sounds, e.g. r**ough**, **c**ough, **d**ough, **pl**ough.

The *First Steps Writing* CD-ROM has a range of teacher reference lists related to teaching graphophonics. These include:

- suggestions for the sequence of introducing graphophonic understandings
- multiple possibilities — common visual patterns and pronunciations
- multiple possibilities — different letter/s used to represent the same sound.

Morphemic Knowledge

Morphemes are the smallest units of meaning in words. For example, the word 'dissolve' contains two morphemes: 'dis' and 'solve'. If students understand how words can be separated into morphemes, it will help them to spell unknown words.

Most English words that have the same meaning base have the same spelling base, e.g. music and musician. If the meaning is different, then the spelling is different, e.g. seen and scenery.

To develop morphemic knowledge, students can explore:
- plurals, e.g. s, es
- comparatives, e.g. er, est
- prefixes
- suffixes
- base words
- compound words.

Etymological Knowledge

Etymology is the study of word origins. Building etymological knowledge is closely linked to building morphemic knowledge, as studying the meaning and origins of non-phonetic words can be a guide for spelling.

Students' curiosity will be enhanced by studying the origins of words — and it will help them to understand why words in the English language are spelt the way they are. Students benefit from knowing that the spelling of words can reflect the origin of that word, e.g. 'bouquet' has a French origin, and 'et' is a common letter pattern used in French words.

The *First Steps Writing* CD-ROM has a range of teacher reference lists related to morphemic and etymological knowledge. These include:
- common prefixes and their meaning
- common suffixes and their meaning
- root or base words from foreign languages and their meaning.

Effective Spellers Understand and Apply Spelling Generalisations

By participating in open-ended activities, students can discover patterns, make observations and construct hypotheses about how words are spelt. If students are given continual opportunities to refine these hypotheses, they will be able to make generalisations and apply these to their own writing. See the *First Steps Writing* CD-ROM for a list of spelling generalisations related to the English Language.

Challenge students to discover spelling generalisations by finding the answer to a specific question, e.g. **What happens to a 'y' at the end of a word when the word is extended?** Give students time to collect as many examples as possible, examine the evidence and develop a generalisation.

Display the list of collected words, then discuss them as a whole class. Invite students to collaboratively suggest a generalisation or 'rule' that applies to the investigation. The generalisation may not always be accurate or adequate; however, students can alter or amend it after collecting further evidence. Involving students in the discovery of generalisations is one way to help them apply new learning to writing tasks.

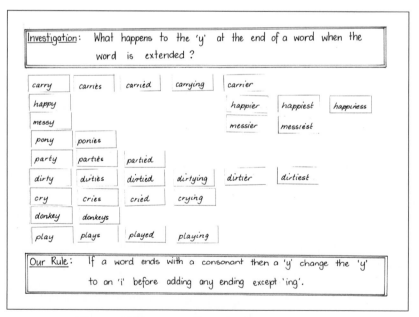

Figure 3.3 Class Spelling Investigation Chart

Effective Spellers Self-Monitor and Generate Reasonable Alternative Spellings for Unknown Words

It is important for students to know that correct spelling enhances the communication between a writer and a reader. There is usually an expectation for the use of conventional spelling in most texts. This usually depends upon the purpose and audience of writing, and the stage of the writing process, e.g. first draft, published piece.

Effective spellers are not necessarily perfect spellers. However, they can identify when a word is incorrect and use a variety of strategies to generate alternative spellings. Effective spellers have developed a 'spelling conscience' and take responsibility for the use of conventional spelling when appropriate.

Students need to have confidence when they are writing to experiment with using words they may not be able to automatically spell. Encourage them to have their best attempt at spelling these words, then to continue writing. Students' attempts at spelling should reflect their phase of development. Rather than 'writing it any way you can', encourage students to have-a-go based on their knowledge of letters, sounds, patterns and meaning.

When students have completed a draft, encourage them to return to the words they attempted to spell and generate alternative spellings for selected words.

Have-a-Go Pads are a tool often used to encourage students to generate alternative spellings to words they misspelt in their writing. Students identify words, select words and then record their alternative attempts on a Have-a Go Pad. Figures 3.3a and 3.3b shows the relationship between students' writing and the use of a Have-a Go-Pad. See *First Steps Writing* CD-ROM for Have-a-Go Pad Formats and Instructions.

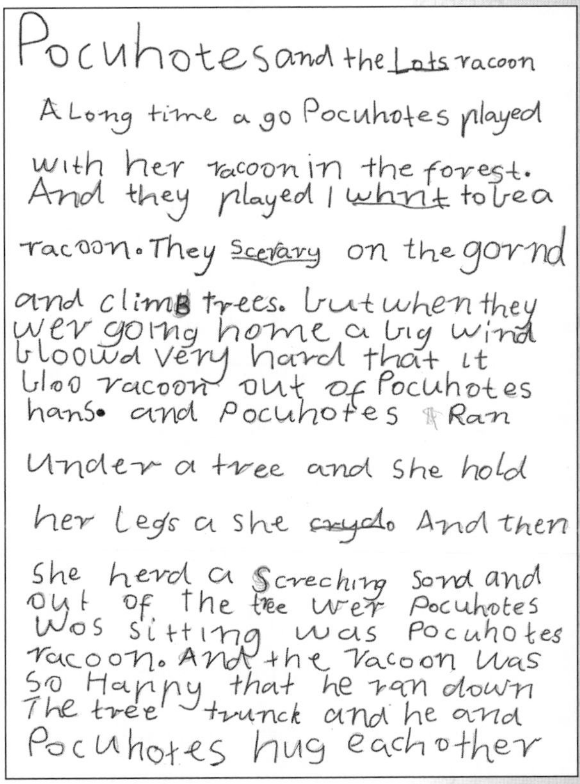
Pocuhotes and the Lots racoon
A Long time a go Pocuhotes played
with her racoon in the forest.
And they played I whrit to bea
racoon. They scerary on the gornd
and climB trees. but when they
wer going home a big wind
bloowd very hard that it
bloo racoon out of Pocuhotes
hans. and Pocuhotes Ran
Under a tree and she hold
her Legs a she cryd. And then
She herd a Screching Sond and
out of the tree wer Pocuhotes
Wos sitting was Pocuhotes
racoon. And the racoon Was
So Happy that he ran down
The tree trunck and he and
Pocuhotes hug eachother

Figure 3.3a Student Writing Sample

After composing a draft text, the student has underlined words that are not spelt correctly. They then selected three to five words to try again on their Have-a-Go Pad.

Have a go	Have another go	Correct Spelling
✓✓✓ Lost ✓✓ Cryed ✓✓ wont ✓✓✓ Scury		cried want scurry

Figure 3.3b Have-a-Go Pad

The student has made an alternative attempt at spelling the unknown words using a Have-a-Go Pad. They then sourced the correct spelling from the teacher or another authority, e.g. **chart, friend, word wall.**

Supporting Spelling Development in the Classroom

Teaching spelling as part of writing — and through explicit and systematic teaching — provides opportunities for students to investigate, discuss, practise and apply spelling knowledge and strategies. It also allows them to learn the words they need to use in their writing. A combination of whole-class, small-group and individual approaches to teaching spelling will enable teachers to support a range of student needs.

Use whole-class mini-lessons to focus on the introduction and modelling of vocabulary, spelling strategies and ways to learn new words. These lessons also provide a forum where you can challenge students to investigate spelling generalisations and patterns.

Small-group sessions allow for more specific instruction and investigations related to students' phases of development.

Providing time for individual work allows students to independently practise what they have learnt in whole-class and small-group sessions and apply it to their personalised spelling lists.

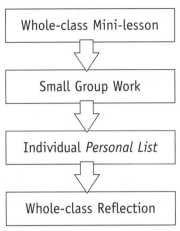

Figure 3.4 Supporting a Range of Student Needs

Reflection time allows students to share what they have discovered during lessons and, when appropriate, to collaboratively construct class charts that represent their new learning.

The following pages explore how to support spelling development in the classroom, with a particular focus on the organisation and management of a student-centred approach.

Using a Student-Centred Approach to Teach Spelling

Using personalised spelling lists is an effective way to meet a range of spelling needs in one classroom. It also helps students to view spelling as an important part of writing. A student-centred approach involves students learning a variety of words, including those words misspelt in their own writing. Words of personal interest can be added to the personalised list, as can class focus words related to a topic or specific learning area.

The structure of a student-centred approach is very flexible. It generally involves students in:
• selecting words they need (or want) to learn to spell
• transferring words into some type of journal
• learning selected words in a variety of ways
• monitoring their own progress and reflecting on spelling strategies used
• accumulating a bank of words that they can automatically spell, then use the words for writing.

Getting Started with a Student-Centred Approach

The successful implementation of a student-centred approach to spelling depends on the following considerations.

1 Select Formats and Create Student Journals.
2 Establish Routines.
3 Introduce a Daily Process.

1 Select Formats and Create Student Journals

Before introducing personalised spelling lists, decide on the type of formats the students will use. A selection of formats is provided on the *First Steps Writing* CD-ROM. These formats can be used or adapted to suit different year levels, student needs and personal preferences. A personal spelling journal for each student can be created by collating the selected formats into a booklet.

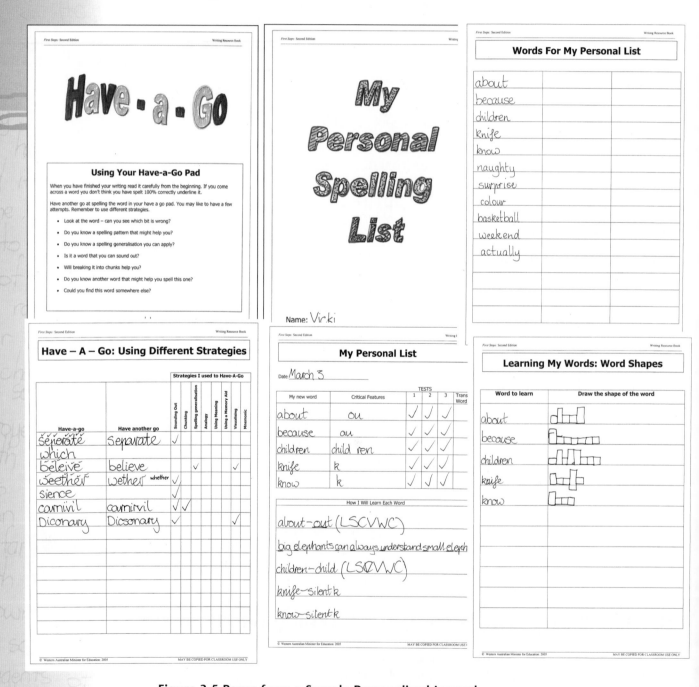

Figure 3.5 Pages from a Sample Personalised Journal

Collecting Words Formats

These formats can be used to record words collected from a range of contexts. Students can then build an ongoing list of words that they want or need to learn to spell.

Figure 3.6 Sample Formats for Collecting Words

Personal List Formats

These formats can be used to record words that will be learnt for the week. These words are selected from students' individual collections.

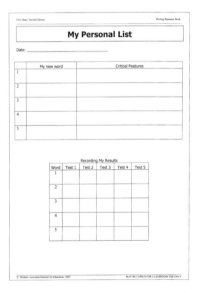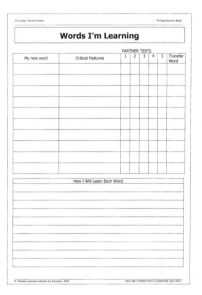

Figure 3.7 Sample Personal List Formats

Ways to Learn Words Formats

These formats can be used to remind students about the different strategies and activities they can use to learn words.

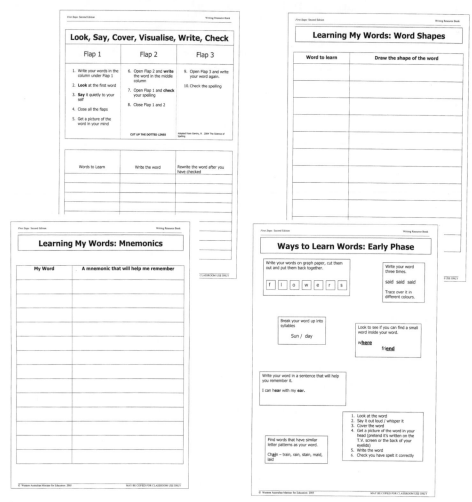

Figures 3.8 Samples of Ways to Learn Word Formats

Testing Words Format

This format can be used to record personal test results.

Personal Word List Test Record Pad					
Word	Partner Test 1	Partner Test 2	Partner Test 3	Partner Test 4	Transfer Word

Figures 3.9 Format for Testing Words

Recording Progress Formats

These formats can be used for keeping a record of the words students have learnt.

Figures 3.10 Sample Formats for Recording Progress

Routine Formats

These formats can be used to help students remember the routines that have been established for using a personalised spelling list.

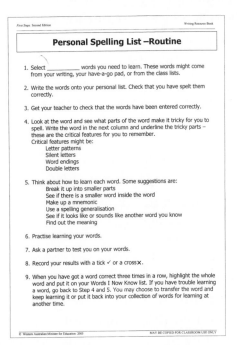

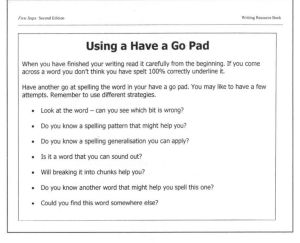

Figures 3.11 Sample Routine Formats

2 Establish Routines

When introducing personalised spelling lists, students need to learn the procedures and routines associated with collecting, selecting, transferring, learning, testing and recording words. Repeated whole-class modelling, discussion and practice time will help students to become independent learners during individualised spelling sessions. Introduce clear routines for the following:
- Collecting Words to Learn
- Selecting and Transferring Words
- Learning New Words
- Testing Words
- Recording Progress.

Collecting Words to Learn

Teaching students how and where to select the most appropriate words to learn is a critical step in using personalised spelling lists. Identifying and selecting words is an ongoing process as students build a cumulative list of words to learn. Make sure that cumulative lists do not become too long or overwhelming for students.

How?

Students need to have the chance to select words that they *want* to learn to spell, but the teacher must also be able to indicate words that a student may *need* to learn. This could include high-frequency words, subject-area specific words or words related to a current topic or theme. The teacher might have a large degree of control over the words selected at first, with the student making limited choices. Responsibility for selecting words to learn can be gradually released to students as they become more familiar with the process.

Where?

Words for personal lists can come from a wide range of sources. They could include words from a Have-a-Go pad, words misspelt in writing from different learning areas, words noticed in literature, pre-tests of high-frequency words, or words of interest heard or seen in real-life events.

It is important that the words on students' personal lists will actually be used by them in future writing events. Students who use a varied and rich vocabulary, and spell accurately when writing, might not benefit from the process of collecting words they need to learn to spell. Instead, challenge these students to explore and play with words through puzzles, crosswords or vocabulary games. See the 'Conventional' and 'Proficient' Phases on the *First Steps Writing Map of Development*.

Selecting and Transferring Words

On a weekly basis, have students select words from their cumulative lists and transfer them to a list of words to learn. The number of words students select to learn each week will vary, depending on their age and level of spelling development. Initially limit new words to no more than five per week. Some students may need a list of only two or three words. As students become familiar with the routines and are capable of learning more words, increase the lists to ten words or more.

Provide a designated time for students to select and transfer words onto a 'words to learn' list in their journal. This could take place at any time and doesn't need to be part of the spelling lesson.

It is important to teach students how to accurately transfer words into their journal. A variety of processes should be used to monitor the accuracy of each student's spelling list. This could be done by:
• having the teacher sight and sign each word
• establishing a 'checking buddy' for each student
• having random list checks
• self-checking.

Learning New Words

Personalised spelling lists help students to build a repertoire of ways they can use independently to learn new words. This is one of the most important features of personalised spelling lists. Learning how to learn words is critical, as is helping students reach the point where they are able to make decisions about the most effective way to learn different words. Not all students will learn a word the same way, and not all words can be learnt in the same manner, so it's important to incorporate a multi-sensory approach to the learning of words.

Use whole-class sessions to introduce, explicitly model and discuss different ways to learn new words. List developmentally appropriate ways to learn new words on a chart, so that it becomes a reference that students can use during independent study time.

The following activities will provide students with a strong foundation for learning new words. Further suggestions can be found in the *First Steps Writing Map of Development* for each phase of development.

Critical Features

Have students circle or tick those parts of the word they can spell correctly and highlight the part of the word that causes them trouble. Have students decide how they can remember the 'tricky' part of the word.

Break Words into Parts

Have students break words into meaningful parts, such as:
• individual sounds
• onset and rime
• syllables
• compound words.

Say the Word as it Is Spelt

Have students play around with words, saying them as they are spelt rather than how they are pronounced, e.g. enunciating the silent k in knife; breaking Wednesday into sections: Wed / nes / day.

Word Shapes

Have students draw boxes around the word to show its shape.

Figure 3.12

Create Mnemonics

Have students create a mnemonic that will help them remember a word. Some mnemonics are a creative sentence or phrase, e.g. because—**b**ig **e**lephants **c**an **a**lways **u**nderstand **s**mall **e**lephants; accommodation—two **c**aravans, two **m**otels and one **t**ent. Other mnemonics use the meanings of the words to provide a clue for the correct spelling, e.g. fourth—the fourth number is four. Sometimes a class-generated mnemonic is helpful; at other times a personal mnemonic is more useful. A list of mnemonics can be found on the *First Steps Writing* CD-ROM.

Use the Senses

Provide opportunities for students to take part in multi-sensory activities.
• Trace over words with their finger.

- Place paper on top of sandpaper and trace over it with a crayon.
- Write into shaving cream or paint.
- Make letters out of clay or playdough.
- Manipulate magnetic letters.
- Write the word and trace over it in different colours.
- Decorate or illustrate the word.

Cut it Out

Students write a word on graph paper, one letter per cell. They can then cut out the letters separately, cut the word into the onset and rime, or cut it so that a letter pattern stays as one unit. They then put the word back together.

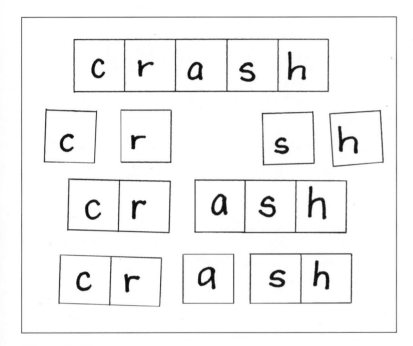

Figure 3.13

Make Connections (Analogies)

Have students make connections between words that have similar visual or sound patterns, e.g. could, should, would.

Build New Words

Have students see if they can make new words by adding prefixes or suffixes to any of their list words, e.g. heat: reheat, heater, heating.

Apply Spelling Generalisations

Have students determine if there are any spelling generalisations they know that they can apply to their new word.

Write the Word in a Sentence

Have students write homophones in a sentence that clarifies their meaning, e.g. I <u>saw</u> the shark. My arm is <u>sore</u>. The eagle can <u>soar</u> above us.

Origin of the Word

Have students research the etymology of the word. There are often clues to the spelling of a word in its origin, e.g. The words aeroplane, aerosol and aerobatics have the spelling 'aero', as that is the Greek word for air.

Meanings of the Word

Have students examine the word meanings, as there is often a visual link between the spelling of related words, e.g. please and pleasant; sign and signature.

Look, Say, Cover, Visualise, Write, Check Process

Teach students the following process.

- **Look** at the word, focusing on any critical features.
- **Say** the word aloud.
- **Cover** the word so it can't be seen.
- **Visualise** the word, imagining it on a blank computer screen or behind their eyelids.
- **Write** the word on a piece of paper.
- **Check** that the word has been spelt correctly.

Additional steps can be included, e.g. trace the word, say the word as you write it, spell the word out loud.

Games and Activities

The *First Steps Writing Map of Development* has further activities appropriate to each phase. They are listed in the Conventions substrand of each phase.

Testing Words

Once students have completed learning activities for their list of words, provide time for some form of testing. Testing can be done in a range of ways, including:

- Self-testing
- Partner testing
- Teacher testing (or testing by another adult).

Testing involves checking the list of words that students are currently studying. Students should check their own work to <u>analyse misspellings</u>. This is a critical element of the testing process, as it supports students as they develop a spelling conscience and allows them to monitor their own development.

Recording Progress

An important part of record keeping is encouraging students to keep a record of their progress. When students have spelt a word accurately at least three times during a self-test or partner-test, have them highlight that word or draw a single line through it. They then record the word onto a 'Words I Know' list. These records can be used for a range of purposes. They provide parents with a clear picture of the words their child has been studying, and a list of words learnt over a period of time. The records will also provide teachers with a tool for monitoring each student's progress and their success in using a personalised spelling list. Teachers can use the collection of words recorded in each student's 'Words I Know' list as a basis for a 'teacher test', if required

3 Introduce a Daily Process

Ideally, students should have time every day to work on their personalised spelling lists. What students do on a daily or weekly basis during this individualised spelling time can be decided collaboratively with the class. The following steps are suggestions of what students might do as they work on a personalised spelling list.

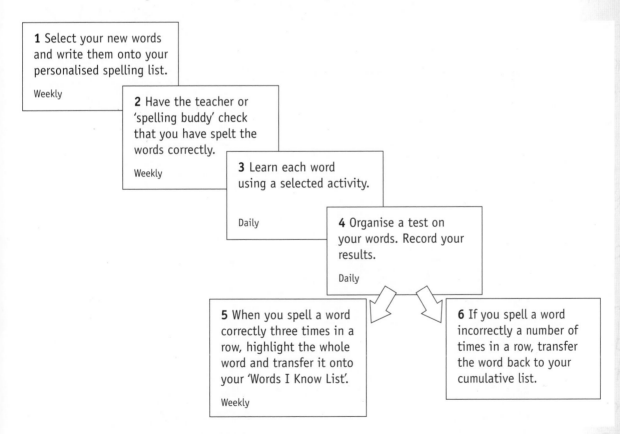

1 Select your new words and write them onto your personalised spelling list.

Weekly

2 Have the teacher or 'spelling buddy' check that you have spelt the words correctly.

Weekly

3 Learn each word using a selected activity.

Daily

4 Organise a test on your words. Record your results.

Daily

5 When you spell a word correctly three times in a row, highlight the whole word and transfer it onto your 'Words I Know List'.

Weekly

6 If you spell a word incorrectly a number of times in a row, transfer the word back to your cumulative list.

Figures 3.14 Sample of a Daily Process

Case Study: Using a Student-Centred Approach in a Year 5 Classroom

Teacher: Rebecca Hough-Neilson

Context: Pasir Ridge International School (9- and 10-year-olds)

I chose a student-centred approach to teach spelling for the following reasons:

- There was a wide range of student spelling ability in my classroom.
- The students were spelling well during 'spelling tests' but not when they were writing.
- It demonstrated the interconnectedness of writing and spelling.
- It catered for individuals.
- It gave me the opportunity to work one-on-one or with small groups.

What I Did to Introduce a Student-Centred Approach

First I reviewed a range of personalised list formats, selected the formats I was going to use and made these into a folder. I then identified what the students needed to be able to do in order to use a student-centred approach. I progressively introduced, modelled and provided time for students to practise the routines, use the folder and learn to work collaboratively with a partner.

1 I talked with the students about the purpose of a personal list. I thought it was really important to let the students know why I had decided to do things a certain way. This helped students understand why a student-centred approach was being implemented.

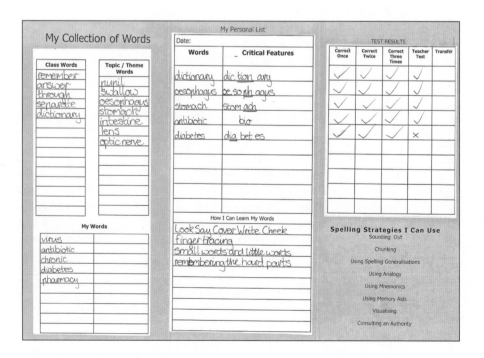

Figure 3.15 Samples from a Personal Spelling Folder

2 I then introduced the folder that we were going to use. This folder included a 'Words to Learn' list, a space for students to write their personal list and a space to record test results. It also included a space for students to record the spelling strategies they were using.

3 I talked with students about where the words to be learnt would be selected. Initially I administered a test of high-frequency words because I wanted to assist the students to identify words that they should be spelling correctly. The misspelt high-frequency words became the basis for their 'Words to Learn' list. Words could also be selected from topic words, class words, words misspelt in previous writing and their Have-a-Go pads.

4 I modelled how to enter words onto the 'Words to Learn' list. Students then entered their words onto their 'Words to Learn' list. I found that it was important for students not to enter too many words, as having a long list was daunting for some students. I initially restricted them to having no more than twenty words on their list at any one time.

5 I modelled how to select and transfer words from the 'Words to Learn' list onto 'My Personal List'. Initially students transferred five words but later the number varied for each student. We discussed the importance of entering the words correctly. I regularly checked each student's folder to ensure they had spelt each word correctly.

6 I modelled how to learn words. I started with teaching students to look for critical features and then to follow a look-say-cover-visualise-write-check process. We kept a record of different ways to learn words on a class chart. As I introduced new ways to learn words, I had students keep a record of these with their folder as a constant reminder.

7 I chose to use partner testing as a way for students to monitor their learning. Three days a week students worked with a partner to test each other on their current list. I had to model this a number of times before students could do it independently.

8 I also had to model how to record results. In my class, students had to spell the word correctly three times and then highlight it. Once they had ten words highlighted I administered a teacher test. All words that were spelt correctly in the teacher test were then transferred to their 'Words I Can Spell Correctly' list.

To assist the implementation, we reviewed the steps and made a class chart to represent what we were going to do each day of the week. This was as much for me as it was for the students!

Day 1	Day 2	Day 3	Day 4	Day 5
Check you have words to learn on your Personal List. Have teacher check the spelling. Choose the most appropriate way to learn each word.	Learn the words. Partner Test. Record the results.	Learn the words. Partner Test. Record the results.	Learn the words. Partner Test. Record the results.	Highlight words 3 × correct. Request a Teacher-Test, if ready. Transfer words to your 'Words I Can Spell Correctly' list.

Figure 3.16 Weekly Class Timetable

Things I Learnt
- Not all students understood each routine at the same time.
- I had to check that words to be learnt had been entered correctly.
- I needed to help students select developmentally appropriate words.
- I had to teach a range of ways to learn words, and help students select the most suitable way for them to learn each word.
- If I identified words that students had spelt incorrectly in other learning areas, this made it easier for them to find words for them to enter on their 'Words To Learn' list.

Where a Student-Centred Approach is Used in My Class
Once we were familiar with using personalised spelling lists, I worked on ensuring that it became part of my whole spelling program. I continued addressing Major Teaching Emphases with the whole class and also managed to work with small groups twice a week. My spelling program was made up of the following elements:
- Whole Class Mini-Lesson with follow-up activity
- Activity from mini-lesson to be completed while teacher works with small group
- Individualised Spelling
- Reflection.

The time allocated to the different elements changed on a daily basis, depending on students' needs.

Conclusions
I found that by using personalised spelling lists, my students:
- developed a spelling conscience and could identify errors in their own writing
- increased the bank of words that they could spell
- entered words that they couldn't spell into their folders on a regular basis
- transferred new learning to their writing
- used varied and rich vocabulary in their writing
- experienced success
- worked at their own level and were being challenged
- shared their learning with each other.

SECTION 2

Developing Grammar

What Is Grammar?

Grammar refers to the rules and systematic relationships that are used to organise a language and its meaning. Grammar is used to make meaning during reading, writing, speaking, listening and viewing.

Although it is widely agreed that grammar needs to be taught in schools and that students need to be able to use Standard Australian English more effectively, there are varied approaches to consider.

The comprehensive approach to grammar reflected in this chapter focuses on the way spoken and written language is structured to suit the context, purpose and audience. It recognises that English is a rich and varied language, and that people use and are exposed to many varieties of English. Those varieties reflect the range of regional and social dialects, as well as different registers used within each context. Each variety of English has its own value and purpose; the most appropriate variation in each context is usually determined by the situation.

Teaching Grammar

Most students come to school having already acquired the basic syntactic, semantic and pragmatic elements of their home language through using oral language on a daily basis. In order for students to build on their understandings and use of grammar, it is important that teachers:

- value the language each student brings to school
- help students become competent users of Standard Australian English
- assist students to construct texts that achieve the intended purpose.

It is important to link the teaching of grammar to the teaching of text forms and to students' needs. This is achieved through reading and discussing a wide range of texts and having students write for authentic purposes. Teaching grammar through writing involves explicit teaching through mini-lessons, providing frequent opportunities to investigate and analyse texts, and giving students daily opportunities to practise and apply new understandings.

It is not necessary for students to learn technical grammatical terms for them to communicate effectively and efficiently. However, students benefit from knowing the metalanguage associated with the functions of language. For example, students need to be able to use the word 'noun', articulate its use and use a noun correctly during their own writing.

'You *know* English grammar if you can read and understand this sentence.

'You *understand* English grammar if you can discuss the ways the language works and check whether your writing can be made clearer by rearranging words, phrases, clauses and sentences that make up the text'.
(Martin, 2000, *Young Writers Guide*, page 175)

It is important at all phases of development to draw attention to the conventions of grammar used in a range of texts. This includes conventions associated with punctuation, parts of speech and their relationships, sentence structure and overall text construction. These conventions need to be introduced, re-visited and practised in meaningful contexts. The explicit teaching of these conventions can occur during a writing mini-lesson. Modelled and Shared Reading and Writing provide a springboard for exploring many of these conventions. Independent Writing allows time for students to apply these understandings in their own writing.

The conventions in Figure 3.17 are outlined on the following pages.

Punctuation	Parts of Speech and their Relationships	Sentences	Paragraphs and Texts
Types of Punctuation	Parts of Speech	Different Types of Sentences	Grouping Related Information
	Relationships Between Parts of Speech	How Sentences are Constructed	Writing a Cohesive Paragraph
		How Sentences are Manipulated	Writing Cohesive Paragraphs to Compose a Coherent Text

Figure 3.17 Conventions Grid

Punctuation

Punctuation is the use of certain marks to break words into groups to clarify the meaning and make the writing readable. It is important to expose students to a range of texts at all phases of development, and to draw their attention to punctuation. Give students time to investigate and analyse the use of punctuation, as this helps them to discover how it is used. Encourage students to apply their discoveries about punctuation when they are creating their own texts.

What Students Need to Know

It is important for writers to be able to talk about, understand and use the following types of punctuation.

Types of Punctuation

Capital Letters are used:
- to begin sentences
- for proper nouns
- for adjectives derived from proper nouns, e.g. Australian
- for the pronoun 'I'
- for emphasis
- for names of special days, titles
- for acronyms, e.g. QANTAS, CSIRO.

Full Stops are used:
- to end statements
- in initials
- in abbreviations that do not end in the final letter of the word, e.g. Mon., Dec.

Question Marks are used at the end of sentences that ask for information. Question marks are not needed when using indirect speech, e.g. I was asked if I wanted to report the incident, or when a sentence is a request, e.g. Can you please hurry.

Exclamation Marks are used to show volume or strong feelings, e.g. What a noise!

Commas are used:
- to separate items in a series, e.g. They collected buttons, needles, material and cotton.
- to separate a word or words used in a sentence for further explanation, e.g. Dean, the tallest boy in the class, helped to put up the poster.

- before conjunctions that join two independent clauses, e.g. **Graham wanted to travel to Japan, but he wanted to learn the language first.**
- to separate independent and dependent clauses, e.g. **When they heard the final siren, the players leapt into the air.**
- to separate the person spoken to from the rest of the sentence, e.g. **Roger, look where you are going.**
- after introductory words such as 'oh', 'yes' and 'no' at the beginning of a sentence, e.g. **No, I don't like those shoes. Oh, I didn't know that.**
- to follow signal words at the beginning of sentences, e.g. **However, I think that … .**
- in front of a direct quotation in the middle of a sentence, e.g. **She asked, 'Where did you get those shoes?'**
- where the quotation is a statement at the beginning of a sentence, e.g. **'Today is Friday,' said Jenny.**

Apostrophes are used:
- for contractions
- to show ownership
- to indicate that letters or numbers have been omitted, e.g. **'04, o'clock.**

Quotation Marks (single or double) are used:
- for words spoken in direct speech
- to show quotations within quotations
- before and after titles
- before and after words that have been used in an unorthodox way, e.g. **slang, the word being explained.**

Colons are used:
- to introduce a list
- to introduce a long direct quotation
- to introduce an explanation, summary or elaboration of the first half of a sentence
- after the headings in memos, journals and faxes
- after the name of a character in a play script, to indicate who is speaking.

Semi-colons are used:
- to join sentences with two or more main clauses
- in a series of three or more items when commas are used within the items
- to separate the main ideas in dictionary and glossary definitions.

Hyphens are used:
- to show that two words should be read as a single word, e.g. one-way
- to join a group of words to form an expression, e.g. Have-a-Go Card
- to write numbers and fractions that consist of more than one word, e.g. one-third.

Dashes are used:
- to introduce a list
- to add or emphasise information
- to add extra details to a sentence (used in the same way as a bracket or comma).

Brackets always appear in pairs and are used:
- to enclose additional non-essential information, e.g. You are required to attend the meeting in Joondalup (avoid the freeway if possible).

Ellipses are used:
- to show incomplete lines of text, e.g. To be or not to be …
- to show words that have been omitted from quotations.

Parts of Speech and Their Relationship

Writers don't just put down words on the page at random; the words are organised in specific ways to convey meaning. By learning about the parts of speech and their relationships, students can begin to understand the use and function of words, and how to use words for meaningful communication.

What Students Need to Know

Developing and refining the following knowledge will help students to make decisions when they are composing texts.
- Parts of Speech
- Relationship Between Parts of Speech

1 Parts of Speech

Each word can be categorised as a part of speech. However, the same word can serve at different times as two or more parts of speech, depending on the context. A word can be a noun in one sentence and a verb or adjective in the next, e.g. I just love roses. Growing them is my love.

It is possible to learn a language without knowing the parts of speech, but knowing *about* the parts of speech makes things easier. There are eight parts of speech in the English Language.

Noun

A noun is a word or phrase that names a person, place, thing, quality or act, e.g. Michelle, New York, table, beauty, execution.

Verb

A verb is a word or phrase that expresses action or existence. Verbs are the heart of a sentence. Unlike other parts of language, verbs change their form, e.g. endings are added or the word itself changes. Verbs are closely related to time and tell if something has already happened, if it will happen later or if it is happening now.

Adjective

An adjective is a word that describes or gives more information about a noun or pronoun. Adjectives describe nouns in qualities such as size, colour, number and type.

Adverb

An adverb is a word that gives more information about a verb, an adjective or another adverb. Adverbs describe qualities such as time, frequency and manner. Adverbs often end in *ly*.

Pronoun

A pronoun is a word that is substituted for a noun. It refers to a person, place, thing, idea or act that was mentioned previously or that can be inferred from the context of the sentence, e.g. he, she, they, it.

Preposition

A preposition is a word that shows the relationship between words in a sentence. The relationships include direction *(to)*; time *(at)*; place *(under)*; and manner *(by)*.

Conjunction

A conjunction is a word that connects other words, phrases or sentences, e.g. and, but, or, because.

Interjection

An interjection is a word, phrase or sound used as an exclamation and capable of standing by itself, e.g. Oh, my goodness.

Article

One of three words that are always used in the presence of a noun: *a, an, the.*

2 Relationship Between Parts of Speech

As well as knowing how to use the parts of speech, students need to know the relationships that govern their use.

Noun/pronoun agreement is linking written ideas by using pronouns that refer to preceding nouns. The pronoun needs to agree in number (singular or plural), in person (first, second or third) and in gender (masculine, feminine or neutral).

Subject/verb agreement: The subject in a sentence must agree in number and in person with the verb to which it is attached, e.g. John and Marilyn <u>were</u> the first to arrive at the party.

Tense: There are three basic verb tenses in English: present, past and future. When using standard English, the tenses fit together in a consistent manner to avoid confusing the reader.

Present tense expresses an unchanging or recurring action or situation that exists now. It can also represent a widespread truth, e.g. The mountains <u>are</u> tall. The council <u>elects</u> a new leader each year.

Past tense expresses an action or situation that began and finished in the past. Most past tense verbs end in 'ed', e.g. The shop <u>closed</u> at 6 pm.

Future tense expresses an action or situation that will occur in the future. This tense is formed by using 'will' or 'shall' or by using 'am going to', 'is going to' or 'are going to', e.g. We <u>are going to finish</u> writing the book by the end of March.

Person is determined by whether writers are referring to themselves; to their readers; or to objects, ideas or persons other than themselves and their readers.

First person is the writer speaking, e.g. I, we, me, us, my, mine, our, ours.
Second person is the person spoken to, e.g. you, your, yours.
Third person is the person or thing spoken about, e.g. he, she, it, his, hers, him, its, they, them, their.

The ultimate aim is for writers to be able to make decisions about their use of punctuation and parts of speech and the relationships between parts of speech. While they are making these decisions, writers need to be reminded of their social obligations to the reader.

Sentences

It is important for students to build knowledge and understandings of the basic types and structure of sentences. Once students have these understandings, they can 'write more syntactically sophisticated and rhetorically effective sentences' (Weaver, 1998) to suit the purpose and audience.

What Students Need To Know

Developing and refining the following understandings will help students decide which sentences to use when composing texts.
• Different Types of Sentences.
• How Sentences are Constructed.
• How Sentences are Manipulated.

1 Different Types of Sentences

It is important to provide many opportunities for students to read and write a variety of sentences, as this will help them to identify different sentence types. There are four basic types of sentences; it's important to model the functions of each sentence, even though students do not need to know the sentence names.

A statement declares or states something. Statements are used to provide information, or to make remarks and assertions, e.g. **It's my turn next. The dog ran down the street.** Written texts consist mainly of statements, unless deliberate interaction with the reader is intended.

A question is used to inquire about something, request information or to gain further information, e.g. **Is it lunchtime? Where is the train station?**

A command directs or gives orders. Commands are used to get things done, to obtain services or goods, e.g. **Mix flour and butter on high. Two tickets to Paris, please.**

An exclamation expresses strong feelings. Exclamations are often used to express emotions, including surprise, fear, excitement and happiness, e.g. **Very exciting! I have just won the lottery!**

2 How Sentences Are Constructed

A sentence is defined as a group of words that expresses a complete thought, begins with a capital letter and ends with some form of punctuation.

Subject and Predicate: A sentence has two parts: the *subject* and the *predicate*.

The subject tells what the sentence is about. The subject can be made up of a word, words or phrases, e.g. <u>The duck</u> swam in the pond.

The predicate contains a verb and tells the reader about the subject, e.g. The duck <u>swam in the pond</u>.

A clause is a group of words that contain a verb; it is often referred to as the basic unit of meaning in the English Language. Students need to understand clauses to be able to construct sentences.

Clauses fall into two main categories: *independent* and *dependent*. *An independent clause* makes sense on its own, e.g. The principal is sick. *A dependent clause* does not make sense on its own and needs the independent clause to complete it, e.g. with the flu.

Sentence Structure

The number of clauses in a sentence helps students to identify the sentence structure. Understanding the structures of different sentences allows students to write more interesting sentences, constructing writing that is more interesting and suitable to their purpose and audience. The three main sentence structures are *simple*, *compound* and *complex*.

A simple sentence contains one independent clause, e.g. We went to the zoo.

Compound sentences contain two or more independent clauses. Each clause must be able to stand alone in conveying a complete message, e.g. We went to the zoo and we saw a tiger.

Complex sentences contain at least one independent clause and one dependent clause, e.g. When we were on holidays we went to the zoo and saw a tiger.

Voice: Sentences can be written in active or passive voice. Students need to be aware of how they can make their sentences active or passive.

Active voice: The subject performs the action, when writing with active voice, e.g. Kerry hit the ball.

Passive voice: The action is performed on the subject, when writing with passive voice, e.g. The ball was hit by Kerry.

191

3 How Sentences Are Manipulated

Once students have an understanding of the different sentence types and structures, model how to combine, expand, reduce and transform sentences. This will help students learn how to manipulate sentences for specific effects.

Sentence Combining

Sentence combining is when students are given simple sentences on a topic, then given time to link the sentences using conjunctions, commas or other punctuation devices. The aim is to compose more complex sentences. Students then compare their sentences with other students' sentences.

Sentence Expanding

Sentence-expanding activities help students to add words and details to existing sentences.

Sentence Reducing

Sentence reducing helps students to compose concise sentences that don't contain any irrelevant details. Challenge students to see if they can take away any parts of the sentence without losing meaning or important information. This activity will help students to understand different structures.

Sentence Transforming

Sentence transforming involves students in rewriting sentences to make their meaning clearer.

Paragraphs and Texts

Just as punctuation helps readers understand what has been written, the organisation of sentences helps the reader to understand the meaning of the text. Once students have an understanding of writing a simple sentence and begin to write for different purposes, the focus is on composing coherent texts.

What Students Need to Know

Students need to develop an understanding of how to compose paragraphs and whole texts by:
• grouping related information
• writing a cohesive paragraph
• writing cohesive paragraphs to compose a coherent text.

1 Grouping Related Information

Students don't initially write texts that are long enough to require paragraphs, although they do develop an awareness of paragraphs through Shared Reading. As a precursor to paragraph writing, provide students with many opportunities to group sentences that contain related information. For example, when writing a scientific report about an animal, students need to be able to sort the gathered information into categories. These categories could be information about where it lives, what it eats, what it looks like, how it moves, how it reproduces and how it protects itself. Once students become familiar with grouping related information together, move the focus to creating paragraphs.

2 Writing a Cohesive Paragraph

A paragraph is a group of sentences that contain related information and work together to clarify the organisation of a text. By constructing paragraphs, the writer assists the reader to 'chunk' ideas and information. There is no one correct way to compose a paragraph; however, the following outline provides a useful structure.

Topic Sentences

A topic sentence expresses the main idea, and is usually found at the beginning of a paragraph.

Supporting Sentences

Supporting sentences explain, expand, illustrate or prove the main point.

Concluding Sentences

Concluding sentences draw a conclusion from what has been said, or provide a summary. The conclusion is left to the very end of the text in texts that are longer than one paragraph.

Paragraph Layout

A new paragraph signals to the reader that there will be a change of focus, a change of time, a change of place or a change of speaker. The break between paragraphs gives the reader time to take in each idea.

A new paragraph can be indicated in two ways.
- *Leave a one-line gap*. This has become more common since the use of word processors.

• *Indent.* The first line of the new paragraph is set slightly in from the left-hand margin. All following lines are set against the left-hand margin. The text is indented each time a new person or character speaks when writing dialogue.

Paragraph Length

The length of a paragraph cannot be specifically defined — except that there should be enough text to fully explore the topic. If paragraphs are too short, there may not seem to be enough detail. If paragraphs are too long, the reader might have difficulty maintaining focus. Sometimes one-sentence paragraphs are used to create a special effect. Use class-generated charts (as shown in Figure 3.18) to help students check and monitor their own writing.

• Is the topic sentence clear?
• Does the topic sentence clearly relate to the whole paragraph?
• Do the details and examples develop the topic sentence?
• Have I provided sufficient detail or support?
• Have I presented the detail or support in some sort of logical sequence?
• Does the concluding sentence summarise or restate the main point of the paragraph?

Figure 3.18 Class-generated Paragraph Chart

3 Writing Cohesive Paragraphs to Compose a Coherent Text

Once students are able to write paragraphs, they need to develop and refine their understanding of the characteristics of cohesive paragraphs. This will help them to construct coherent texts. A cohesive paragraph is one that 'hangs together'. Cohesion can be created through the use of conjunctions and signal words and phrases.

It is important for students to understand that different sentence connectors or conjunctions are used to link and organise information. These include words and phrases related to:

• *Compare and Contrast* These involve attempting to explain how two or more objects, events or arguments are similar or different.
• *Cause and Effect* These involve showing causal relationships between events.
• *Problem and Solution* These involve identifying a problem, then attempting to generate solutions or ways of overcoming the problem.
• *Listing* Involves explaining characteristics of people, animals, objects or places by drawing on lists, collections of details and sequences.

COMPARE AND CONTRAST
• similarly
• on the other hand
• otherwise
• but
• yet
• the opposing view
• not only ... but also ...
• in spite of
• in contrast
• instead
• however
• meanwhile
• although
• compared with

PROBLEM AND SOLUTION
• one reason for that
• a solution to this
• the problem is
• one response is
• this leads to

• to prevent
• question
• answer
• trouble
• difficulty
• solved
• propose

CAUSE AND EFFECT
• because
• as a result of
• then
• so
• therefore
• accordingly
• due to
• consequently
• nevertheless
• this resulted in
• if
• cause
• effect

LISTING
Collection of Details:
• an example
• for instance
• such as
• another
• in fact
• several
Sequence:
• earlier
• finally
• after this
• next
• firstly
• in addition
• eventually
• to begin with
• on (date)
• below

Figure 3.19 Sentence Connectors Table

Another way to form coherent texts is to use words that refer back to other parts of the text. This includes the use of synonyms, pronouns and repetition.

Synonyms: Substituting words with similar meanings for words already used, e.g. **Honey Bees <u>collect</u> nectar from flowers to make honey. These insects travel many miles to <u>gather</u> the nectar.**
Pronouns: A pronoun is used to refer to a previously used noun, e.g. **<u>Denise</u> was having a coffee. <u>She</u> had ordered a latte.**
Repetition: Deliberately repeating key words or related words.

A cohesive text can use synonyms, pronouns and repetition but still lack coherence. In a coherent text, the evidence and examples relate to the rest of the text and the reader can easily follow its meaning. For a text to be coherent, it has to maintain a topic, use appropriate text organisation and structure a logical sequence of sentences and paragraphs. Consistency in point of view, verb tense and number are also important substrands of coherence.

Coherence is one of the most important substrands of a text and one of the most difficult for writers to manage. A writer may believe that a text is coherent because of their closeness to it, whereas a reader might not make the same connections without considerable thought.

CHAPTER 4

Processes and Strategies

Overview

This chapter focuses on applying knowledge and understandings to compose texts. Some processes and strategies are employed intuitively, particularly when writing for familiar purposes and audiences. However, unfamiliar contexts, sophisticated purposes or wider audiences require the deliberate selection and manipulation of processes and strategies.

The intent of this chapter is to provide teaching and learning experiences that can be applied to all phases of writing development, with the aim of helping students use processes and strategies in their writing. These processes and strategies are not hierarchical or specific to a phase. A variety of processes and strategies need to be introduced, developed and consolidated at **all** phases of development. The ideas and suggestions provided can be easily adapted to meet the needs of students across a range of phases.

This chapter contains one section:
• **Section 1 – Writing Processes and Strategies**

Figure 4.1

SECTION 1

Writing Processes and Strategies

Effective teachers understand how writing occurs; they plan learning experiences and instruction that support students, helping them to become more successful writers. A variety of writing processes and strategies need to be introduced, developed and consolidated at all phases of development. This chapter is designed to support the Major Teaching Emphases listed under the Processes and Strategies substrand at each phase of development in the *First Steps Writing Map of Development*.

Teachers play an important role in ensuring that all students build up a bank of knowledge they can access when they are crafting texts. Instruction should be planned so that students have knowledge of:
• a growing list of sight words
• graphophonic elements
• grammatical features of the English language
• text structures and organisation
• topics and concepts
• cultural and world matters.

Explicit teaching of the processes and strategies used when composing texts is an important element in supporting writing development. Teaching writing processes provides students with a structure they can follow to help them craft text from beginning to end. The writing processes include planning, drafting, conferring, refining and publishing. Strategies can be introduced for students to use and apply as they plan, draft, confer, refine and publish texts for a range of social purposes.

What Are the Writing Strategies?

Being able to control a wide range of strategies is vital to successful writing. Writers use various strategies as they compose texts and spell unknown words. Students need to understand that some strategies will be more appropriate to use during planning or drafting, while others will be more suited when conferring, refining or publishing. Students should apply writing strategies as needed, throughout the process of writing. For example, students may use the Determining Importance strategy during planning, drafting or refining.

The following seventeen writing strategies are not phase-specific or hierarchical. During any part of the writing process, a number of strategies can be used simultaneously to compose texts and spell unknown words.

- Predicting
- Self-questioning
- Creating Images
- Determining Importance
- Paraphrasing/Summarising
- Connecting
- Comparing
- Re-reading
- Synthesising
- Sounding Out
- Chunking
- Using Visual Memory
- Using Spelling Generalisations
- Using Analogy
- Using Meaning
- Consulting an Authority
- Using Memory Aids.

Predicting

Writers predict which content, form, format and conventions are appropriate for their audience, purpose and context. For example, they anticipate whether:

- the content of their text will be too easy or too hard for the audience
- a narrative form will best suit the purpose of entertaining a reader
- a joke they heard can be effectively shared as a text message or whether it would be more suited to email
- colloquial language will be suitable in a job application.

Writers made predictions on a cyclic, ongoing basis as they consider word choices and sequences, and the impact they might have on a reader. Following reflection, initial predictions are often rejected or refined, requiring alterations to drafts — and sometimes even abandonment of the writing task.

Students in the early phases of development often display a limited capacity to predict. For example, they may include characters without introduction, not anticipating that the audience is unfamiliar with them.

Self-questioning

Effective writers continually form questions in their mind before, during and after writing. They use these questions to help them confirm or reject their predictions, and to compose text. Often these questions are formed spontaneously and naturally, with one question leading to the next.

As they make more sense of how language is used, young writers ask more questions with increasing sophistication. They initially might ask themselves:

- will my reader understand this?
- does this sound right?
- will this achieve my purpose?

Later they may ask:

- is there a better word I can use?
- is a limerick the best form for persuading Dad to let me go to the movies?
- is it appropriate to fax this to Mum's workplace?

Helping students to become aware of questions they naturally ask is an important part of supporting writing.

Creating Images

Writers use all five senses to create images in their mind; they then use these images to describe characters, events and phenomena in a wide range of forms. The images that individuals create are based on their prior knowledge. They visualise detail and sequence as a means of selecting appropriate words and phrases. Often writers draw on visualised images to create powerful similes, metaphors and analogies.

Students in the early phases of development regularly use images to underpin their writing. They become motivated by television and computer images they have seen, then draw their own pictures as a rehearsal for, and an accompaniment to, their first writing attempts.

Writers in later phases benefit from being able to mentally create images that can work in a similar way. It is important to give students the opportunity to share their images, and to talk about how creating images helps them compose better texts.

Determining Importance

The key to effective writing is making the greatest impact with the fewest possible words. To achieve this, writers need to master the strategy of determining importance. Determining Importance in writing extends far beyond word choice; it includes selecting content, form, format and conventions to suit the intended purpose and audience. The impact of information and communications technology also demands that writers make choices about sequence, positioning and linking.

Students in early phases of development display a limited ability to determine importance and often include irrelevant details, e.g. Giving all elements of description equal prominence in a retell.

Teaching students about text organisation and text structure makes patterns of writing explicit — and helps developing writers determine the importance of different parts of the text, including paragraphs, sentences and words.

Paraphrasing and Summarising

As developing writers assume greater control of the Determining Importance strategy, they become more able to paraphrase and summarise. Paraphrasing is the strategy writers use to restate a text (or part of a text) in a way that retains the sense and meaning of the original.

Paraphrasing often requires the writer to summarise, or to restate the gist of the original text in a more concise form. Determining Importance is one strategy that a writer can use to paraphrase and summarise; they can also use others, such as the predicting and synthesising strategies.

There are many strategies that underpin Paraphrasing and Summarising, making it a complex strategy to learn. However, the incredible volume of text in a growing range of modes, multi-modes and formats students are exposed to which make this strategy an essential part of writing.

Connecting

Effective writers often compose text about subjects and topics they know and care about. This allows them to make strong connections between their prior knowledge and the information they present in their texts. Activating each student's prior knowledge before writing allows them to consider what they know about the content, form, format and conventions to be used.

The type of connections made by effective readers, as outlined by Keene and Zimmerman (1997), can also be applied to support writers as they make connections. Encourage writers to make the following connections.

Text to Self Connections
Involves writers thinking about their life, and connecting their own personal experiences to the information they wish to present in a text.

Text to Text Connections
Involves writers thinking about texts they have previously composed, as well as texts written by other authors. They may make connections to common themes, styles, organisations, structures, characters or content.

Text to World Connections
Involves writers thinking about what they know about the world outside their personal experience, their family or their community as they compose texts. Effective writers also gather additional information about topics that are not directly related to their own experiences.

Comparing

Making comparisons relates closely to, and is an extension of, the connecting strategy. As students make connections to their prior knowledge, they also begin to make comparisons with what they know, helping them to decide what they will include in a text.

Making comparisons involves students thinking specifically about the similarities and differences between the connections they are making and what they will include in a text, e.g. **How can I make this text have a different ending to the one I read? How is what I have written different to what I saw happening in real life?**

Re-reading

Re-reading is a strategy that all writers use to maintain sense. Re-reading operates at the word, sentence, paragraph and text level. It is a recursive strategy, returning to a point in the text to read it through again before adding to the text. Re-reading enables students to confirm that a draft piece of text is coherent and cohesive. It is a strategy writers use to check that they have maintained the thread of meaning.

Writers may initially vocalise and sub-vocalise as they re-read, progressing later to rapid, mental skimming of large sections of text, and more focused scanning of areas of potential concern.

Synthesising

When composing text, effective writers use synthesising to bring together information from a variety of sources. Synthesising involves piecing information together, much like putting together a jigsaw. As students write, they synthesise by stopping at selected places in their text and thinking about what has been written; this allows them to keep track of what is happening in their text.

Students who are consciously aware of using the synthesising strategy are able to continually monitor the meaning being created in their text. When synthesising, students may be re-reading, connecting, comparing, determining importance, self-questioning and creating images.

Sounding Out

Writers use their knowledge of letter/sound relationships to take words apart, attach sounds to the parts and blend the parts back together to spell unknown words. Sounding out phonemes is a strategy students often use to spell unknown words in the early phases of development.

Chunking

As students encounter greater numbers of multi-syllabic words, they need to be encouraged to break words into units that are larger than individual phonemes. Writers chunk words by pronouncing word parts such as onset and rime, letter combinations, syllables, or parts of the word that carry meaning.

Using Visual Memory

Students need to understand that words not only need to sound right but also need to look right. Writers who recall the visual features of a word are using visual memory as a strategy to spell unknown words. Students use graphic patterns, critical features, length of words, little words within big words or word shapes when using visual memory. The 'look, say, cover, visualise, write, check' routine is based on improving students' visual memory for words and letter strings.

Using Spelling Generalisations

Using spelling generalisations is a strategy that can be used to spell unknown words during writing. However, students are often confused by the many exceptions to spelling 'rules'. Encourage students to explore words and to make their own self-generated spelling hypotheses; this is an effective way to lead students to make spelling generalisations and apply them in their own writing.

Using Analogy

When writers manipulate or think about words they already know how to spell in order to spell unknown words, they are using analogy. They transfer what they know about familiar words to help them identify unfamiliar words. When using analogy, students transfer their knowledge of common letter sequences, onset and rimes, letter clusters, base words, word parts or whole words that carry meaning.

Using Meaning

Most English words that have the same meaning base are spelt the same, e.g. **nation, nationality.** When the meanings of the words are different then the spelling is different, e.g. **seen** and **scenery.** Using knowledge of word meanings is an effective strategy for spelling unknown words.

Writers are also using meaning as a strategy when they use knowledge of the function of different parts of words, e.g. **past tense can be represented by 'ed' or 't'.**

Consulting an Authority

This strategy supports students as they unlock the spelling of unknown words. Consulting an authority is a secondary strategy; encourage students to use other strategies prior to consulting an authority. Teach students how to use resources such as a dictionary, Word Wall or spellchecker, and how to consult a human resource, such as an adult helper.

Using Memory Aids

Memory aids, such as mnemonics, help writers to remember the correct spelling of particular words. Creating rhymes or making personal associations are simple but effective ways that could help students memorise the spelling of words.

What Are the Writing Processes?

Writing processes are the 'how' of writing. There is not, as is sometimes thought, one 'process approach'. There are many useful writing processes that feed into a recursive cycle. Consciously or not, all writers go through a series of stages or use predictable paths to compose a text. Writers move back and forth between stages, making the process fluid and dynamic.

The number and type of processes that are documented may vary, but they usually reflect a similar outcome. This resource presents the following writing processes.

- Planning
- Drafting
- Conferring
- Refining
- Publishing.

Effective writers understand that writing occurs over time, and that a single final copy is not always produced immediately. They also understand that some writing may not go through all processes. The need for multiple drafts, refining and publishing may vary from writer to writer, or vary according to the purpose and audience of the writing event. Sometimes a first draft is the final piece of text and does not go through any further processes, e.g. shopping list, greeting card message.

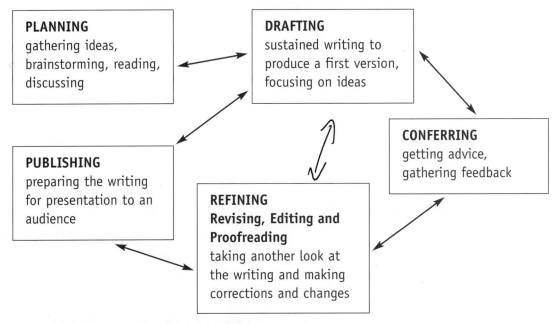

Figure 4.2 Processes Used During Writing

Teaching Writing Processes and Strategies

At all phases of development, the processes of writing — and the strategies used within those processes — are most effectively introduced through the sequential and recursive use of four effective teaching practices. These teaching practices are modelling, sharing, guiding and applying.

Figure 4.3 is based on The Gradual Release of Responsibility model originally presented by Pearson and Gallagher (1983). Teachers can use this framework to help them plan for the effective introduction of the writing processes and strategies. The framework involves moving students from a supportive context where the teacher has a high degree of control (modelling), to a more independent context where the student has more control (independent application). The long-term goal is that all students can select and use writing processes flexibly and independently during any writing event.

Teachers can help students achieve this goal by giving them opportunities to:

- actively attend to demonstrations of writing processes and strategies
- hear the thinking behind the use of each writing process and the strategies used within each process
- contribute ideas about the use of processes in supportive whole-group situations
- work with others when using writing processes
- receive feedback and support about their writing processes from the teacher and peers
- independently use writing processes to compose a range of texts
- apply writing processes in authentic writing situations.

	Modelling	**Sharing**	**Guiding**	**Applying**
Role of the Teacher	The teacher demonstrates and explains writing processes being introduced. This is achieved by thinking aloud the mental processes used when planning, drafting, conferring, refining or publishing.	The teacher continues to demonstrate the use of the writing processes to compose a range of texts, inviting students to contribute ideas and information.	The teacher provides scaffolds for students to use the writing processes. Teacher provides feedback.	The teacher offers support and encouragement as necessary.
Degree of Control			Students work with help from the teacher and peers to practise the use of the writing processes to compose a variety of texts.	The students work independently to apply the use of writing processes in contexts across the curriculum.
Role of the Students	The students participate by actively attending to the demonstrations.	Students contribute ideas and begin to practise the use of the writing processes in whole-class situations.		

Figure 4.3 A Gradual Release of Responsibility Approach to Teaching Writing

Modelling

Some teachers overlook modelling — or consider it unnecessary — but modelling is the most significant step in explicitly teaching writing processes and strategies. It is essential to conduct regular, short sessions that involve modelling and thinking aloud about how an effective writer uses the selected writing process to compose a text.

Using modelling to introduce writing processes allows teachers to articulate what is happening inside their heads, making the strategies used throughout the processes evident. This 'thinking aloud' is a vital part of the modelling process. Teachers need to plan for multiple demonstrations when introducing writing processes.

Modelling sessions need to be well planned and thought out. It is more effective to think through what needs to be modelled than to make spontaneous comments as the text is being composed.

It is essential to compose a variety of texts used for different purposes during modelling sessions.

Planning Modelling Sessions

Consider these questions before modelling for students, to ensure that the sessions are deliberate and effective.
- How do I use this process in my own writing?
- What strategies do I use throughout this process?
- What is important for students to know about this process?
- What language can I use to best describe what I am doing and thinking?

Sharing

Sharing sessions give students and teachers opportunities to think through texts together. Sharing allows the teacher to continue to demonstrate the use of the selected writing process. The major difference between modelling sessions and sharing sessions is that students are now invited to contribute ideas and information.

Thinking aloud during sharing sessions allows the teacher to demonstrate the use of the selected processes and strategies. It is also a time when individual students can be invited to have a go.

Use ongoing sharing sessions to work collaboratively with students, composing a variety of texts used for different purposes.

Planning Sharing Sessions

Consider these questions before sharing sessions, to provide a focus for the session.
- What facets of the process do I need to demonstrate further?
- What strategies are used during this process that need further demonstration?
- What type of text might be the most appropriate to reinforce this facet of the process?
- What language associated with this process do I want to review?

• What's the best way to get students to contribute to the demonstrations?

Guiding

Guiding sessions give students the opportunity to use writing processes to compose a variety of texts. Guiding sessions involve the teacher providing scaffolds as students use the process. Make sure that ongoing feedback and support is provided to students as they move towards taking responsibility for the use of the processes.

Planning Guiding Sessions

Consider these questions before students complete any practice activity, to ensure that the sessions are deliberate and effective.
• Have I provided multiple demonstrations, thinking aloud about the use of the process?
• Have I provided many opportunities for sharing sessions where students and I have discussed and used the process?
• What texts do I want the students to compose so they can use the process?
• What grouping arrangements will be most suitable for the students?
• How will I provide feedback to the students during the writing event?
• How will I provide the opportunity for students to reflect on and share their learning?

Applying

It is essential that students have opportunities to work independently and apply the writing processes. It is also important to encourage students to use writing processes when working in other learning areas. Continue to talk about and demonstrate the application of writing processes when creating texts together in other learning areas. Encourage students to use the processes beyond planned classroom writing activities.

Suggestions for Ongoing Scaffolding and Support

The remainder of this section focuses on each of the writing processes. Each process contains information outlining what effective writers do, as well as suggestions for providing ongoing scaffolding and support.

Suggestions for Ongoing Scaffolding and Support	Planning	Drafting	Conferring	Refining	Publishing
Make a List (page 211)	✔				
Ideas Journal (page 212)	✔				
Brainstorming (page 212)	✔				
Storyboarding (page 212–213)	✔				
Start at the Beginning (page 213)	✔				
Roll the Dice (page 213)	✔				
What's Important? (page 214)	✔				
Graphic Organisers (page 214–216)	✔				
Partner Sharing (page 221)			✔		
Teacher Conferencing (page 221)			✔		
Sharing Circle (page 221)			✔		
Whole Class Sharing (page 222)			✔		
Highlighting (page 224–225)				✔	
Have I Captured the Action? (page 225)				✔	
Remove the Rubble (page 225)				✔	
Let's Hear It (page 225–226)				✔	
Using a Spellchecker or Grammar Checker (page 226)				✔	
Collaboratively Created Charts (page 226–228)				✔	
What's Included? (page 230)					✔
Setting it Out (page 230)					✔
Design This! (page 231)					✔
Publisher's Palette (page 231)					✔
That Catches My Eye (page 232)					✔
Screen-Based Publications (page 232–233)					✔
How Can I Publish? (page 233)					✔

Figure 4.4 Suggestions for Ongoing Scaffolding and Support

Writing Process: Planning

All writers face a series of decisions before they begin writing. Planning involves writers considering their topic for writing, the purpose and audience for their text and making some choices about the form that the writing will take. It also involves anything that helps writers figure out what they will say and how they will say it.

Effective writers don't always use formal pre-writing activities to plan prior to writing. This is particularly true in cases such as writing a personal letter or greeting card. However, larger texts often involve some level of planning and thinking before starting. Invite students to consider and record their thinking before writing an initial draft; this helps them to organise their thoughts. Students can plan for writing in a wide range of ways. This might include simple techniques, such as recording by sketching or writing random thoughts, to more complex techniques such as creating word webs or note making.

Effective Writers Know How to Plan

Effective writers are able to make choices about how to plan, depending on the purpose, audience and context of their writing. Effective writers are able to do the following.

- Select a topic.
- Identify the purpose and audience for the text.
- Select the most appropriate form and format to suit the purpose, audience and context.
- Build their own knowledge about the topic.
- Gather and record possible ideas about a topic, e.g. **take notes from a variety of sources.**
- Talk with others about what might be written.
- Use a variety of techniques to organise ideas before writing, e.g. **brainstorming, drawing, listing, using graphic organisers.**
- Consider the writing processes that will be used to complete the text.

Supporting Writers to Plan

It is important to expose students to a range of planning techniques; these techniques can be introduced and experimented with over a period of time. When focusing on the different facets of planning, include a combination of demonstrations, think-alouds and opportunities for students to apply the techniques in real planning situations.

The goal is for all students to be able to select from a large repertoire of techniques to suit the specific needs of each writing event. The following planning techniques will help students to make informed choices about how to plan when they are composing texts independently.

- Make a List
- Ideas Journal
- Brainstorming
- Storyboarding
- Start at the Beginning
- Roll the Dice
- What's Important?
- Graphic Organisers
  — Mapping
  — Clustering
  — Retrieval Charts
  — Venn Diagrams
  — Tree Diagrams.

1 Make a List

Make a List is a technique that students can use for developing a list of topics to write about (www.ttms.org). Provide students with a stimulus heading to consider, then have them write a list of associated thoughts about it. They can use these ideas as a springboard for future writing events.

- Provide students with a selected stimulus heading, e.g.
  — Things I Like/Things I Dislike
  — Things I'm Good At and Things I'm Not Good At
  — Things That Are Easy and Things That Are Hard
  — Things That Make Me Laugh/Things That Make Me Cry
  — Things I'm Scared Of/Things I'm Not Scared Of
  — Things That Bother Me/Things That Don't Bother Me
  — The Person I Most Admire
  — Places I've Been

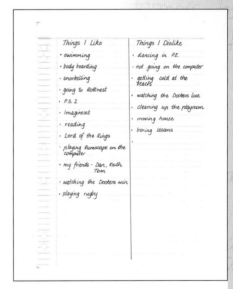

Figure 4.5 A Student's 'Make a List' Sample

- Provide time for students to write a list of associated thoughts. They could record their thoughts in an Ideas Journal.
- Encourage students to refer to their recorded ideas as a springboard for future writing events.
- Encourage students to create further lists based on their own criteria.

2 Ideas Journal

An Ideas Journal is a personal notebook or journal in which students record their thoughts, feelings, responses, sketches, observations, conversations, and interesting or unusual words or opinions. The Ideas Journal becomes an ongoing planning document, and may become the stimulus for future writing events.

- Talk with students about the purpose of an Ideas Journal.
- Share a personal Ideas Journal and discuss the types of entries that can be made. Alternatively, provide examples from previous students' journals.
- Provide opportunities for students to notice the world around them, e.g. sit outside and take note of what they hear; discuss community issues.
- Provide time for students to share what they have noticed.
- Encourage students to write in their journal on an ongoing basis.
- Invite students to share their recordings at regular intervals.

3 Brainstorming

Brainstorming is a technique used to record, in a limited time, all that is known about a topic. Ideas are written down immediately they spring to mind, and there is no need to categorise what is written. All ideas should be accepted and recorded. Brainstorming is a technique that can be used with the whole class, small groups or on an individual basis.

- Discuss the selected topic.
- Provide time for students to record anything they know about the topic.
- Invite students to share brainstormed ideas.
- Have students use the brainstormed ideas as either a springboard for further research or as the impetus to write.

4 Storyboarding

Storyboarding involves identifying the main ideas to be included in a text, then using them to plan. Storyboarding helps students to consider what pieces they want as the key parts of the text.

- Provide time for students to think about their topic. Some students will find it useful to talk about their ideas with a peer.
- Have students write down words associated with their topic, or sketch images.
- Ask students to categorise their words or images into related information. Each category should then be labelled to indicate the main idea.
- Have students place the main idea labels to make a storyboard sequence.

- Ask students to consider if there are any missing pieces.
- Provide time for students to find further supporting information for each category, if necessary.
- Encourage students to use the storyboard as a plan when they begin their draft.

5 Start at the Beginning

This is a planning technique where students consider purpose, audience, form, specific vocabulary and ideas prior to writing.
- Give students a copy of the Start at the Beginning format from the *First Steps Writing* CD-ROM.
- Have students consider the purpose, audience, form and topic for their writing, and record this information.
- Allow time for students to record initial ideas and specific vocabulary they could use in their writing.
- Direct students to consider the outline of their text, recording the possible sequence of information.
- Remind students that the ideas and outline can be changed and adapted as they compose their text.

6 Roll the Dice

Roll the Dice is a planning technique that helps students think about what information needs to be included in their writing. Create a dice by listing questions or statements on each face of the dice. The questions and statements should be related to that particular form. Students throw the dice, then plan responses to the questions. This technique helps students begin investigating and planning their text.
- Provide students with a Roll the Dice format from the *First Steps Writing* CD-ROM. Make sure the questions are applicable to the form the students are writing, e.g. **A Roll the Dice format for a scientific report could include questions or statements related to the classification, description (where it is found, what it looks like, what it eats, special characteristics) and a concluding statement.**
- Have students use the questions as a basis for planning their text.

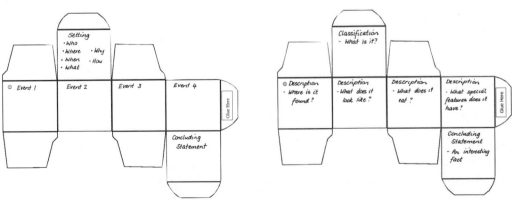

Figures 4.6a and 4.6b Student Samples From 'Roll the Dice'

7 What's Important?

What's Important? is a technique that helps students determine what information is important to include in the text, and what is not. It works most successfully when creating informational texts. This technique gives students the opportunity to consider and record the most relevant and irrelevant information prior to writing.

- Provide students with a What's Important? format from the *First Steps Writing* CD-ROM. Have them record the purpose and audience for writing on the format.

- Provide time for students to consider their ideas about their topic. Each idea should be considered for its level of importance.

- Students should record each idea in either the relevant or irrelevant column.

- Encourage students to refer to their What's Important? format when composing their text.

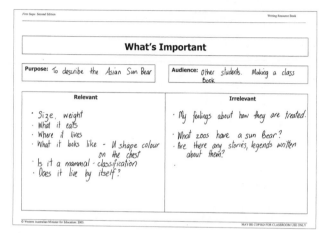

Figure 4.7 Student 'What's Important?' Sample

8 Graphic Organisers

Graphic Organisers are visual representations of information. They are a useful planning technique, helping students to identify key information and interrelationships between the ideas they are presenting in their writing. Students need to be introduced to a wide range of graphic organisers; this allows them to select the most appropriate way to record information for a particular writing purpose. Types of graphic organisers that support students' plans for writing include:

- Mapping
- Clustering
- Retrieval Charts
- Venn Diagrams
- Tree Diagrams.

Mapping

Mapping uses strong single words and meaningful phrases to help students focus clearly on the idea being developed.

- In the middle of their page, have students write the most

important word, short phrase or symbol to represent the idea they are writing about, then draw a circle around it. The circle forms the centre of their map.

- Encourage students to write single words and simple phrases (or draw pictures) that relate to the concept in the circle. The new ideas should be written around the outside of the circle, using different colours to represent different ideas.
- Direct students to draw lines to show the links between different ideas. This will help students see how one part affects another.
- Have students reflect on their map to decide if they have grouped things together correctly and make any necessary changes.
- Have students number the order in which they will introduce ideas into their writing.
- Allow time for students to use their map to begin composing their text.

Clustering

Clustering is a graphic organiser that helps students focus on and develop particular sub-topics of a piece of writing. It requires students to explore a sub-topic until all options have been exhausted, then to move onto another sub-topic.

- Have students write the topic, using a word or phrase, in the middle of a page and draw a heavy circle around it.
- Provide time for students to look at the word or phrase and write another associated word close to the centre circle.
- Encourage students to continue to add to the associated word in a string leading out from the centre. This should continue until all options are exhausted.
- Students then look back at the centre word again and produce another string of words related to a new sub-topic.
- Ask students to continue with their sub-topic strings until they have no more ideas.
- Have students review their clustering of sub-topic ideas, then have them use the clustering to begin composing their text.

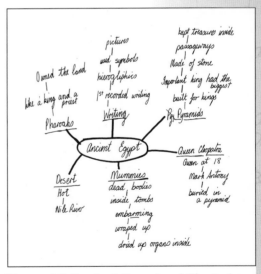

Figure 4.8 Student Sample of Clustering

Retrieval Charts

A Retrieval Chart is used to organise information about a topic according to a number of categories. This information can be used to make comparisons and to help students compose texts that compare and contrast.

- Provide time for students to construct the appropriate headings for their Retrieval Chart, based on the type of information being sought, e.g. where it lives, what it eats.
- Allow time for students to collect relevant information, recording it as key words on the Retrieval Chart.
- Encourage students to use the Retrieval Chart to verbalise the similarities and differences within categories.
- Have students use the recorded information as they compose their compare and contrast text.

Venn Diagrams

Venn Diagrams consist of two or more overlapping circles. They can be used as a planning technique to consider how events, people, characters or ideas might be represented in a text. Considering the similarities and differences of an element helps students choose how to represent that element in the text.

- Have students identify the element they wish to consider, e.g. characters.
- Have students consider the two options for comparison, e.g. boy or girl.
- Direct students to identify what the options have in common and record the common elements in the intersecting oval.
- Provide time for students to identify the differences between the options and record these in the non-intersecting portions.
- Complete this process for further elements of the text, e.g. setting.
- Encourage students to use the completed Venn Diagram to make choices and decisions about the text to be composed.

Tree Diagrams

Tree Diagrams are used to record information that might be included in a text and show how this information might be linked. Tree Diagrams start with a focal point, e.g. main idea or main character or person. Subordinate (or lesser-order) information then branches out from this point.

- Have students determine the topic for their writing. This should be recorded at the focal point of the tree diagram, e.g. firemen.
- Students then need to consider some subheadings about the topic, e.g. clothing, equipment, training, dangers.
- Direct students to brainstorm their sub-topics with additional detail, e.g. hard hat, boots, jackets, glove, goggles.
- Have students use their completed Tree Diagrams as a framework for composing their text.

Writing Process: Drafting

Drafting is the process of transferring initial ideas or plans into texts. The focus when drafting is on content, rather than the mechanics or conventions of writing. It is important that students have the freedom to get down their initial thoughts and ideas fluently without being too preoccupied with neat handwriting, perfect spelling or precise grammar. Students continue to plan what ideas might be included or deleted from the text during the drafting process, but they do not need to formally proofread or edit the text. The notion of sustained writing is important when creating a first draft, as it allows students to capture the main ideas, maintain fluency in their thinking and create meaning.

Effective Writers Know How to Draft

Effective writers are able to make decisions about the number of drafts that are necessary, depending on the purpose, audience and context of their writing. Effective writers are able to do the following.

- Consider audience and purpose.
- Generate, explore and develop topics and ideas.
- Record ideas rapidly in order to capture the essence of what it is they want to say.
- Explore additional ideas during drafting.
- Use planning notes to support drafting.
- Make critical choices about which content to include.
- Experiment with style, tone and voice.
- Read and re-read as part of drafting.
- Add to or delete from the text during drafting.
- Use strategies to spell unknown words within the text.

Figure 4.9

Supporting Writers to Draft

It is important to provide students with multiple opportunities to use drafting for real writing situations. A unit of work focusing on the different facets of drafting is also appropriate, and might consist of a combination of demonstrations and think-alouds. These demonstrations should focus on getting ideas down as quickly and as fluently as possible, rather than the mechanics of writing.

Activities such as 'Ready, Steady, Write' or 'Drop Everything and Write' are designed to encourage students to write on a selected topic for five to ten minutes. Using such activities on a regular basis supports students to focus on getting their ideas down on paper.

Collaborative charts can also be created to help students with the process of drafting.

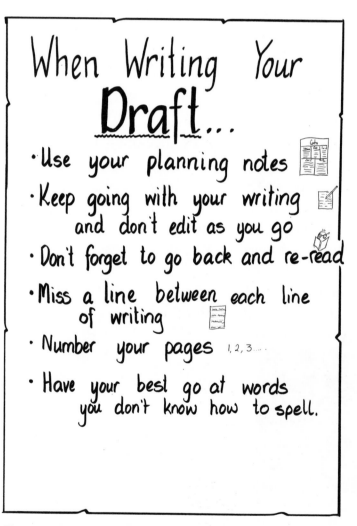

Figure 4.10 Teacher Chart Supporting Writers as They Draft

Writing Process: Conferring

An important goal of conferring is receiving feedback from others; this feedback can then be used to help improve and polish drafts. Discussing drafts with others helps students to move their draft closer to a final version of text. Collaborative efforts play an important part in this process. Students benefit from both formal and informal opportunities to provide and receive feedback. Peer sharing, teacher conferences or short small-group sharing sessions all help students to obtain constructive feedback.

Feedback helps students to reflect upon initial drafts and to confirm or adjust the direction of their writing. Obtaining feedback often generates new ideas. Peers, teachers, parents or other adults can provide feedback about students' writing.

Effective Writers Know How to Confer

Effective writers are able to respond helpfully to others' writing by providing positive comments and constructive suggestions for improvement. Effective writers can also identify those areas of their own writing that they would like to receive feedback about.

Effective writers are able to do the following.
- Identify areas in their own writing that they want feedback about.
- Share their writing with others.
- Request and obtain constructive feedback from others.
- Listen to and keep track of suggestions made by others.
- Make decisions about what feedback to incorporate.
- Read others' writing with a critical eye.
- Identify and share the strengths of others' writing.
- Provide constructive feedback in an appropriate way.
- Ask probing questions that help other writers reflect on their text.

Figure 4.11

Supporting Writers to Confer

The goal is for all students to be able to select from a variety of sharing forums to suit their needs and the needs of other writers. These forums might include partner sharing, small-group conversations, teacher conferences or whole-class sessions. Students need to be able to participate successfully in each of these forums. When focusing on the different facets of conferring, include a combination of demonstrations, think-alouds and opportunities to apply the techniques in real sharing sessions.

It is important to expose students to a range of questions and statements that will help them to give and receive constructive feedback. Collaboratively created charts will provide support to students as they work in a variety of sharing forums.

Get the Background Information From the Writer

- What form are you writing in?
- Who is your audience?
- What reaction do you want your reader to have?
- How do you feel about what you have written so far?
- What is the part that you like the most / least? Why?
- Do you think you have got your message across clearly?
- How can I help you?
- What would you like me to listen for?

Make Some Positive Comments

- I really like the way ...
- I enjoyed ...
- You have used a great hook to get people interested here ...
- This sentence clearly explains ...
- This section reminded me of...

Provide some Constructive Suggestions for Improvements

- I'd like to suggest ...
- I think you need to ...?
- Have you thought about ...?
- One idea you may like to think about is ...
- What do you mean by ... ?
- Can you explain more about ...
- Does this sentence, word or phrase make sense to you?

Asking for Constructive Feedback

- Today I'd like you to help me with ...
- My writing is about ...
- The purpose of my writing is ...
- The audience for this piece is ...
- I'd like you to listen for ...
- Can you suggest how ...
- I'm not sure about this point ...
- I'm stuck on ...
- Do you think I'm showing or telling?
- Should I include ...?
- Where do you think I need to ...?

Figure 4.12 Sample Charts Supporting Students as They Share Their Writing

Forums for Sharing Writing

1 Partner Sharing

Partner sharing is an opportunity for students to talk about their writing with a peer.

- Have the writer decide how to share their text with their conference partner. They might decide to read the piece aloud. Or they might give it to their partner to read either silently or aloud.
- Have the writer tell their partner what they want to focus on during the sharing time.
- Provide time for the partner to ask open-ended questions that help the writer talk about their writing and consider possible changes.
- Encourage the writer to take notes about the partner's feedback so that they can refer back to it when making changes during the refining process.
- Have the writer thank their partner for their feedback and sharing.

2 Teacher Conferencing

Teacher conferences provide an opportunity for students to receive feedback from an adult. They operate in a very similar manner to partner sharing.

- Ask the student to identify the focus for the conference.
- Invite students to read their work aloud as you listen.
- Comment on the overall message of the writing, identifying any strengths.
- Ask questions and talk about the selected focus area.
- Provide suggestions that will help the student improve their writing.
- Record notes if necessary.

3 Sharing Circle

Sharing Circle gives students an opportunity to talk about their writing with a small group of peers.

- Organise students into groups of four or five.
- If appropriate, give students a Sharing Circle format from the *First Steps Writing* CD-ROM for recording the group's feedback.
- Together, review the appropriate way to respond to others' writing.
- Provide time for students seeking feedback to share their writing.
- Encourage the writer to record their feedback.
- Have students use the feedback when they begin to refine their work.

4 Whole Class Sharing

Whole Class Sharing is an opportunity for students to share their writing and receive feedback in a whole class forum. This type of forum benefits all students, as they can adapt the feedback given to others and apply it in their own writing.

- Select a student. Invite them to identify the area they would like feedback about.
- Have the student read their writing aloud while the class listens.
- Invite class members to ask questions, provide praise and give constructive feedback.
- Summarise the major suggestions given that will help the writer improve their work.
- Invite another student to share.

For further information, see Author's Chair on pages 23–25.

Two Stars and a Wish

The Two Stars and a Wish format gives students a simple framework for recording feedback for others. It provides the opportunity to reflect on positives (the stars), as well as making suggestions for improvement (the wish).

- Give students a Two Stars and a Wish format from the *First Steps Writing* CD-ROM for recording feedback.

Writing Process: Refining

After creating a draft and receiving helpful feedback from a range of sources, students need to work at bringing their text closer to completion. This process is referred to as refining; students take a closer look at their drafts to make decisions about whether to move text, add text, cut text or leave things alone. The refining process consists of revising, editing and proofreading.

Revising

Revising generally refers to changes made to ideas and organisation at the text level. This could involve students rearranging the order of paragraphs or sentences to improve the text sequence.

Editing

Editing involves clarifying meaning at the sentence level. Students might add, change, delete or rearrange words to enhance meaning.

Proofreading

This involves reading to check conventions, rather than the content. Proofreading involves rereading a draft to check on the use of punctuation, spelling and grammar.

It is important to help students build a positive attitude towards the refining process, and to help them value the time they spend in improving their own writing. Developing a revision consciousness (Routman, 2005) involves students looking at their writing from a reader's point of view. Students consider their audience needs as a priority for making changes to their draft texts.

Figure 4.13

Processes and Strategies

Effective Writers Know How to Refine

Effective writers are able to identify the types of changes they wish to make; they also have the techniques that allow them to make those changes in a text. Effective writers are able to do the following.

- See writing from a reader's point of view.
- Know the difference between revising, editing and proofreading.
- Identify changes to be made.
- Demonstrate an awareness of audience.
- Revise ideas and organisation.
- Rearrange paragraphs to produce a more convincing order.
- Remove unimportant details.
- Add missing information.
- Rearrange or add words, phrases and sentences for shades of meaning.
- Add dialogue, if appropriate to the form.
- Re-read and then re-write for clarity and detail.
- Use appropriate tools to adjust punctuation, grammar or spelling.
- Use a proofreading guide or editors' checklist to refine their own writing.
- Continue refining until satisfied.

Supporting Writers to Refine

It is important to expose students to a range of refining techniques; these techniques can be introduced and experimented with over a period of time. When focusing on the different facets of refining, include a combination of demonstrations, think-alouds and opportunities to apply the techniques in real refining situations.

The goal is for all students to be able to select from a large repertoire of techniques to suit the specific needs of each writing event. The following refining techniques will help students make informed choices about how to improve their texts.

- Highlighting
- Have I Captured the Action?
- Remove the Rubble
- Let's Hear It
- Using Spellcheckers and Grammar Checkers
- Collaboratively Created Charts

1 Highlighting

Highlighting is a technique students can use to consider what information needs to be added to their text. Students highlight specific parts of their text, then review it to add further detail or any information that has been omitted.

- Have students read and re-read their texts to highlight where specific information has been included. For example, in a retell, students could highlight the setting, events, and conclusion.
- Have students consider what further information and details could be added.
- Have students check the order of the information, e.g. **Are the events listed in the order they happened?**
- Discuss how adding information has improved the text.

2 Have I Captured the Action?

This technique helps students to consider and refine how they have described actions in a text.

- Have students choose a piece of text they have previously composed. The text should contain events with some kind of action occurring.
- Ask students to read the text, highlighting any sentences that describe an action.
- Provide time for students to consider whether the words effectively convey what or how something happened.
- Encourage students to add words that help to describe the event more effectively, e.g. **adding adverbs.**
- Provide time for students to make changes, then talk about how the changes have made the action pieces clearer.

3 Remove the Rubble

Remove the Rubble is a technique students can use to delete excess information from their texts.

- Have students choose a piece of text they have previously composed.
- Arrange students in pairs. Ask them to re-read each text to help each other identify any 'rubble', or unnecessary information.
- Students then work individually to delete any repeated or excess information.
- Compare the final text to the original piece.
- Together, discuss how students decided what to delete from their texts.

4 Let's Hear It

Let's Hear It is a technique that supports students as they refine their writing. The teacher reads the text aloud, then the class contributes ideas to help the selected student revise, edit or proofread. It is best to focus on one or two selected areas, e.g. **use of punctuation, use of verbs.**

- Select a student who has a piece of text to be refined.

- Enlarge the text so that all students can see it, e.g. **overhead projector, chart paper.**
- Identify the focus for the session, e.g. **proofreading for punctuation.**
- Read the text aloud, inviting the class and the writer to make suggestions for refining.
- Have the writer act as editor to change the text according to class recommendations.

5 Using a Spellchecker or Grammar Checker

Spellcheckers and Grammar Checkers are tools that writers can use when using word-processing programs to compose texts. Students using word-processing programs should be taught to use a spellchecker and a grammar checker as proofreading tools.

Make sure the spellcheck and grammar checker functions are switched off while students are composing, as they are a distraction. Turn these functions back on when students are ready to refine their texts.

As spellcheckers often list suggestions for misspelt words, students will need to draw upon their spelling knowledge in order to choose the correct word. Students will also need to be aware that spellcheckers will not recognise certain errors, e.g. **homophones; unknown words, such as place or family names; American spellings; typographical errors, such as use and sue.**

Grammar checkers also offer suggestions. However, students need to read their work carefully before deciding whether to accept the suggestions. Teach students that the green squiggly line suggests that there might be a problem with the structure of the sentence, but that it is up to them to determine if the sentence makes sense or requires changes.

Students also need to understand that spellcheckers and grammar checkers are not totally foolproof — they should not be relied on as the only form of proofreading.

6 Collaboratively Created Charts

Collaboratively created charts remind students of the routines and questions they need to consider during revising, editing and proofreading. These charts can be compiled progressively. The charts help students work through the refining process in a logical way.

- Work with students to create charts they can use during independent refining.
- Ask students to suggest questions they could ask when revising,

editing or proofreading.

- Record the questions on a chart. Progressively add to the chart as students discover new ideas and further questions.
- Encourage students to use the questions as a guide when refining their texts.

Revising and Editing Our Writing

When revising and editing we concentrate on the 'big picture'. This is the time to see if you need to add, cut, move, change or leave things alone to make the piece of text the best it can be.

Look at the whole text
- Have I read my writing aloud to myself or to someone else?
- Does my writing make sense?
- Does my writing flow?

Look at paragraphs
- Do I start with a strong hook that will get people interested?
- Do I have an interesting topic sentence?
- Do the other sentences have relevant details?
- Are the ideas in a logical sequence?

Look at words
- Have I used a variety of words?
- Have I used words that convey exactly what I mean?
- Can I substitute a more interesting word?

Look at sentences
- Does each sentence make sense?
- Are there any sentences that are too long and need to be broken up?
- Can I combine any sentences?
- Can I add more detail to any sentences to make them more interesting?
- Do I need to delete words to make my writing clearer?

Figure 4.14 Sample Revising and Editing Chart

Proofreading My Work

Concentrate on the 'little details' when you proofread. This is the time to check spelling, punctuation and grammar.

- Did I underline the words I'm not sure I spelt correctly?
- Have I checked the spelling?
- Does every sentence begin with a capital letter?
- Does every sentence finish with a full stop, question mark or exclamation mark?
- Have I used punctuation correctly, e.g. commas, speech marks?
- Have I used the right grammatical structures, e.g. verb-subject agreement?
- Have I been consistent with the use of tense?

Figure 4.15 Sample Proofreading Chart

Our Editor's Code

^	Insert something
ⓟ	Check punctuation
=	Capital letter needed
/	Make this a small letter
ⓢⓟ	Check spelling
↶	Check order
ℓ⁄	Delete
\\	New paragraph
?	Clarify meaning

Figure 4.16 Editor's Code

Writing Process: Publishing

Publishing is the process of preparing a text for final presentation to (or sharing with) the intended audience. For the publishing process to be meaningful, students need to be writing for real purposes and authentic audiences. Not every piece of text students compose needs to be published; texts written for purely personal reasons might never be shared with an audience.

Modern technology makes it much easier for students to publish their work — and it also makes it possible to reach audiences beyond classroom boundaries. The Internet enables students to publish their writing for real audiences worldwide.

Effective Writers Know How to Publish

Effective writers are able to make choices about how to publish, depending on the purpose and audience of their text. Effective writers are able to do the following.

- Use a variety of publishing formats, e.g. books, pamphlets, cards, posters, electronic.
- Identify the most appropriate format for purpose and audience.
- Use word-processing programs or legible handwriting to prepare published work.
- Compose a piece of writing which is both readable and appealing to an audience.
- Add artwork, graphics or photographs to enhance texts.

Supporting Writers to Publish

It is important to expose students to a range of publishing techniques; these techniques can be introduced and experimented with over a period of time. When focusing on the different facets of publishing, include a combination of demonstrations, think-alouds and opportunities for students to publish their writing in a variety of ways.

The following experiences will help to build students' understandings about publishing options. The most powerful way for students to build this understanding is by analysing a variety of formats, exploring features such as layout, design, use of colour, font size and type, and use of graphics. Analysing different examples of the same format will enable students to develop guidelines that they can refer to as they publish their own texts. The following are suggested analysing experiences.

- What's Included?
- Setting It Out
- Design This!

- Publisher's Palette
- That Catches My Eye
- Screen-based Publications
- How Can I Publish?

1 What's Included?

What's Included provides students with the opportunity to analyse published texts and make decisions about what is important to include when publishing texts in a book format.

- Have students gather a range of texts published in book format, including commercially published texts and texts published by students.
- Invite small groups of students to examine the texts and list all the features of the published books. These could include:
  — Cover or jacket (with illustration or photograph)
  — Title page
  — Publication details
  — Dedication page
  — Information about the author
  — Contents page
  — Index
  — Bibliography.
- Have students discuss the features that should be included when publishing in a book format.
- Create a class chart of features for future reference.

This outline can also be used to explore the features of other publishing formats.

2 Setting It Out

Setting It Out gives students an opportunity to investigate a variety of publishing formats, and to compare how their layout impacts on the audience.

- Provide students with a variety of texts published in the same format, e.g. **posters**. These could be commercially bought posters or posters published by students.
- Have students work in small groups to examine each text, ranking them according to the level of visual appeal. Ask questions such as the following to assist students examine and rank the texts.
  — Where has print been positioned?
  — Where have illustrations been positioned?
  — What lettering or font style has been used?
  — What do you notice about the size of the font, typeface, headings, illustrations?
  — How have diagrams or illustrations been labelled?

— How are the pages numbered (or labelled)?

- Provide time for the whole class to discuss each group's rankings and justifications.
- Create a class chart of features to include when publishing in the chosen format.

3 Design This!

Design This! encourages students to add graphics to a piece of text and to design an appealing layout for a given audience.

- Provide groups of students with a cut-up piece of text, with organisational features such as headings and graphics removed.
- Have students organise the text into an appropriate order, then work on designing the layout of the text to suit the given audience. Students will need to consider:
  — where the text should be positioned
  — where illustrations, diagrams or pictures should be positioned
  — the size and position of titles, headings, labels and captions.
- Have students add headings, graphics and other text features that will enhance the appeal and readability for their audience.
- Have students share their text with the whole class. Invite them to discuss their rationale for design features and text alterations.

4 Publisher's Palette

Publisher's Palette helps students to think about the use of colour when publishing texts. Students need to understand how the use of colour can impact on the reader.

- Ask students to think about the feelings or moods that different colours create, e.g. yellow: bright, sunny; blue: calm.
- Have students analyse a variety of texts that have been published in the same format, looking specifically at which colours have been used and how many of them.
- Encourage students to look for any colours that:
  — are difficult to read
  — are used to emphasise a point
  — create a particular feeling
  — distract the reader.
- Encourage students to discuss and determine the most effective use of colour in the chosen format. Suggestions could include the use of colour in:
  — the cover page or title block
  — large initial letters
  — quotes pulled from the text, e.g. in flyers or newspaper stories
  — borders
  — graphics, e.g. illustrations, graphs or logos.

- Challenge students to publish a piece of text in the chosen format using only black, white and three other colours.
- Invite students to share and discuss where they used colour, and its effect on the readability and visual appeal of the text.

5 That Catches My Eye

That Catches My Eye is an opportunity for students to experiment with different lettering and font styles. It helps students to consider what is the most effective and suitable style to use for title pages and headings.

- Invite each student to select a title from something they have written.
- Challenge students to use different lettering and font styles to create several different designs for the same title.
- Encourage students to experiment with different media and materials. This could include:
  — using word-processing software
  — using stencils
  — creating their own alphabet design
  — cutting letters from different materials, e.g. **fabric, paper, cardboard, plastic**
  — incorporating materials or objects related to the title, e.g. **if the title was 'gold' students might use golden glitter to fill each letter; a title related to the sea might incorporate shells or sand.**
  — using different drawing implements, e.g. **pens, markers, crayons, chalk.**
- Display all designs. Invite students to comment on which designs they think are the most effective, and why.
- Remind students about these discussions when they are publishing their own texts.

6 Screen-based Publications

Provide time for students to explore a range of screen-based publications; this will help them to understand how different features are used to help or hinder the readability of texts.

- Provide students with web addresses of a range of suitable websites.
- Provide time for small groups of students to examine each homepage, and to discuss the following questions.
  — What is the focal point? How do you know this?
  — How has emphasis been achieved? e.g. **use of bold or italicised font, white space, colour.**
  — How have text or graphics been aligned?
  — How have items been grouped?

— What font or lettering style and size has been used? Is it easy to read?

— How does the spacing between words (and between letters in a word) help you to read the text?

— How many different fonts or lettering styles have been used in the same piece? Why do you think this has been done?

— What colours have been used?

• Encourage students to apply their discoveries when creating their own screen-based texts.

7 How Can I Publish?

How Can I Publish? is an opportunity for students to publish the same text in a variety of formats. Students can then compare the different publications and determine which is the most effective and why.

• Divide students into groups.

• Select a piece of text that has been composed as part of a class session.

• Allocate each group a different format for publication, e.g. letter, poster, electronic presentation, newspaper, book, pamphlet.

• Provide time for students to complete their group publication.

• Have each group present their publication.

• Discuss the effectiveness of each publication of the text.

Sample Publishing Charts created collaboratively in a Year 6 Class are shown in Figures 4.17 and 4.18.

How Will I Publish My Work?

• Book
• Newspaper
• Electronic Bulletin Board
• Screen Saver
• Magazine
• Web Page
• Brochure
• Letter
• Pamphlet
• Chart
• Journal
• Card
• Display Board
• Multimedia Presentation
• Game Board
• Mobile
• Internet

Figure 4.17 Sample Publishing Chart

When I Publish My Work I Need to Think About ...

• Who is the audience for my text?

• What is the purpose of my text?

• What would be the most effective publishing format to use?

• What features will I include to enhance my publication?
  — objects related to the theme or subject of the text
  — special effects, e.g. fold outs or pop ups
  — borders that relate to the theme of subject, e.g. shade or singe the edges for an historical look
  — multimedia, e.g. animation, 3-D models, video or audiotape

• What colours and typographical elements will I use? e.g. font style and size

• Do I have a time line for creating my publication?

Figure 4.18 Sample Publishing Chart

first steps

Glossary

affidavit   a statement in writing made under oath or before an authorised officer

autobiography   the biography of a person, narrated by themselves

automaticity   bringing information to mind with little or no effort because a skill or understanding is so well known

ballad   narrative poem composed of short verses intended to be sung or recited, frequently of unknown authorship

bias   a prejudiced view or one-sided perspective

biography   an account of someone's life written by another person

blurb   a short piece of writing, often on the cover or jacket of a text, designed to interest the reader in the text

brochure   a format for writing, containing descriptive or advertising material

contents page   a list of what is included in a book; usually at the front of the book

context   the broad linguistic, social and cultural experiences that are brought to a situation

dialect   a variety of a language which belongs to a particular social group or geographical area

editorial   an explanatory form of writing used in newspapers and magazines to discuss current news events and express opinions

epitaph   text added to an inscription on a tombstone to tell something more about the deceased

eulogy   a speech, oral or written, that praises someone or something

experiment   an operation carried out under controlled conditions in order to discover an unknown effect or law, to test or establish a hypothesis, or to illustrate a known law

explanation   factual writing that explains how something works or happens

exposition   a text that intends to persuade or gives an argument

fable   a short tale in prose or verse that teaches a moral, often with animals and inanimate objects as characters

fantasy   an imaginative story about characters, places and events that do not exist

homographs   words that are spelt the same but pronounced differently and have different meanings, e.g. **tear and tear, minute and minute**

homonyms   words that are spelt the same and pronounced the same but have different meanings, e.g. **scale (fish), scale (music)**

homophones   words that are pronounced the same but spelt differently and have different meanings, e.g. **here and hear; aisle and I'll**

hybrid text   using a combination of forms in one text

hyperlink	a link from a hypertext file to another location or file, usually activated by a highlighted word or icon
hypertext	machine-readable text that is not sequential, but is organised so that related items of information are connected
legend	a traditional tale handed down initially in oral form before later becoming a written form
memo	an informal record; *also* a written reminder
memoir	an account of one's personal experiences and observations
metalanguage	language used to describe and analyse natural language; language about language
minutes	an official record of the proceedings of a meeting
multi-modal texts	utilising more than one mode of text, i.e. visual, spoken or written
narrative	a story, actual or fictional, expressed orally or in writing
phrase	two or more words in sequence forming a grammatical expression, but not containing a finite verb, e.g. in the kitchen
policy	a plan of action adopted by an individual or group
sidebar	a short news story, often boxed, printed alongside a longer article; typically presents additional, contrasting or late-breaking news
site map	a textual or visual index of a website's contents
summons	to command to appear in court
synopsis	a brief summary
travelogue	a text about travel; can be written, spoken or visual
word stem	the part of a word to which a suffix is or can be added

Bibliography

Atwell, N., 1998, *In the Middle—New Understandings About Writing, Reading, and Learning*, 2nd Edition, Boynton/Cook, Portsmouth New Hampshire, USA

Barratt-Pugh, C., Rohl, M., 2001, *Literacy Learning in the Early Years*, Allen and Unwin, Crows Nest, Australia

Bear, D.R., Invernizzi, M., Templeton, S., Johnston, F., 2000, *Words Their Way, Word Study for Phonics, Vocabulary and Spelling Instruction*, 2nd Edition, Prentice-Hall, New Jersey, USA

Booth, D., 2001, *Reading and Writing in the Middle Years*, Pembroke Publishers, Ontario, Canada

Brand, M., 2004, *Word Savvy*, Stenhouse, Portland, Maine, USA

Brownjohn, S., 1994, *To Rhyme or Not to Rhyme? Teaching Children to Write Poetry*, Hodder and Stoughton, Abingdon, UK

Bruce, B.C., (ed.) 2003, *Literacy in the Information Age: Inquiries into Meaning Making with New Technologies*, International Reading Association, Newark, Delaware, USA

—— 2001, *Illuminating Texts*, Heinemann, Portsmouth, New Hampshire, USA

—— 2003, *Writing Reminders*, Heinemann, Portsmouth, New Hampshire, USA

Buss, K., and Karnowski, L., 2002, *Reading and Writing Nonfiction Genres*, International Reading Association, Newark, Delaware USA

Collerson, J., 1997, *Grammar in Teaching*, PETA, New South Wales, Australia

Covich, S., (ed.) 2003, 2004, *A Circle in a Room Full of Squares*, John Curtin College of the Arts, Fremantle, Western Australia

Cunningham, P., Moore, S., Cunningham, J., Moore, D., 2004, *Reading and Writing in Elementary Classrooms*, Pearson, Boston, MA

Derewianka, B., 1990, *Exploring How Texts Work*, Maryborough, Victoria, Australia

Dougan, J., & Gorman, R., (eds.) 2005, *Critical Literacy and Inquiry Learning in Action*, AISWA, Perth, Western Australia

Downes, T., & Fatouros, C., 1996, *Learning in an Electronic World: Computers and the Language Arts Classroom*, Heinemann, Portsmouth, NH, USA

Education Department of Western Australia, 1997, *Writing Resource Book*, Rigby Heinemann, Port Melbourne, Victoria, Australia

Fay, K., & Whaley, S., 2004, *Becoming One Community—Reading and Writing with English Language Learners*, Stenhouse Publishers, Portland, Maine, USA

Fehring, H., & Green, P., (eds.) 2001 *Critical Literacy: A Collection of Articles from the Australian Literacy Educators' Association*, International Reading Association, Newark, Delaware, USA

Gee, R., & Watson, C., 1990, *The Usborne Book of Better English*, Usborne Publishers, London, UK

Graves, D.H., 1994, *A Fresh Look at Writing*, Heinemann, Portsmouth, NH, USA

Gentry, J.R., 2004, *The Science of Spelling*, Heinemann, Portsmouth, NH, USA

Glazer, S.M., 1998, *Phonics, Spelling and Word Study: A Sensible Approach*, Christopher-Gordon Publishers, Inc, Norwood, Massachusetts, USA

Harris, P., McKenzie, B., Fitzsimmons, P., & Turbill, 2003, *Writing in the Primary School Years*, Social Science Press, Australia

Bibliography

Harwayne, S. 2000, *Lifetime Guarantees: Towards Ambitious Literacy Teaching*, Heinemann, Portsmouth, New Hampshire, USA

Healy, A., & Honan, E., 2004, *Text Next*: *New Resources for Literacy Learning*, Primary English Teachers Association, NSW, Australia

Heffernan, L., 2004, *Critical Literacy and Writer's Workshop: Bringing Purpose and Passion to Student Writing*, International Reading Association, Newark, Delaware, USA

http://as1.seattleschools.org/alt_ed/social_action.htm

http://curry.edschool.virginia.edu/go/clic/nrrc/reinking.html

http://nadabs.tripod.com/ghaith-writing.html

http://www.sasked.gov.sk.ca/docs/ela20/teach4.html

http://www.sasked.gov.sk.ca/docs/mla/write.html#write

http://www.ttms.org/PDFs/04%20Writing%20Process%20v001%20(Full).pdf

Jago, C., 2002, *Cohesive Writing — Why Concept Is Not Enough*, Heinemann, Portsmouth, New Hampshire, USA

Johnson, T.D., 1988, *Unriddling The World*, Western Australian College of Advanced Education, Mount Lawley, Western Australia

Keene, E.O., Zimmerman. S., 1997, *Mosaic of Thought — Teaching Comprehension in a Reader's Workshop*, Heinemann, Portsmouth, New Hampshire, USA

Knobel, M., & Healy, A. (eds.) 1998, *Critical Literacies in the Primary Classroom*, PETA, Newton, NSW, Australia

Lankshear, C., & Knobel, M., 2003, *New Literacies: Changing Knowledge and Classroom Learning*, Open University Press, Buckingham, UK

Lazar, A., 2004, *Learning to be Literacy Teachers in Urban Schools*, International Reading Association, Delaware, USA

Lewis, B., 1998, *The Kid's Guide to Social Action: How to Solve the Social Problems You Choose and Turn Creative Thinking into Positive Action*, Free Spirit Publishing, Minneapolis, Minnesota, USA

Lyon, A. & Moore, P., 2003, *Sound Systems*, Stenhouse Publishers, Portland, Maine, USA

Mansutti, E., 2004, *The Poetry Detectives*, Oral Presentation, Australian Literacy Educators' Association, State Conference, Perth, Western Australia

Marten, C., 2003, *Word Crafting*, Heinemann, Portsmouth New Hampshire, USA

Martin, R.D., 2000, *Young Writers Guide*, 3rd Edition, Era Publications, Flinders Park, South Australia

McCarrier, A., Pinnell, G.S., & Fountas, I.C., 2000, *Interactive Writing: How Language and Literacy Come Together*, K-2, Heinemann, Portsmouth, New Hampshire, USA

Mooney, M. E., 2001, *Text Forms and Features*, Richard C. Owen Publishers Inc., Katonah, New York, USA

Murdoch, K., & Wilson, J., 2004, *Learning Links: Strategic Teaching for the Learner-Centred Classroom*, Curriculum Corporation, Carlton South, Victoria, Australia

Olness, R., 2005, *Using Literature to Enhance Writing Instruction*, International Reading Association, Delaware, USA

Parsons, L., 1992, *Poetry Themes and Activities Exploring the Fun and Fantasy of Language*, Pembroke Publishers Ltd., Ontario, Canada

Pearson, P.D., and Gallagher, M.C., 1983, 'The Instruction of Reading Comprehension', *Contemporary Educational Psychology*, 8: 317–344

Pinnell, G.S., & Fountas, I.C., 1998, *Word Matters: Teaching Phonics and Spelling in the Reading/Writing Classroom*, Heinemann, Portsmouth, New Hampshire, USA

Rogovin, P., 2001, The *Research Workshop: Bringing the World into Your Classroom*, Heinemann, Portsmouth, New Hampshire, USA

Romano, T., 2004, *Crafting Authentic Voice*, Heinemann, Portsmouth, New Hampshire, USA

Routman, 2005, *Writing Essentials*, Heinemann, Portsmouth, New Hampshire, USA

—— 2000, *Conversations: Strategies for Teaching, Learning and Evaluating*, Heinemann, Portsmouth, New Hampshire, USA

Simon, L., 2004, *Strategic Spelling*, Heinemann, Portsmouth, New Hampshire, USA

Snowball, D., & Bolton, F., 1999, *Spelling K–8*, Stenhouse Publishers, York, Maine, USA

Stahl, S.A., & Murray, B.A., 1994, 'Defining Phonological Awareness and its Relationship to Early Reading', *Journal of Educational Psychology*, 86, 221–234

Stanovich, K.E., Cunningham, A.E, & Cramer, B., 1984, 'Assessing Phonological Awareness in Kindergarten Children: issues of task comparability', *Journal of Experimental Child Psychology*, 38, 175–190

Stead, T., 2001, *Is That a Fact? Teaching Nonfiction Writing K–3*, Stenhouse, Portland, Maine, USA

Tannenbaum, J., 2000, *Teeth, Wiggly as Earthquakes: Writing Poetry in the Primary Grades*, Stenhouse Publishers, Portland, Maine, USA

Tiedt, I., 2002, *Tiger Lilies, Toadstools, and Thunderbolts: Engaging K-8 Students with Poetry*, International Reading Association, Newark, USA

Tompkins, G.E., & Collom, C., 2004, *Sharing the Pen: Interactive Writing With Young Children*, Pearson, Merrill Prentice Hall, Upper Saddle River, New Jersey, USA

Tompkins, G.E., 2004, *Literacy for the 21st Century: Teaching Reading and Writing in Grades 4 Through 8*, Pearson Education Inc., Upper Saddle River, New Jersey, USA

Weaver, C., 1998, *Lessons to Share—On Teaching Grammar in Context*, Boynton/Cook Publishers, Heinemann, Portsmouth New Hampshire, USA

Wepner, S., Valmont, W., Thurlow, R., 2000, *Linking Literacy and Technology A Guide for K-8 Classrooms*, International Reading Association, Delaware, USA

Westwood, P., 1999, *Spelling — Approaches to Teaching and Assessment*, ACER Press, Victoria, Australia

Whitehead, D., 2003, *Writing Frameworks*, Pembroke Publishers, Ontario, Canada

Wilson, L., 1994, *Write me a Poem: Reading, Writing and Performing Poetry*, Eleanor Curtin Publishing, Armadale, Australia

First Steps Second Edition Professional Development Courses

First Steps Second Edition texts form a critical part of the *First Steps* professional development courses that promote a long-term commitment to educational change. Together, the professional development and the materials provide a strategic whole-school approach to improving students' literacy outcomes.

First Steps offers a full range of professional development courses that are conducted at the invitation of a school or education sector. Given the breadth of literacy, schools generally choose to implement only one strand of literacy at a time. A strand should be selected on a needs basis in line with the school's priorities. Schools can select from two-day courses in any of these strands:

• Reading
• Writing/Spelling
• Viewing
• Speaking and Listening.

Each participant who attends a two-day course receives:
• a *Map of Development* in the chosen literacy strand
• a *Resource Book*
• the *Linking Assessment, Teaching and Learning* book
• a Course Book of professional development reflections
• practical activities for classroom use.

Within each strand, a selection of additional sessions, beyond the regular course, will also be available to meet the needs of teachers in different schools and contexts. These sessions can be selected in consultation with a *First Steps* Consultant.

For further information about or registration in *First Steps* courses contact your nearest Steps Professional Development and Consulting Office.

UNITED STATES OF AMERICA

Steps Professional Development
80 Washington Square
Unit F-30
Norwell
MA 02061 USA
Phone: 001 978 927 0038
Fax: 001 978 759 9990
Toll Free: 1 866 505 3001
www.stepspd.com

AUSTRALASIA

Steps Professional Development
234 Great Eastern Highway
Ascot
Western Australia 6104
Phone: 0061 8 9373 2200
Fax: 0061 8 9373 2299
www.stepspd.com

UNITED KINGDOM

Steps Professional Development
Unit 78
Shrivenham Hundred Business Park
Majors Road, Watchfield SN6 8TY
Phone: 01793 787930
Fax: 01793 787931
www.stepspd.com

CANADA

Pearson Professional Learning
26 Prince Andrew Place
Don Mills, Ontario M3C 2T8
Canada
Phone: 416 447 5101
Fax: 416 447 3914
Toll Free: 1888 867 7772
www.pearsonprofessionallearning.ca

Professional Development Notes

Professional Development Notes

Professional Development Notes

Professional Development Notes